1991

PARK PLANNING GUIDELINES
3RD EDITION

by George E. Fogg

Published by
National Recreation & Park Association

TABLE OF CONTENTS

ACKNOWLEDGEMENTS AND CREDITS

The original idea for *Park Planning Guidelines* was based on a manual entitled *State Park Planning Guidelines* which was contributed to by members of Pennsylvania's former Department of Forests and Waters, Bureau of State Parks, Division of Planning and Development and written by the author.

The Commonwealth's Department of Environmental Resources is acknowledged and thanked for the use of its data developed by the Office of Resources Management, Bureau of State Parks which was used in the initial writing and its first revision. Data for the second revision has been received from several sources including the National Golf Foundation, the National Rifle Association, and the National Recreation and Park Association. The National Recreation and Park Association, through its continuous support, has made it possible to keep this document current. Without the continued interest of the users of this book, however, the ongoing research and updating would not be possible.

The author wishes to expressly thank the following for their efforts and participation in the development of *Park Planning Guidelines* and its various revisions: Original contributing authors - Brij Garg (utilities and engineering); Clayton Kritschgau (hunting and fishing); E. James Tabor (golf courses); Michael W. Fogg (white water boating). Of particular assistance in preparation of this revision have been Brij Garg and his input on utilities, Michael W. Fogg for his help on white water boating, river and stream access, downhill skiing and cross-country skiing, Dennis Pagen for his preparation of the material on hang gliding and para-gliding, Dick Green of Green's of Golden Gate for the typesetting and layout work.

Finally, a very special thanks to my wife Rebecca for her help, encouragement, translation of my handwriting and her untold hours of typing, proofing, and editing.

George E. Fogg

Dedicated to Mom
who shared her love with all those she came to know
and made their lives a little brighter.

INTRODUCTION

Parks, recreation and leisure time facilities are provided by various public, quasi-public and private agencies and companies for use during people's leisure time. Each individual's leisure time is currently being used for something (fishing, going to parties, watching T. V., bicycling, art classes, doing crossword puzzles, etc.).

The only sources of additional leisure time and, therefore, users for any leisure time facilities and programs are increased population and/or increased amounts of leisure time. Leisure time for most segments of the population is not, and probably will not be, increasing in the near future (most families actually have less aggregate leisure time due to the rapidly increasing number of households where both parents are working). Population increases are generally due to immigration from other countries, increases in the older segment of our society, and migration from other areas of the country. This migration, of course, has a corresponding opposite effect on the area being left.

If an existing park is to be rebuilt or expanded, or if a new park facility is being proposed, careful consideration should be given to who is going to use the facilities. Where are the users coming from? Are you competing with other already established leisure time patterns? *A Site Design Process* by this author and published by the National Recreation and Park Association will be helpful in approaching this aspect of preparing the design of the proposed park/leisure time facility.

Park Planning Guidelines is intended to provide information on the physical aspects of planning large-scale, resource-oriented parks. This 3rd Edition includes new information gathered since 1981. Five new chapters have been added on Environmental Impacts, Mechanical Vehicle Facilities, Archery, Firearm Ranges, and Non-Consumptive Wildlife Recreation. New or expanded information has been included on salt water beaches, golf courses, scenic roads, handicapped accessibility, charter boating, surfboarding, surfsailing and winter use. Personal observations, new research and available reference information have been incorporated throughout the text. A special emphasis has been placed on environmental aspects throughout the revisions. The text has been expanded by 50 percent and 110 new drawings have been added.

The sources from which data were gathered are footnoted [00] and shown in the bibliography. Unfortunately, there is, after fifteen years, still little research and documentation available in the physical aspects of park planning. Data developed by a number of agencies and organizations, plus the Commonwealth of Pennsylvania's Department of Environmental Resources, is used at the beginning of each applicable chapter. There are other activities that could have been included but there was insufficient information or too little use at this time to consider them, i. e., mountaineering, hot air ballooning, etc. Planning guidelines for facilities normally provided in smaller, urban park and recreation areas will soon be available in a companion publication currently being compiled by this author to be entitled *Urban Park Planning Guidelines.*

This resource book cannot assure good design or plans. It does present, however, some of the tools necessary to plan parks for people. To make full use of the material, it is necessary to conduct a thorough, in-depth study of the park site and its setting in the surrounding region. Such a study must include, among other items, information and analysis of soils, geology, hydrology, climatology, ecology, cultural features, history, vegetation, utilities and access. Please refer to *A Site Design Process* referenced above.

Planners and managers should consider several alternatives to achieving the goals set for the resource use. They should question the end results and the side effects of the proposed project. In particular, they must look at the requirements for operating and maintaining the park. New approaches, ideas, and concepts which might solve problems not adequately handled through existing and/or conventional techniques should be investigated not only for development but, more importantly, for reducing ongoing operations and maintenance costs, including vandalism. Please refer to *Management Planning for Park and Recreation Areas* by this author published by the National Recreation and Park Association.

If it is concluded that a specific activity is necessary, the question should be asked, "Is it necessary within the park boundaries?" If the development is necessary, it should not exceed the capacity of the land resources to sustain use without deterioration. Basically, the greater the number of users, the greater the management effort that will be needed (staff and dollars) to maintain a quality facility.

It should be clearly understood that these planning guidelines are just that -- guidelines. The information presented should not be used as final answers to park development but rather as a point of departure for innovative and imaginative design solutions.

Chapter 1
METHODS FOR DETERMINING VISITOR DEMAND

One of the first steps in planning facilities for any park is determining the visitor demand, or design load; that is, who the visitors are, how many are likely to use the facility and when they will come. Design load and characteristics should be determined for the present and projected for future years to permit the proper kind and phasing of development.

Beach with little use -- Naples, Florida.

Fishing Pier with heavy use -- Cape Hatteras, N.C.

The following are some of the methods of projection of recreation demand which have been developed to assist planners. The success of each method depends, of course, on the relative accuracy of the input data.

MAXIMUM CARRYING CAPACITY METHOD

When a park is located in an area of obvious heavy use, the capacity of the land to sustain recreation use without deterioration of the resource should be determined. This method assumes a thorough and comprehensive site analysis by knowledgeable professionals. (See *A Site Design Process*, Chapter 4.) [87] The maximum carrying capacity method should be considered for all parks in urban areas. Effective utilization of this approach is dependent on a corresponding analysis of the potential park users and an inventory of the regional leisure time services currently available and the level of their use. [65, 87] This is necessary in order to be able to develop a realistic program of the kinds of facilities needed. Without the knowledge and understanding of what people need/want in a park, even new urban parks may be underused.

COMPARABLE DEMAND METHOD

One or more existing recreation resource is selected to be, as closely as possible, comparable to the resource under consideration. Expected recreation use at the proposed resource is computed by analogy with the existing, comparable project(s).

The process of analogy involves several steps:

(1) Determine the population of travel time zones around the proposed park and the existing park(s) for comparison.

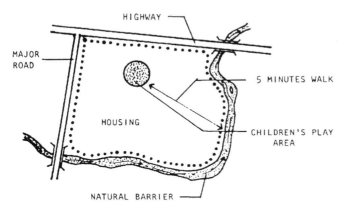

Service Area -- Children's playground and for special user groups.

(2) Determine the per-capita use at the existing area from the total population served and attendance figures from the park.

$$\frac{Use}{Population} = \text{per capita use}$$

Check attendance trends in the park(s) and population trends in the proposed service area. If specific activity use figures are available, an even more accurate projection tailored to the specific proposed program would be possible.

Example

150,000 population within 1/2 hour's driving time of the facility (the area served by the neighborhood park) and 10,000 within 15 minute's walk -- number of users is 1,500 on a maximum day or a per day, per capita use of 0.01.

(3) After establishing a ratio using the population and attendance of the existing park(s), apply this to the proposed park, which will give a projected attendance for the new facility.

Example

If the population in the proposed park's one-half hour service area is 100,000, then the number of users would be 100,000 x 0.01, or 1000.

(4) Adjust the figures to account for the influence of existing and proposed recreation developments in the zone of influence. Please note that the results of these findings may show that the facilities planned are not needed! Go back to the users and find out their desires.

The reliability of this method depends largely upon the degree of comparability between the two resources, both as to intrinsic recreation potential and as to distribution and type of population.

BURSLEY'S FORMULA [46]

Formulas and equations have been developed to determine demand and/or projected use. Bursley's Formula was one of the best early ones for projecting demand for an individual park or recreation area. This formula reflected an attempt by some members of the National Park Service in the early 1950's to establish a method for prediction of day-use demand in eastern parks. It is no longer used because of extreme variability of results.

FACILITIES DETERMINE DEMAND AND/OR
LEADERS DETERMINE DEMAND

It is believed by some resource researchers and planners that the provision of recreation facilities and/or recreation leaders themselves can create visitor demand. This is particularly true for organized sports and other supervised activities.

DETERMINATION OF VISITOR DAY CAPACITIES

Most large parks can be reached only by car. Therefore, the daily capacity of these parks can generally be determined by multiplying the number of cars times the average turnover rate times the number of people per car. It should be clearly understood that a visitor day usually consists of more than one activity day.*

*In Pennsylvania in the 1970's the average was 2.2 activity days/visitor day.

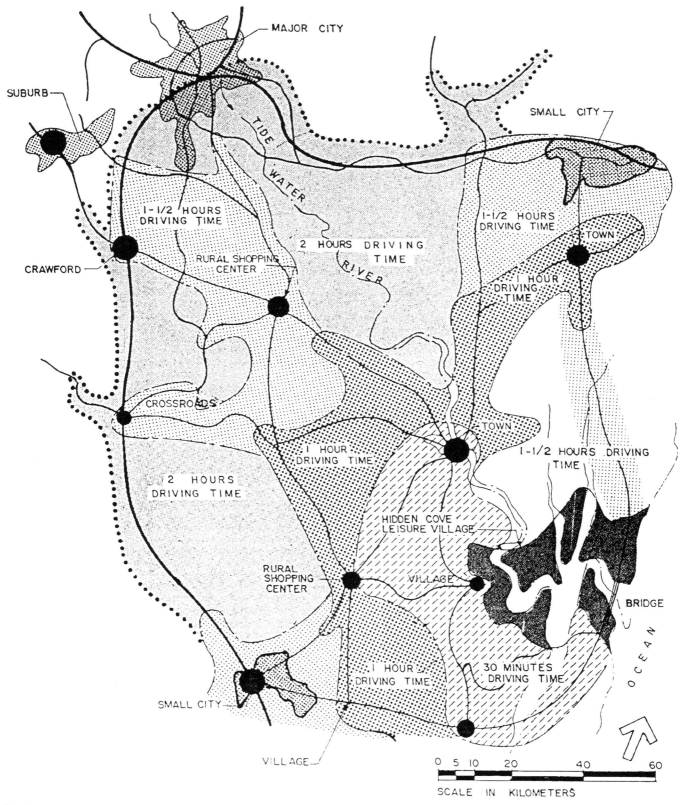

MAJOR CITY

SUBURB

SMALL CITY

1-1/2 HOURS DRIVING TIME

TIDE WATER

2 HOURS DRIVING TIME

RIVER

1-1/2 HOURS DRIVING TIME

TOWN

CRAWFORD

RURAL SHOPPING CENTER

1 HOUR DRIVING TIME

CROSSROADS

TOWN

1-1/2 HOURS DRIVING TIME

1 HOUR DRIVING TIME

2 HOURS DRIVING TIME

HIDDEN COVE LEISURE VILLAGE

RURAL SHOPPING CENTER

VILLAGE

BRIDGE

30 MINUTES DRIVING TIME

OCEAN

SMALL CITY

1 HOUR DRIVING TIME

VILLAGE

0 5 10   20   40   60

SCALE IN KILOMETERS

Service area -- large-scale park.

Maps from *A Site Design Process* by George E. Fogg, 1986. Please refer to this book for further details on ''service area.''

3

Formula

Number of cars + turnover x's number of people/car = daily capacity

Example

1000 cars + 0.05 turnover = 50 extra cars would use the facility or 1050 cars

$$1050 \times 2.8 = 2940 \text{ people per day}$$

It should be noted that if space permitted and use (people turned away) indicated, capacity could be increased by increasing the number of parking spaces. This may also necessitate increasing other site facilities.

Type of Activity	No. of People per Car (Summer)*	Average Turn-over Rate**
Sightseeing	3.2	Variable 1-10 or more
Family Picnic	3.3 to 3.5	1.0 to 1.5
Family Camping	4.0	1.0
Group Picnic	4.0	1.0
Group Camping	4.0	1.0
Boat Ramp	2.0 to 2.5	1.0 to 2.0
Freshwater Beach/ Pool Areas	3.5 to 4.0	2.0 (for pool or beach only - not for multi-use beach/ picnic etc. areas)
Coastal Beach Areas	2.7 to 3.5	1.3 to 2.0
Boat Concession	3.0 to 3.5	2.0
Overlook	3.5	Variable 1-10 or more
Golf (During main use season)	2.0	2.0 Private 3.0 Public
Restaurant	3.0	4.0
Stables	2.0	2.0 to 3.0
Equestrian Area	2.0	1.0
Fishing	2.5 to 3.0	1.0
Hiking	2.0	1.0 to 1.5 depending on trail length

* The average number of people/car using Pennsylvania State Parks was 2.8 in 1978/79 and rose to 3.3 in 1980. This figure will probably continue to vary with changes due to cost of travel, car size and type. The number of people per party is frequently larger than the number of people/car indicating that there is more than one car per party with about a 6-person-per-party the average in Pennsylvania State Parks. (21, 38, 50)

** Judgment should be used in applying turnover factors since little data is available to substantiate these turnover rates. These numbers still have not been accurately verified but are the best available.

ANNUAL CAPACITY

The annual capacity of a park can be determined by multiplying the daily capacity by the number of capacity days per year. Each area of the country has a different number of capacity days per year per facility. In Central Atlantic States a typical park might enjoy fifty capacity days of use determined as follows: three days of use per week (40 percent during the week, 20 to 25 percent on Saturday and 35 to 40 percent on Sunday) x 13 weeks summer season + 30 percent off-season use (3 x 13 + 30 percent =51). In milder areas there might be as many as 100 capacity days, while in colder climates only 40 days. These figures must be adjusted to take into consideration differences in traveling time, variety and kinds of facilities and local weather.

Example

(people/day x number of capacity day/year) + off-season use = Annual use

$$(2940 \times 50) + 30\% =$$
$$147{,}000 + 44{,}100 =$$
191,100 people/yr. would use the park.

Chapter 2
VISITOR DATA/TRENDS

Activities at a given recreation area vary over the year with cool weather (spring and fall) high in sightseeing, hiking, fishing; fall, hunting; and summer, in much of the U.S., high in picnicking, water skiing, boating and swimming.

- Length of stay in day-use areas averages 3 to 5.1 hours [21, 22, 34] With parks closer to peoples' homes, the visitors stay a shorter length of time, three to four hours. A typical state park user may experience a five to six hour stay, sightseeing only about 3.2 hours. Sundays average one-half hour longer than the rest of the week.

- Length of stay for camping is three days and two nights. [20, 35, 51]

- Numbers of day-use visitors per car vary between Sunday, 3.3; all others 3.0; spring, 2.8 to 3.0; summer 3.0 to 3.6; and fall, 2.6 to 3.0. [2, 5, 8, 12, 38, 50]

- Peak-use night for camping is Saturday -- approximately 10 to 20 percent more than Friday. [6, 34]

- The average day-use party size has been declining steadily over the last several years from 6.7 in 1971 to 4.35 in 1977 (4.06 on week days and 4.80 on weekends). This is higher than the average car capacity -- 3.3. [13, 21, 28, 35, 50, 51] There was a steady decline in the number of people per car from a high of 4.0 in 1965 to a low of 2.82 in 1979. [50] A major change to the current figure of 3.3 people per car occurred in 1980. [50] It is projected that this figure will level off at approximately 3.3 to 3.5 people per car. The average picnic party size is steadily declining and now is six. [51]

- Park satisfaction increases with age. [51]

- Transportation is a significant limitation to teenagers' attendance to parks at greater than walking/biking distance from their homes. [51]

- The major reason people do not attend parks is the availability of time. Over 90 percent of all people who say they would like to attend parks more often do not do so because, according to them, they do not have the time. [52]

- Wildlife viewing is a year-round activity which usually peaks when the objects viewed are present in their greatest numbers (the migratory season for each species).

There are ten activities which account for most recreation time for "natural-type" park users: camping, fishing, hiking, picnicking, relaxing, sightseeing/pleasure driving, swimming, sunbathing. In addition, wildlife viewing (birds, animals, plants) is strongly involved both as a primary and secondary activity.

In the teenage bracket the activities rank in this order: sunbathing (19.4%); swimming (15.3%); biking (10.3%); picnicking (8.9%); hiking (8.3%); sightseeing/pleasure driving (6.6%); camping (5.9%); relaxing (5.5%); fishing (4.8%); nature walk (4.8%). [50, 51, 52]

In the 20-29 age bracket the activities rank in this order: sunbathing (43.5%); nature walk (33.3%); camping (31.0%); sightseeing/pleasure driving (28.9%); biking (28.2%); swimming (26.8%); picnicking (26.0%); relaxing (23.2%); hiking (22.7%); fishing (16.3%). [50,51,52]

In the 30-44 age bracket the activities rank in this order: camping (42.5%); fishing (38.9%); relaxing (38.2%); hiking (37.0%); swimming (36.6%); picnicking (36.5%); sightseeing/pleasure driving (33.1%); nature walk (28.6%); biking (25.6%); sunbathing (15.7%). [50,51,52]

In the 45-64 age bracket the activities rank in this order: fishing (33.7%); biking (33.3%); relaxing (29.7%); hiking (26.0%); picnicking (25.4%); nature walk (21.4%); sightseeing/pleasure driving (20.7%); swimming (19.6%); sunbathing (19.4%); camping (17.6%). [50, 51, 52]

In the 65+ age bracket the activities rank in this order: nature walk (11.9%); sightseeing/pleasure driving (10.7%); fishing (6.3%); hiking (6.1%); relaxing (3.4%); picnicking (3.2%); camping (2.6%); biking (2.6%); sunbathing (1.9%); swimming (1.8%). [50, 51, 52]

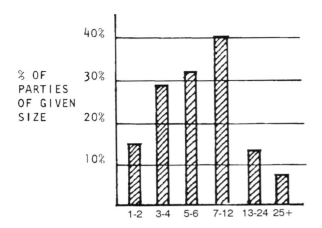

PICNICKING PARTIES

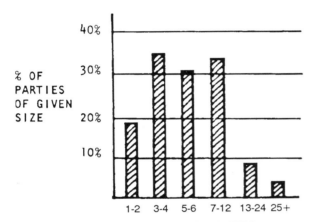

SWIMMING & BOATING (RENTAL) PARTIES

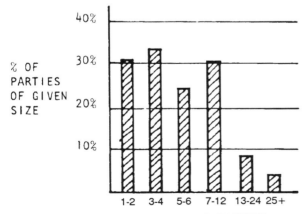

FISHING & BOATING (NON-RENTAL) PARTIES
Group size and Activities (Selected Activities)
(generalized pattern)

Picnicking parties tend to be the largest -- fishing and non-rental boating parties the smallest. [42]

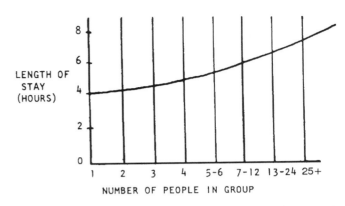

Group size and length of stay (generalized pattern).

In parks with facilities designed for large group activities, longer stays and lower turnover of visitors can be expected. [42]

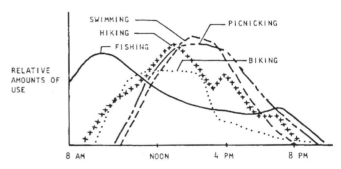

Activity and time of day (generalized pattern).

Swimming has the severest peaking in activity, and in a sense, the most excess capacity during the rest of the day. Fishing, in contrast, is fairly evenly distributed throughout the day. [42, 51]

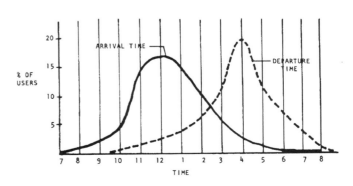

Typical arrival/departure time.

Chapter 3
PARKSCAPE

A park visitor experiences with all his senses. Therefore, park planning should enhance desirable attributes, i.e., views, pleasant odors, and eliminate or minimize obtrusive elements such as sewage plant odors, highway noise, etc.

ENHANCEMENT OF DESIRABLE ATTRIBUTES

The visual environment is of major importance to most park users. This visual experience can be enhanced by coordinating all aspects of the park development. All man-made elements should relate to the resource, either blending with it or enhancing it. Some areas to be considered are:

(1) A planned sequence of visual experience for all roads and trails.

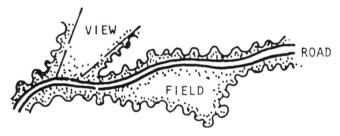

A planned sequence of views.

(See Chapter 10, "Roads and Parking".)

(2) Plantings that will harmonize with existing vegetation. Wherever possible native plant material should be used in rural and natural-type parks. A proper balance of forests and open spaces is one of the prime requisites in the overall planning of parks. The desirable amount of open space varies greatly between parks.

(3) Lands formerly used for farming and other man-controlled activities generally have straight lines of plant materials and frequently have large, unforested fields. An early planning/management decision should be made in regard to revegetation due to the long time needed to get effective results. In many areas of the country, open fields will, within ten years, be well on the way to reverting to forested spaces. It is, therefore, necessary to make an early decision to keep fields open or the decision will have been taken out of your hands by the natural successional growth.

Spring Flowers (Lupin) -- These flower fields will remain only as long as the cattle grazing continues. No cattle, few flowers. Oroville, Calif.

(4) Odors are also important in park planning. Pleasing odors can be provided by planting (pine, other evergreens, flowering plants, etc.) and by taking advantage of existing natural elements.

SCREENING UNDESIRABLE AREAS

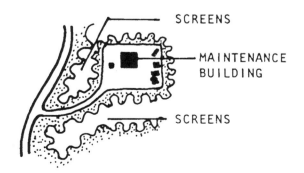

Screening.

CONSIDERATION FOR NOISE ABATEMENT

Sound waves travel in a straight line.

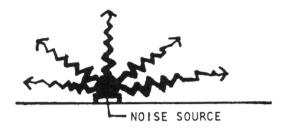

Direction sound travels.

The basic methods for noise abatement are land use planning and sound barriers.

- Land Use --

  (1) Noise sensitive developments should be located as distant from sources of noise as possible. [79]

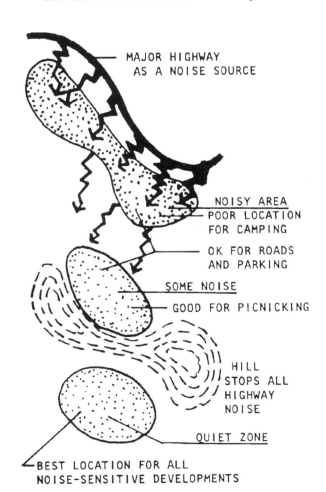

Location of activities in relationship to noise source.

  (2) Noise-compatible uses such as entrance stations, interior park roads, parking lots, park office, park maintenance, utilities, etc., should be placed in areas subject to excessive noise. [79]

  (3) Use buildings as sound barriers. [79]

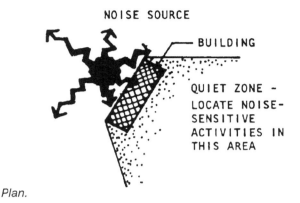

Plan.

- Noise Barriers --

"Noise barriers can be erected between noise sources and noise sensitive areas." [79] Barriers must be solid and should be easy to maintain and aesthetically pleasing. They can be made of earth (earth berms would be typically used in large-scale parks) or constructed from concrete, wood, or other solid building materials.

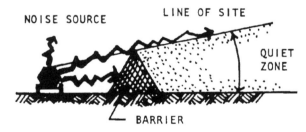

Section.

To be effective, a barrier must block the line of site. The closer the barrier to the noise source, the greater the area it will protect. [79]

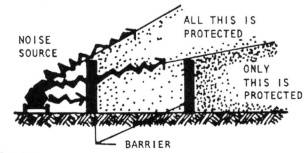

Section.

8

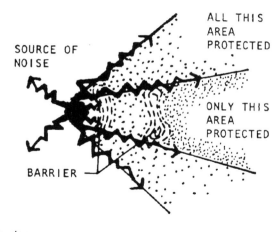

SOURCE OF NOISE

ALL THIS AREA PROTECTED

ONLY THIS AREA PROTECTED

BARRIER

Plan view.

The use of plant material for sound reduction is of limited value with only an additional 3 to 5 dBA reduction per 100' (30 m) of width of dense planting likely. The main effect of planting is psychological -- if you can't see the source of noise, it doesn't bother some people as much. Basically, plant material is useful in conjunction only with other sound abatement techniques, and then, primarily and importantly from an aesthetic standpoint.

Care should be taken to minimize offensive noises and smells through proper site selection, the provision of buffers, and the zoning of park uses, i. e., campgrounds should be located away from noise and offensive odors; sewage treatment plants should be downwind from all development areas.

Chapter 4
ENVIRONMENTALLY SENSITIVE DESIGN

The environment is composed of two basic interactive parts -- living (plants and animals) and non-living (rocks, water, climate).

LIVING + NON-LIVING = ENVIRONMENT

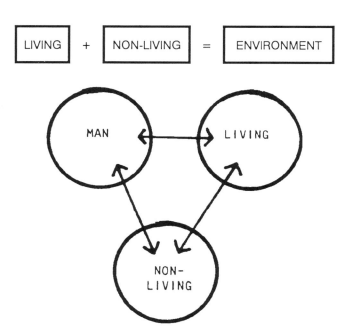

Man and the environment.

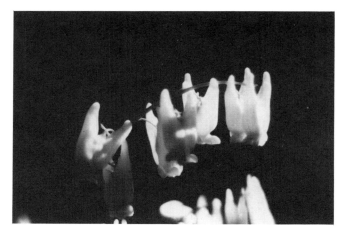

Dutchman's Breeches, Penn.

Bryce Canyon National Park, Colorado.

Man is an integral part of the environment. Everything which we as people do has an impact, either positively or negatively, on the environment.

If we choose to ignore this fact, we do so at our own peril. The development of barrier islands and coastal wetlands and the removal of mangrove forests are examples of man's actions in coastal areas which have led to major problems. Every year throughout the world billions of dollars of damage and hundreds and sometimes thousands of lives are lost due to storm damage in inappropriately developed coastal areas. On the opposite end of the environmental spectrum is the destruction of vegetation in arid environments through overgrazing and its use for fuel. This has resulted, and continues to result, in desertification (the increase of desert lands) around the world, including the United States.

In addition to these well known natural reactions to man's actions, there are many almost unnoticed examples of well meaning actions which have occurred due to little things that people have done which have had major impacts on the environment. One example of such actions is the importation of African bees into Brazil for experimental purposes. Since their escape in

11

Man and the natural environment can be successful. Wind Cave National Park, South Dakota.

South America they have multiplied and taken over the more docile local European bees used throughout Europe and the Americas for crop pollination and the making of honey. The resulting losses in crop pollination and honey production have been substantial. A second example is the use of Australian pine (Casuarina sp.) for windbreaks in Florida. Unfortunately, the pine was a very successful adaptation which has naturalized throughout the southern part of the state and is forcing out, together with two other imports (Melaleuca and Brazilian Pepper), much of the native vegetation in some areas of the state. This invasion of non-native plant material is profoundly affecting the ecology of this Southern state while similar biological invasions affect other areas of the country, i.e., gypsy moth, tumbleweed, Dutch elm disease and starlings to name only a few.

Parks are generally places where man and nature co-exist in harmony. They are, because of this, one of the prime resources for teaching the public by example about the man/environment interrelationship. It is, therefore, imperative that **ALL** development and management practices within parks be carefully evaluated in relationship to the consequences of these actions for their impact on the environment.

The Federal government and many state and local governmental jurisdictions have laws or rules governing the preparation of Environmental Impact Assessments (EIA) and Environmental Impact Studies (EIS) for any major project, and some have requirements for such studies for management actions.

An EIA is simply an analysis of the impact of a proposed action by man on the affected and surrounding environments. An EIS is a proposed course of action to be taken with the alternatives considered which must include the alternative of "no action."

Utilization of proper site planning procedure will automatically provide the necessary data with which to know the environment, the use(s) and the users. These steps are:

(1) **Research** into the needs of the users and the proposed activities.

(2) **Regional Analysis** -- data on off-site surrounding areas that may affect the site.

(3) **Site Analysis,** including existing man-made features (both historical and cultural), natural features (living and non-living), and climatic factors.

(4) **Programming and Relationships** -- What is to be built? Who is to be served? How many people? How much space do they need? The relationship between the various proposed elements should be in both written and graphic form.

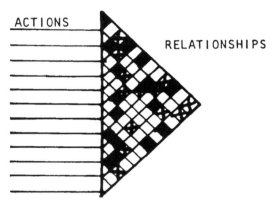

Relationship diagram.

(5) **Functional Analysis**

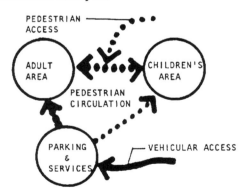

Functional analysis.

(6) **Land Use** -- The critical step where the synthesis of the site information and user needs occurs. All too frequently, the site analysis and/or programming are disregarded, and a non workable development, either for the users or the site, is the result. [87]

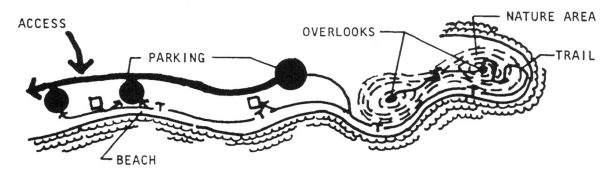

Land use concept.

For more detailed information on the site planning process, please refer to *A Site Design Process* as previously referenced.

The title of this chapter infers that design and development should be environmentally sensitive. It acknowledges that development is necessary, but further indicates that man must work with nature, not fight it.

Some factors to be considered in developments are:

- Disposal of sewage -- can it be treated and reused?
- Protection of primary and secondary dunes at beach areas.

Section through beach and dune.

- Use of elevated boardwalks in wet areas and swamps. See Chapter 8, "Trails" for additional information.

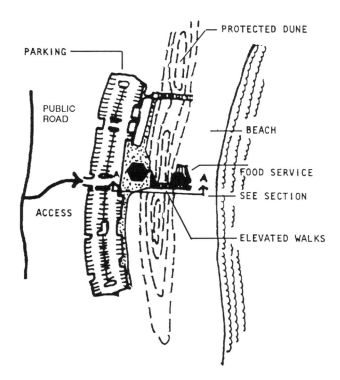

Coastal development.

Boardwalk connecting parking lot to coastal beach. Clam Pass County Park, Naples, Florida.

- Securing detailed topographic information so that parking lots, buildings and other physical developments will fit the land, not change it.
- Retention on site of surface water run-off generated by the development.
- Use of porous pavements, where possible, to permit water to penetrate to the aquifer. See Chapter 10, "Roads and Parking" for additional details.

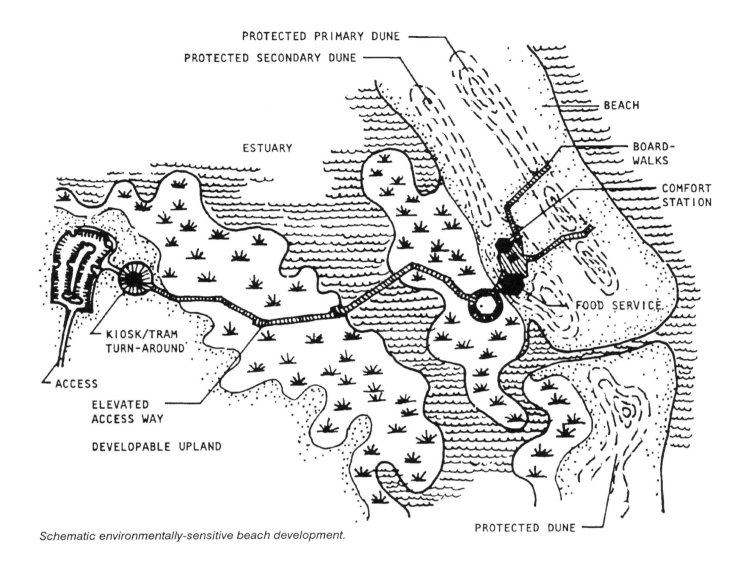

PROTECTED PRIMARY DUNE

PROTECTED SECONDARY DUNE

BEACH

BOARD-WALKS

COMFORT STATION

ESTUARY

FOOD SERVICE

KIOSK/TRAM TURN-AROUND

ACCESS

ELEVATED ACCESS WAY

DEVELOPABLE UPLAND

PROTECTED DUNE

Schematic environmentally-sensitive beach development.

• Use of xeriscape practices. This is especially important in the desert, arid and semi-arid environments, and those areas where supplemental watering is commonly done. Wherever possible plants that will grow in the environment without additional water being required for their maintenance should be used. Minimize the use of turf where irrigation will be required.

• Provision of educational displays and exhibits to help people understand their environment and how man affects the environment by his actions. See Chapter 7, "Interpretive Facilities."

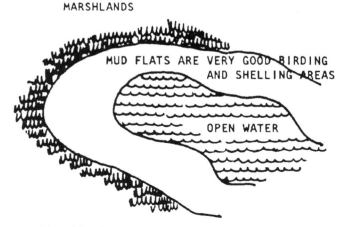

MARSHLANDS

MUD FLATS ARE VERY GOOD BIRDING AND SHELLING AREAS

OPEN WATER

Marsh/mud flats/open water.

14

- Preparation of an environmentally sensitive management plan to accompany any development. See *Management Planning for Park and Recreation Areas* as previously referenced for detailed information on what a management plan is and how to prepare it. [65]

- Provide, where possible, for a diverse habitat which will encourage a wide variety of bird and animal life. This would put an emphasis on the edges and transition zones, i.e., fields/forests, swamps/open water, river and estuarine tidal flats, ocean water.

THE EDGE IS MOST PRODUCTIVE AREA FOR WILDLIFE

Woods/Field edge.

Chapter 5
PARK ARCHITECTURE

Most park development requires structural elements. All park structures must relate in a proper manner to their functions and reflect a meaningful and logical concept based upon the environment of the specific area involved. Buildings should also relate to the topography and "feeling" of the land and should be designed as an integral part of the setting; not forced upon it.

Building form reflects the land, comfort stations, Bluffer's Park, Toronto, Canada.

The buildings must show concern for the scale of particular sites; relationships to existing and proposed facilities reflected by the master plan; and a design continuity throughout the park including such elements as benches, fountains, play areas and other features.

Considerations include:

- Need or use the building is to serve.
- The existing topography and its future planned development.
- Subsurface conditions.
- Wind directions.
- Orientation to the sun.
- Drainage conditions (air and water).
- Availability of utilities.
- Means of access.
- Locations of trees to be preserved and other natural features such as rock formations or overlook areas.
- Necessary winterizing and/or off-season "mothballing" for facilities of summertime use such as bathhouses, pools and picnic areas, comfort stations.
- Materials -- maintenance, durability, economy.
- Aesthetics.
- Handicapped accessibility.
- Energy self-sufficiency, where possible.

BUILDING CONSTRUCTION IN FLOOD PLAIN AREAS

The ideal design for buildings to be located in flood areas would be such that all portions of the structure are above the maximum flood level ("C" curve). In order to minimize construction, operations and maintenance costs, yet provide recreation facilities at a desirable location, the following should be considered:

(1) All major permanent buildings, especially restaurants, should be located above the "C" curve flood level.

(2) Minor-type concession buildings in which limited food and/or novelties are sold, and bathhouses which can be subject to occasional flooding, should be placed at or above the 100-year flood level.

(3) Buildings such as boat houses, pavilions and comfort stations may be considered for levels where flooding occurs at greater frequency than 100 years.

In all cases, structures constructed below "C" curve flood level should be anchored to prevent flotation and should be constructed of materials which can withstand submergence and can be easily cleaned.

An alternate approach to constructing permanent structures within flood plains is to use portable buildings and/or floating structures.

17

Factors to consider would include:

(1) Aesthetics.

(2) Modular construction for expansion and ease of movement.

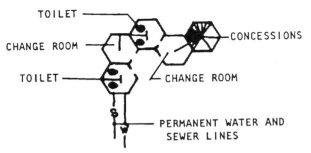

Portable structures.

(3) Anchorage of floating or portable structures where stream currents are not likely to cause damage.

HURRICANE AND STRONG WIND PRONE AREAS

Most coastal areas on the East and Gulf coast are subject to occasional and sometimes frequent hurricanes, and many areas in the middle Western plains experience frequent strong winds and sometimes severe tornadic activity. Any buildings to be constructed in these environments must, in addition to designing for flooding covered in previous sections, consider the following:

(1) Wind protection --

    • Building orientation for protection of user areas from strong winds.

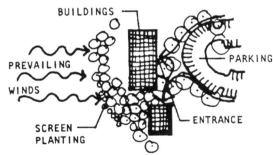

Buildings as a wind screen.

Sun/wind screen.

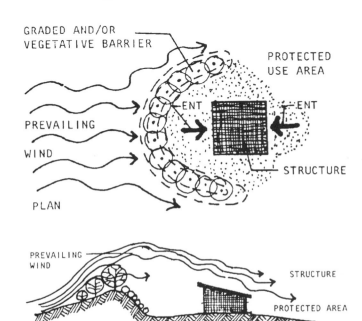

Movable picnic facilities. White Sands, New Mexico. Photo by George Medlicot.

    • Storm shutters on window openings to prevent window breakage from wind driven debris.

    • Grading to direct wind flows.

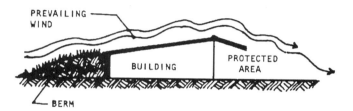

PREVAILING WIND

BUILDING

PROTECTED AREA

BERM

Grading and/or planting and/or building design can provide protection from strong winds.

- Planting of wind tolerant species.

(2) Electrical failure --

- Provision of emergency generators.

(3) Storm shelters in locations subject to tornadic activity must be provided.

BUILDING RENOVATIONS

Many park areas, when first acquired, contain one or more buildings which have some use potential. Unless a structure is architecturally or historically significant or it adds significantly to the aesthetics/character of the park, it should be used for park purposes only if it will economically satisfy a need, i.e., will it be cost effective? Building renovation and repair for public use is expensive, frequently costing more than a new structure, and is time consuming.

Blue Ball Inn, restored and turned over to Historic Society to use and maintain as headquarters for Society. Little Buffalo State Park, Penn.

Factors to consider:

(1) Complete evaluation of existing condition and repairs necessary to put or keep it in good condition.

(2) Intended use.

(3) Changes needed to meet building code requirements.

(4) Changes required to make building cost effective - insulation, water, lighting, heat, etc.

ENERGY REDUCTION IDEAS

All architectural elements must consider every feasible means to minimize the use of energy.

(1) Orientation is critical. Factors to consider:

- Orientation to sun -- maximum winter heat gathering and retention; minimum summer heat absorption; maximum heat dissipation.
- Wind direction by seasons.

(2) Design

- Minimum windows facing north and into most frequent winter storm winds.
- Adequate ventilation.
- Adequate insulation, the "R" factor.
- Consider low profile and depressed buildings to take advantage of the insulating qualities of earth.

(3) Heat Sources

- Solar -- active
          -- passive - preferable.

  Show the systems off through integration with the interpretive program.

- A variety of types of heating -- firewood, electrical, fuel oil, gas.

(4) Landscaping

- Screen planting (evergreen) for reducing strong winds.
- Deciduous planting for summer shade and winter sun.
- Grading to divert winds, eliminate cold pockets.

Chapter **6**
HANDICAPPED ACCESSIBILITY

International Symbol for Handicapped Accessibility

Park and recreation areas and facilities must be made accessible to the handicapped. Approximately 12 percent of Americans are handicapped in some manner requiring physical modifications in typical construction techniques, with less than 1 percent of the population confined to wheelchairs (the single group most likely to require the full range of accessibility features). [18] These modifications not only will make the facilities accessible to the handicapped, they will make them much more usable by the elderly. This is particularly important since those fifty-five and over make up the most rapidly expanding segment of our population. [65] Although reference is made throughout this book to making facilities accessible to the handicapped, this chapter is intended to focus attention on the subject.

GENERAL

The handicapped/disabled do not desire to be segregated from the mainstream of society. Do not provide separate special facilities for them for this only draws attention to their disability, frequently causing negative attitudes by them and the rest of society about their disabilities. In addition, most handicapped people arrive at the park accompanied by friends and/or family who frequently have no handicaps.

Prior to determining the type, location and extent of the facilities to be made accessible, work closely with those individuals and organizations who are disabled and who would be likely users. In addition, consult:

American National Standard Specifications for Making Building and Facilities Accessible to and Usable by Physically Handicapped People A. N. S. I. A117.1 - 1980 or its latest revision.

The Uniform and Federal Accessibility Standards distributed by the National Recreation and Park Association.

Not **all** activities and facilities (i.e., backpack camping accessible to wheelchairs) need to be made accessible to **all** handicapped, but at least some of each **kind** of activity or facility should be made accessible (i.e., typical family campsite).

PARKING

- A reasonable number of surfaced parking spaces but at least one located as close to and on an accessible route to the desired facility/activity as possible. The following number of handicapped parking is required to meet federal accessibility standards:

Total Parking	Minimum Spaces
1 to 25	1
26 to 50	2
51 to 75	3
76 to 100	4
101 to 150	5
151 to 200	6
201 to 300	7
301 to 400	8
401 to 500	9
501 to 1000	2% of Total
1001 & over	20 + 1 for each 100 over 1000

- Parking overhang shall not reduce the accessibility route to less than the 36 inch (915 cm) minimum.
- A curb break or ramp must be provided to the accessibility route.
- Slopes shall be 2 percent or less in handicapped parking section of parking lot.
- The handicapped parking can be distributed throughout the lot to provide the best accessibility to the site and facilities.
- All handicapped parking spaces shall be signed with the international symbol of accessibility as reserved for the handicapped and visible when the space is filled.

Handicapped Access -- Also works as a bicycle access.
Washington, D.C.

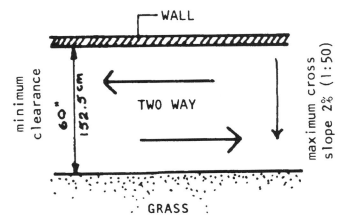

Two-way walk.

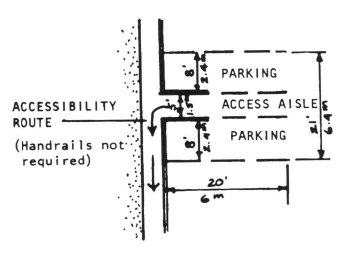

Parking.

ACCESSIBLE ROUTE - There shall be at least one accessible route within the boundary of the site from the point(s) of access to the site to the accessible facility(ies). [78]

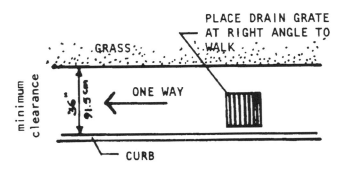

One-way walk.

- No objects shall protrude more than 4 inches (10 cm) into an accessible route if they are mounted between 27 inches and 80 inches high (68 to 200 cm). If objects are built they shall not, however, reduce the clear space to less than the required 36 inches (91.5 cm) minimum. [78]

- Ground surfaces along accessible routes (including floors, walks, ramps, stairs and curb breaks) shall be stable, firm and slip-resistant and shall not exceed 5 percent (1:20). Soft loose surfaces (sand, clay, etc.) and irregular surfaces (cobbles, rough stone, etc.) should be avoided.

- Changes in level up to 1/4 inch (6 mm) are "OK"; 1/4 to 1/2 inch (6 to 13 mm) can be handled with a 1:2 slope and anything greater will be treated as a ramp.

- Drainage grates -- Place perpendicular to the direction of travel with the openings no greater than 1/2 inch (13 mm).

- Emergency Egress -- Where fire codes require more than one emergency exit, then more than one exit shall be provided for the handicapped. [78]

- Stairs on accessible routes must have a minimum of tread of 11 inches (28 cm); no open risers shall be permitted; and handrails shall be provided on both sides of the stairway.

- Elevators may be provided for elevation changes in lieu of ramps and stairs.

RAMPS

- Make all ramps with the least slope possible.

- Maximum slope 1:12 with the maximum rise of 30 inches (760 cm).

- Ramps with a rise of over 30 inches (760 cm) will have landings at the top and the bottom of each run.

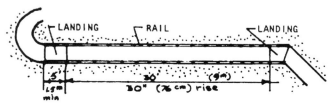

Ramp/Handrails.

- Handrails are required on both sides of all ramps (except curb ramps) of greater than six inches (150 cm) or six feet (1.8 m) in length.

DOORWAYS

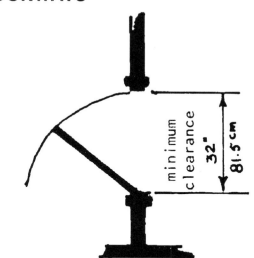

Doorways.

TOILET FACILITIES

Each public or common use toilet building shall have toilet facilities for handicapped. [78] Reference Federal Accessibility Standards for required details. Also see Chapter 11, "Utilities".

DRINKING FOUNTAINS

Accessible drinking fountains must be provided with a clear paved space in front of 48 inches (120 cm) wide and 30 inches (76 cm) deep, and the fountain shall be no higher than 36 inches (91.5 cm) with a clearance under the fountain of at least 27 inches (68.5 cm) of a minimum depth of 17 inches (43 cm).

Chapter 7
INTERPRETIVE FACILITIES

The purpose of an interpretive program is to relate and explain to people the natural, historic and/or cultural values of the park and the surrounding lands and waters through various means so that these values will be made more meaningful and enjoyable.

Interpretive information -- Alice Springs Natural History Park, Australia.

Before including interpretive programs and facilities in a park plan, an inventory of interpretive opportunities should be made and a program concept developed. It should be clearly understood that it takes a great deal of research and time to prepare a good interpretive program plus adequate staff and operating funds to keep it in operation.

OBJECTIVES OF THE
INTERPRETIVE PROGRAM [1]

• To help the visitor enjoy the park through better understanding and appreciation of its purposes and resources.

• To promote intelligent use of park resources and facilities through educational programs and activities.

139,940

• To help the visitor develop a sense of responsibility concerning the conservation and use of our natural resources.

• To instill in the visitor a sense of appreciation for the natural and man-made resources of the park in order to reduce willful destruction and vandalism of park property.

• To help the visitor increase his knowledge and understanding of his role in the natural environment.

• To help the visitor understand, enjoy, appreciate, and develop respect for his environment.

• To develop a knowledge and understanding of ecology.

• To help the visitor develop an interest in past history.

CONSIDERATIONS

• Adequate access to the interpretive facilities is a pre-requisite for use.

• Heavily used areas may require substantial parking and often need sanitary facilities and other support facilities.

• Handicapped accessibility is necessary for all buildings and should be provided to as many on-the-ground sites as design will permit. (See Chapter 6, "Handicapped Accessibility".)

FACILITIES

Nature Centers — should be used where necessary for the purpose of displaying materials associated with flora, fauna and other phases of the natural resources relative to the park environment. Should only be considered where adequate staff is available. Usually only the very largest parks can afford a separate nature area (s). Generally combined in a limited form with "visitor center" or park office.

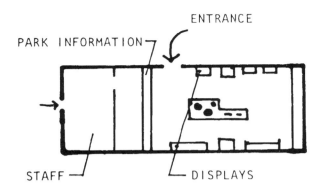

Nature Center/Park Office.

Museums — to be constructed in appropriate situations. They combine the features of a Nature Center with other exhibits explaining the "history" of a site. These buildings are even more expensive than a Nature Center to build and equally as expensive, dollar-wise and in manpower, to operate.

Guided and Self-Guided Nature and Historic Trails — should be studied for inclusion in all parks. This is the "heart" of most park interpretive programs.

GUIDED & SELF-GUIDED TRAILS
REQUIREMENTS

- Trailside information displays and/or, where appropriate, self-guiding brochures coordinated with trail markers are a necessity for visitor enjoyment of educational trails. They permit use during all seasons and do not require the services of a trained staff person on a regular basis.

Interpretive marker on coconut shell. Self-guiding brochure tells about the exhibit. (A traditional Hawaiian game.) City of Refuge National Park, Hawaii.

- Width -- adequate to provide for anticipated use with wider areas at interest points along trail.

- Nature trails should be kept as inconspicuous as possible to keep the effect of the natural surroundings.

- Make the trail interesting, but do not fake what is not there.

- Do not connect areas of heavy use in parks with a nature trail; it will become a thoroughfare and lose its natural character.

- Avoid switchbacks or doubling back -- they invite shortcutting.

- Consider rest areas along the way on longer trails.

- Surfacing depends on amount of use -- varies from wood chips to blacktop.

- Trails should be loop types, ending at the point of beginning and generally one-half to two miles (.8 to 3.2 km) long.

- Where possible, provide for handicapped access. When handicapped access is provided the trail surface must be hard, firm and smooth (no sand, clay or cobbles).

GUIDED AND SELF-GUIDED CAR TOURS OR TRAILS — can be effectively used to interpret the scene in areas where this form of locomotion is the most effective means of interpretation. Self-guiding vehicular trails are frequently used in large parks, both along major through roads and in specially designed interpretive trails. See Chapter 25, "Non Consumptive Wildlife," for a typical vehicular trail. The only addition to such a layout would be interpretive signs or markers.

Interpretive signs.

Trail markers keyed to interpretive brochures.

BICYCLE BOAT AND BRIDLE TRAILS — can be constructed in appropriate situations.

INTERPRETIVE SHELTERS (KIOSKS) AND WAYSIDE EXHIBITS — to be installed where on-site interpretation can be effectively utilized. Keep them simple and vandal-resistant.

Park information.
Sydney Botanical Gardens, Australia.

SCENIC OVERLOOKS AND OBSERVATION TOWERS — as appropriate. Consider incorporating in park structures, including water towers.

EVENING CAMPFIRE PROGRAMS — can be effectively utilized in any area of 150+ units for overnight park use. Campfire facilities should be so located as to minimize disturbance of those not desiring to participate. They can vary in size and complexity from a simple campfire circle to formal amphitheaters. Space may serve also for Sunday morning church services (see Chapter 13, "Overnight Use").

Campfire.

AMPHITHEATER

- Location

    (1) Within 500 feet (150 m) of adequate parking. Possibly combined with concession parking or day-use parking, thus making dual use of this resource.

    (2) Within walking distance of the overnight accommodations when possible -- 1000' (300 m).

    (3) Adequate visual and sound separation from campsites.

    (4) Can sometimes utilize visitor center facilities.

    (5) Accessible to handicapped.

Amphitheater -- Craters of the Moon National Monument, Idaho.

- Design
  (1) Capacity is determined by the planned type of program, potential day-use audience and proximity to the overnight accommodations. Approximately one-quarter to one-half of the overnight-use capacity (varies with quality of the evening program and distance from the campground) will participate.

  (2) Orientation -- screen must be in evening shade, facing east.

  (3) Projector stand -- 40 feet (12 m) from screen for most areas, greater distance for larger audiences.

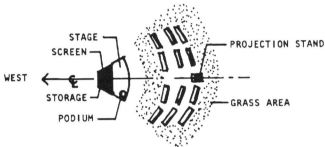

Amphitheater layout.

  (4) Sloping site is desirable, or major earth work will be necessary to get proper visual exposure.

  (5) Facilities needed:
      (a) benches for normal capacity audience - level space for handicapped on handicapped-accessible routes;
      (b) stage;
      (c) screen (rear projection is best but not required).

  (6) Facilities desirable:
      (a) Lighting -- along walks, flood lighting in seating area;
      (b) Drinking fountain(s).

  (7) Utilities
      (a) Electricity -- needed;
      (b) Water -- desirable.

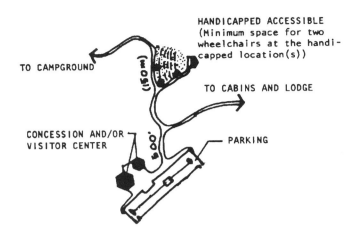

Amphitheater location.

ENVIRONMENTAL EDUCATION CENTERS – Some governmental agencies and private non-profit organizations have developed facilities that will supplement school education programs in environmental education. These facilities are for in-depth training of young people. Another major function is to educate the teachers in the potential of using the total environment in their teaching process. They exist to provide a way for society to become aware of the potential for both good and bad that man can experience within his environment.

VISITOR CENTER – Most large parks require some type of visitor contact point where information about the park, its facilities, and its programs can be secured. A simple counter in the park office may suffice; however, major parks may benefit from a more elaborate visitor center with displays covering the park's natural and cultural heritage. In most instances the facilities should be combined with the park's administrative activities permitting the clerical staff to provide a dual function during low-user periods. The visitor center should be located on the major access road and as close to the park entrance as possible.

DEMONSTRATION FARMS – Major park systems, especially those serving urban populations, should consider developing a demonstration farm. They are of great interest to adults as well as children. Children from three to ten, together with their parents and teachers constitute the major clientele during the week, with families and older people the major users on the weekends. Main use occurs during the good weather seasons, generally April to November in the northern half of the country. Summers frequently will see a significant reduction in use during the week days. A demonstration farm can only be effective when adequately interpreted. Visitors and farming activities do not readily mix and careful planning in conjunction with the farm staff and the interpretive personnel is a necessity. Some factors to consider in addition to the interpretive ones are the need for adequate staffing, including both maintenance and interpretive personnel, availability of existing land and buildings, parking (both car and bus), sanitary facilities, food and other concession operations.

Demonstration farm -- Toronto Harbor Park, Canada.

Chapter 8
TRAILS

There are nine commonly identified trail types: hiking, biking, equestrian, cross country skiing, water (canoe, raft, boats), all terrain vehicles (ATV), motorcycle, off-road vehicles, and snowmobiles. They have been divided into motorized and non-motorized categories. This chapter will cover only hiking, biking and equestrian trails. Water trails is covered in Chapter 17, "Boating"; cross country skiing and snowmobiles are covered in Chapter 20, "Winter Use Areas"; and motorcycle and off-road vehicles are covered in Chapter 9, "Special Use Facilities."

NON-MOTORIZED TRAILS
GENERAL

Trails should be provided where they enhance public enjoyment of the environment and utilization of fish and wildlife resources. Trails provide enjoyable, safe, and environmentally sensitive passage for foot travelers, equestrians and bicyclists. There is no better way to convey the true spirit of the out-of-doors to the park user than to provide an opportunity to see the park by trail.

There are two kinds of trails; one is primarily for trail activities -- the experience of being on the trail -- and the other is to provide effective and economical access to and between the areas of recreation development and/or points of interest.

Important factors to consider when designing either type of trail are alignment, terrain, topography, cover, aesthetic value, points of interest, road crossings or other potential dangers, and final destination.

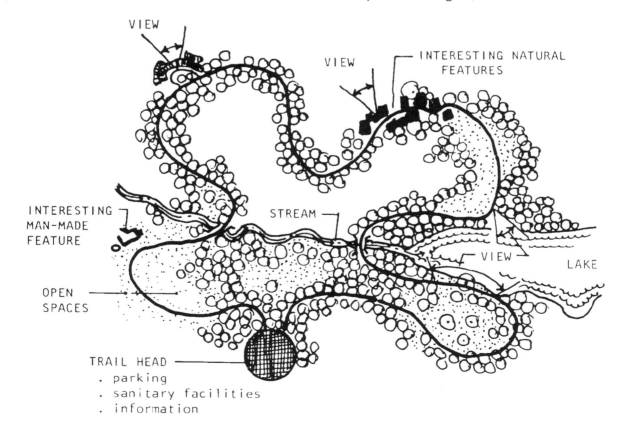

Conceptual trail layout.

Zoning of trails for the types of use intended is necessary, i.e., motorized vehicles are not compatible in primitive areas and snowmobiles conflict with skiers.

Parks can serve ideally as trailheads (terminus points) for comprehensive trails systems; such trail systems are complemented by the park facilities. A park-administered contact point can provide for user safety, control of use, and trail information.

Trail use is subject to a continuous series of seasonal changes which must be considered in any trail planning.

Whenever possible, hikers and horseback riders should be kept separate for sanitary as well as safety reasons. Consideration should be given to developing trails with adequate width -- minimum of six feet (1.8 m) -- for service and emergency vehicles. Trails can serve as fire trails but must then have a minimum width of eight feet (2.4 m) for emergency fire equipment access.

LAYOUT -- Trails should have a variety of experiences taking advantage of views (vistas and intimate), traversing ridges and valleys, open spaces and forested areas, and, where possible, water bodies. [55]

- Vary trail alignments.
  - Avoid "sameness."
  - Take advantage of natural features.
  - Vary vegetative cover.
  - Change grade.

- Trails should fit the land -- don't fight contours unless there is no other choice. All construction should be inconspicuous.

- Consider all the senses: sight, touch, hearing (both good sounds and annoying sounds), and, where possible, smell.

- Avoid straight lines (monotonous).

- Avoid poor soil conditions (wet areas, erosion prone areas).

- Utility lines.
  - Avoid where possible. In urban and suburban areas, however, utility R/W may be the only relatively undeveloped space where trails can be constructed.
  - Cross as quickly as possible and screen from view with topography or vegetation.

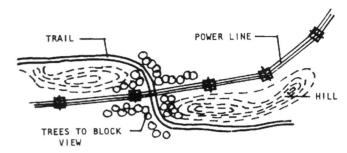

Trail crossing of utility line.

DRAINAGE -- Drainage is one of the most important items in trail construction and is often the most neglected.

Water must be kept within manageable limits to prevent damage from erosion and keep a trail usable during the travel season.

- Sheet water drainage, which occurs where water drains from a short uphill slope and is drained across the trail in a sheet, is most desirable.

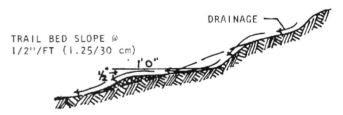

Trail bed (all low-use density trails).

- Water stops and gutters (made from natural materials) are necessary on many trails which traverse steep hills.

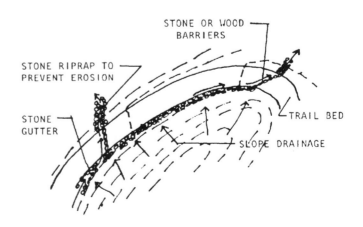

Trail surface drainage.

- Wet areas should be avoided if at all possible; if you must cross such areas, it takes care and they are expensive to build and maintain. If wet areas are not avoidable, foot trails can be made of large flat rocks 18 inches (45 cm) o.c. or elevated wood walkways.

- All natural drainage must be considered for a minimum of a 100-year flood. Drainage structures **must** be kept inconspicuous and all end sections should be finished in native materials.

- Make sure that trails do not become drainage channels.

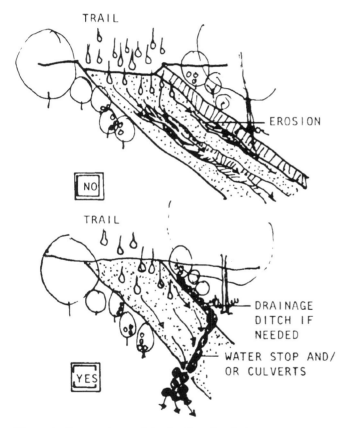

Steep trails need special attention to drainage to prevent erosion.

STREAM CROSSINGS -- Trail users, as almost all recreationists, like to see bodies of water. Where trails come in contact with water, special care must be taken, especially at crossings. The preferred crossing will minimize the visual and physical intrusion on the stream environment; fords for horses, inconspicuous bridges for all others.

HIKING TRAILS

USER CHARACTERISTICS

Short hikes, or nature walks, appeal to all age groups. However, longer hikes and backpacking tend to be the domain of the younger and the more educated recreationists. [42, 51]

ACTIVITIES [42]

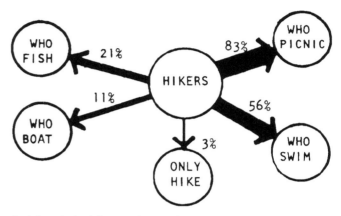

Activity mix for hikers using parks.

Trail use as an activity by itself has become one of the areas of recreation growth.

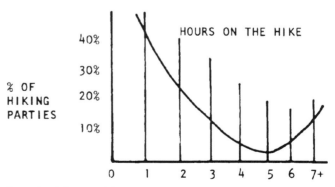

Length of time on hike by percentage of hikers.

In national parks, the "average" hike is a four-to-five hour, one-day trip. Only one in ten hikers stays overnight.

ATTITUDES [43]

Half the hikers in wilderness areas preferred not to meet horsemen.

Crowding on trails is not a serious problem in terms of hiker satisfaction even in wilderness areas. However, loss of solitude at campsite does lower satisfaction.

Hikers feel that trails should be designed to provide:

(1) Maximum scenic beauty.

(2) Large rock outcrops where hikers can observe the surrounding landscape.

(3) Natural openings in forest stands where there is variety in lighting, color, temperature and view distances.

GENERAL -- Hiking trails, where possible, should be for hiking only. Under no circumstances are motorized vehicles compatible with non-motorized uses. Barriers such as logs, stairways, and narrow stream crossings can be utilized to discourage non-pedestrian users.

LENGTH -- Trails are generally classified as short (pleasure walking), long loop and cross-country. They should be loop-type returning to the point of beginning except for cross-country ones.

Short trails: frequently urban/suburban in nature and connecting parks or other facilities -- generally 30 minutes to 2 hours maximum, 1 to 3 miles long (1.5 to 5 km).

Long loop: 7 to 14 miles (10 to 20 km), a one-day hike.

Cross-country: 20 miles (30 km) or longer with as few road crossings as possible and one or more overnight stops.

TRAILSIDE CAMPING -- Cross-country trails should have overnight stopping points every 7 to 10 miles (10 to 15 km). These areas require a source of potable water, sanitary facilities and rubbish containers. They should be located off the main trail far enough away to give the camper privacy from the trail users and sufficiently far away or screened from any noise source to provide the desired solitude. They also should be at least one mile (1.5 km) from the nearest parking area to discourage their use as a "hike-in" type campground. Access for service vehicles is also desirable. (See Chapter 13, "Overnight Use" - Primitive Camping.)

Trail shelters are particularly desirable in areas having frequent precipitation during the use seasons. Shelters should blend into the countryside.

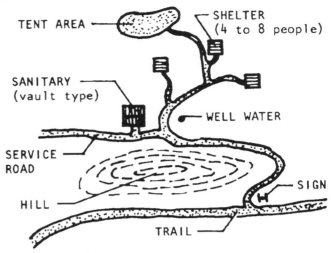
Trailside camping.

Trailside shelter.

Trailside shelter -- Laural Ridge State Park, Pennsylvania.

GRADIENTS -- Trail gradients that are satisfactory from the standpoint of erosion prevention and control will ordinarily be suitable for hiking use. Maximum sustained gradient should not exceed ten percent. When

34

pitches in excess of ten percent must be used, the length and steepness of these should be governed by sound engineering judgment and cannot be defined by formula or arbitrary limitations. The extent of such pitches should be broken at short intervals by gently sloping sections of trail and the number of these sharp pitches should be kept to a minimum. To avoid steep gradients considerable trail distance can be side hill construction with variable side slopes. Avoid switchbacks wherever possible since this leads to short cutting and ultimately to erosion problems.

SHORT CUTS

WIDTH OF TRAILS -- The width of the trail varies according to its use. Short trails within heavily used recreation areas will normally be considerably wider than the trails removed from heavily used areas.

Tread width: 2 feet (60 cm) minimum; 6 to 8 feet (1.8 m to 2.4 m) for pleasure walking or in areas with steep dropoffs.

Clearing width: 4 feet (1.2 m) minimum.

Height of clearing: 7 feet (2.1 m) minimum.

Clearing for trail construction should be kept to a minimum. All vegetation removed should be cut flush with the ground. Remove all hazardous material. Some obstruction such as fallen logs and large rocks at trailheads are desirable to discourage vehicular use.

Trails for winter use should have a correspondingly higher clearing line depending on snow depth. (See Chapter 20, "Cross-Country Skiing".)

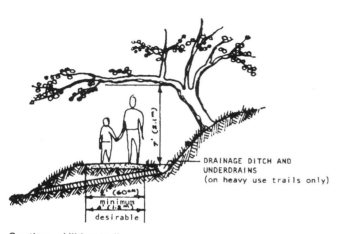

DRAINAGE DITCH AND UNDERDRAINS (on heavy use trails only)

minimum
desirable

Section -- Hiking trail.

CUT SLOPES -- The cut slopes may be as steep as the material will stand without serious erosion. Most soils will stand with a 1/2:1 or 3/4:1 cut slope. Care must be taken to establish an angle or repose that will insure a stable slope condition indefinitely and which will permit vegetation to grow.

SURFACING -- Surfacing is a costly item in trail construction and natural materials should be used where feasible, especially in back country trails. Basically the finish should discourage erosion and encourage natural cover. Bituminous or other materials may be needed on trails in highly used recreation areas or at points of concentrated use.

SIGNING -- Adequate signing is essential at trailheads, intersections, and at locations on the trail where the direction is not readily discernible. Trail signs should include mileage to various points of interest along the way, along with the total trail mileage. Frequent mileage markers along the trail are helpful to the hiker and useful in the operations and maintenance of the park.

Interpretive markers and information are desirable features on any type of trail.

VIEWS -- Selective clearing to enhance views is sometimes desirable, especially in areas of dense understory vegetation.

BICYCLE TRAILS

Class 1 bike path.
Cape Cod National Seashore, Massachusetts.

Bicycling as a recreation activity has remained at a relatively high level for the last 19 years with approximately 10 million new bicycles per year being sold of all types. The only significant trend appears to be a substantial increase in all terrain bikes which appears to be increasing dramatically as a percentage of sales from 9.2 percent in 1987 to 21 percent in 1988. With the continuation of high energy costs and the physical fitness awareness, bicycling will undoubtedly continue as the most popular recreation activity with approximately forty to fifty percent of the population involved.

BIKEROUTE (Class 3) -- A shared right of way located on lightly traveled streets and roadways designated solely by "bikeroute" signs. These signs help encourage use and warn motorists that bicyclists may be using the road. This is the least expensive route but it is dangerous especially on narrow back country roads where it is most frequently used.

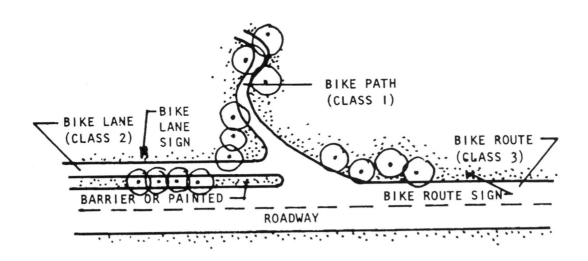

Use classification of bikeways.

USE CLASSIFICATION [55]

Bikeways encompass a wide range of development options from shared right-of-way with other vehicles to trails reserved exclusively for bicyclists. The following are nationally accepted classifications:

BIKEPATH (Class 1) - The safest system of bicycle use completely separated from motor vehicle traffic and where conflicts with pedestrians, equestrians, and motor vehicles are limited. The bikepath is often located within parks and neighborhoods and is often used to connect shopping centers, schools and areas of scenic interest. Approximately 50 to 80 bikers per mile of trail per day can be accommodated on such a trail. [70]

BIKELANE (Class 2) -- A restricted segment of a shared street or roadway for use by bicycles where, at least, a colored stripe serves as a separation between the two users. The stripe provides psychological rather than physical protection. The barrier may also be physical, such as the placement of plant materials, guardrails or a type of low curbing.

Both the bikelane and the bikeroute are dependent upon existing roadways for their alignments as they either share or closely follow these vehicular corridors. They should be developed in conjunction with new or reconstructed roadways, and therefore would be used mainly as transportation routes. Close coordination with the appropriate transportation department is a necessity to make Class 2 and 3 bikeways a reality.

With the significant increase in all terrain type bikes, it may be desirable to consider special challenging all terrain riding areas similar to mechanized ATV trails.

GENERAL -- Trails should be so designed that the rider can have many interesting and exciting visual experiences. In addition, consideration should be given to adding interpretive information along the trail.

LOCATION -- When determining the location of Class 1 Bikepaths, consideration should be given to utilizing abandoned canal towpaths, abandoned railroads, utility R/W and utility corridors. Close coordination of planning efforts with transportation officials in the various jurisdictions traversed by the trail is a necessity. [15]

LENGTH – The average cyclist can easily sustain speeds of 10 mph (16 kmh) on level terrain. Trails should be designed with varying lengths and preferably with a loop system. Three to five miles (5 to 8 km) would be a minimum length with trails of 10 to 30 miles (15 to 50 km) desirable. Touring trails can be much longer and can tie into youth hostels and campgrounds for overnight stopovers.

GRADIENT -- Bicycle trails should follow the contour wherever possible. Bicycle gradients should not exceed 10 percent and pitches from four to eight percent should occur for short intervals only. When long grades are unavoidable, provide frequent, wide, level areas where the less-than-average cyclist can dismount without difficulty and rest.

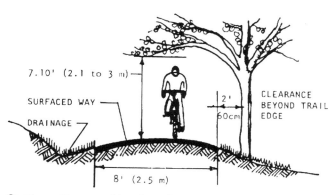

7.10' (2.1 to 3 m)

SURFACED WAY

DRAINAGE

2' 60cm

CLEARANCE BEYOND TRAIL EDGE

8' (2.5 m)

Section -- Two-way bicycle trail.

WIDTH OF TRAILS -- A desirable width for a two-way trail is eight feet (2.4 m) with a minimum recommended width of five feet (1.5 m) and then only on trails with low use. Curves should be widened by four feet (1.2 m) if not banked. To add variety, divided trails could be used to bypass boulders, trees, a descriptive marker, etc.

CLEARING -- *Vertical:* All obstructions under seven feet (2.1 m); desirable - everything under 10 feet (3 m).

Horizontal: All obstructions beyond the trail edge for a minimum of two feet (60 cm) with additional clearing to four feet (1.2 m) on the inside curves to improve site distance.

TURNING RADIUS -- Care must be taken when laying out trails to avoid sharp angles and short radius curves, particularly in an area where higher speeds might be attained. A bicycle going quite slowly can be turned in a twelve-foot (3.6 m) space; a six-foot (1.8 m) radius. The recommended minimum turning radius is 10 feet (3 m) with 15 feet (4.5 m) desirable except in areas where high bicycle speeds are expected. Turns should be banked where possible.

DRAINAGE -- The paved bicycle trail is very similar to a road in construction and the same general conditions and solutions for drainage would apply as for road construction. The better the drainage, the longer-lasting the bikeway.

SURFACING -- The design sections of the bicycle trail are generally the same as sidewalk design sections. The recommended surfacing material is bituminous paving; other acceptable choices are concrete (very expensive), soil cement, and compacted gravel. A widely used trail section is 4 inches (10 cm) or more of crushed stone choked and rolled with fines (quarry dust).

SIGNING -- Utilize standard highway department bikeway markers and signs.

SAFETY MEASURES -- Safety measures must be taken to protect the bicyclists such as realigning drainage grates at right angles to the bike path.

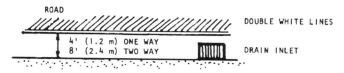

ROAD

DOUBLE WHITE LINES

4' (1.2 m) ONE WAY
8' (2.4 m) TWO WAY

DRAIN INLET

Bicycle trail safety measures.

BICYCLE RENTAL -- Park trails with heavy use by non-local people should probably include bicycle rental facilities. These can be developed in conjunction with other concession facilities (boat rental, food services) for more economical operation. Bicycle rental facilities should be located only where there is sufficient pedestrian traffic or vehicular parking to insure adequate customers for a viable financial operation.

EQUESTRIAN TRAILS AND FACILITIES

Horseback riding -- Tyler State Park, Pennsylvania.　　　　Photo: William Forrey.

USER CHARACTERISTICS [41]

Riding is a short-time activity. "A few available hours" account for about half of all rides, while slightly over one-quarter of all rides are one-day outings.

Most riding is done close to home, but where opportunities exist for overnight horse camping, it has been popular.

TRAIL DESIGN -- See Hiking Trails.

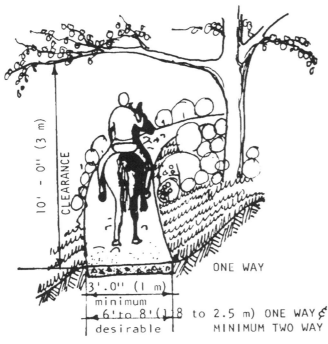

Section -- Equestrian trail.

SPECIAL EQUESTRIAN CONSIDERATIONS [55]

- Loop trails are best - 7 to 10 miles (10 to 15 km), 1/2 day; 10 to 20 miles (15 to 30 km), one day.

- Trips of two or more days are usually destination trips. Vehicular access points near overnight stops are required so that food and water can be provided for the horses. A shuttle arrangement for cars and trailers is required.

- Adequate car/trailer parking facilities are required at all trailheads.

- Short stretches - 1/2 mile (1 km) of straight alignment are desirable to provide for running the horse.

- Grades to 15 percent are permissible.

- Trail surfacing should be of native material. Where heavy use occurs, a mixture of sand, sawdust and oil can be utilized.

MULTIPLE USE -- Multiple use of equestrian trails for hiking is recommended for low volume use facilities only. Horses and hikers do not mix well due to horse excrement, accelerated erosion, spooking of horses, and different lengths of required trails.

Winter use of equestrian trails for ski touring or snowmobiling is compatible.

EQUESTRIAN FACILITIES -- Most successful stables depend on boarding horses as their main source of income. This activity can be combined with a rental (hack) operation. Rental of horses is difficult to make financially self-sustaining due to high insurance costs.

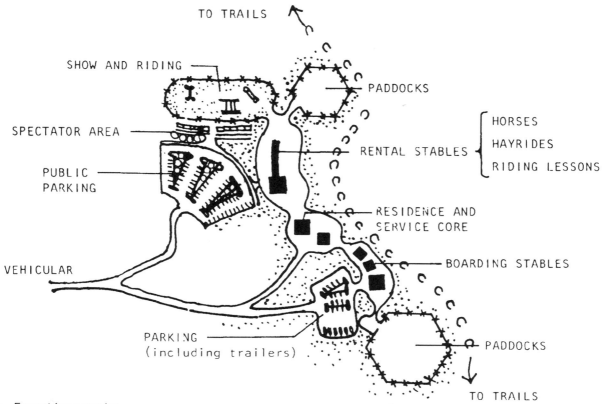

TO TRAILS

SHOW AND RIDING

PADDOCKS

SPECTATOR AREA

RENTAL STABLES { HORSES HAYRIDES RIDING LESSONS

PUBLIC PARKING

RESIDENCE AND SERVICE CORE

VEHICULAR

BOARDING STABLES

PARKING (including trailers)

PADDOCKS

TO TRAILS

Layout -- Equestrian complex.

Items to be considered:

(1) Is there a need, and if so, how big should the facility be and what should it contain?

(2) Kind of stable(s).

- boarding (30 horses minimum or multiples thereof).*

- rental (30 horses minimum or multiples thereof.)*

*Thirty horses is the approximate number one person can take care of.

Equestrian Center Boarding Stables -- East Bay Regional Park District, California.

(3) Types of activities.
- show*
- rodeo
- hunting (not normally done in most of the U.S.)*
- cross-country*
- show jumping*

Show jumping -- East Bay Regional Park, California.

- dressage*
- hayrides
- trails
- equestrian assembly area.

(4) Parking (including horse trailers).
- boarding -- one car/two horses
- rental -- one car/one horse
- spectators if equestrian events are planned.

(5) Availability of trails or land for trail development. Without trails an equestrian center is likely to fail.

*See Equestrian Sports [84] for additional details on the design of these elements.

(6) Corrals.

(7) Sanitary facilities.

(8) Picnic areas.

(9) Food service.

(10) Employee housing -- a necessity for safety purposes.

(11) Overnight accommodations for users -- not normally provided.

(12) Utilities -- water, sewage, electrical and communications.

(13) Indoor riding ring -- a necessity in areas with many days of inclement weather.

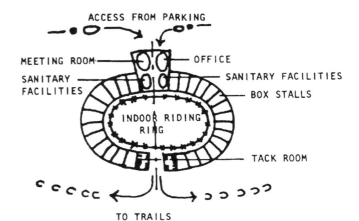

Indoor riding ring surrounded by stables.

(14) Removal of manure.

(15) Storage of feed.

(16) Tack room.

(17) Meeting, lounge and office space.

40

Chapter 9
SPECIAL USE FACILITIES

There are a number of leisure time activities which do not fit the traditional concept of "parks." This chapter will cover some of them including hang gliding and para-gliding, both quite, non-polluting uses. It will also cover off-road recreation vehicles, motorcycles, all terrain vehicles and motorized models of all kinds, all of which are noisy, and many which cause severe site erosion problems. They will be covered in two groups – hang gliding and motorized vehicles.

HANG GLIDING (88)

The recreation activity which uses non-powered fixed-wing flying vehicles and/or modified parachutes.

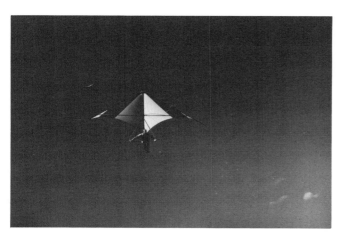

Hang gliding. Denver, Colorado.

GENERAL

Where suitable conditions exist, hang gliding can be an attractive addition to the traditional park uses, both for the flyers and for the park's other users who become spectators.

Hang gliding in its modern form is a far cry from the popular conception of a daredevil activity. It requires the participant to be a rated pilot under the close scrutiny of the United States Hang Gliding Association (USHGA). The association's equipment certification program and its standard operating procedures are a large part of the current good safety record of hang gliding. Sites are rated I, II, III and IV (similar to boating waters) with IV being for advanced pilots.

SITE REQUIREMENTS

There are two sites required for hang gliders -- take off (launching area) and landing. They do not, and frequently are not, directly connected.

LAUNCHING

Consider using overlooks, ski slopes and sledding areas for launching sites, wind direction permitting.

Hang gliders require an elevated launch site facing the wind. This will be best satisfied by having multiple launch points oriented in different directions to increase the number of days when flying can occur. The largest would be facing into the prevailing wind.

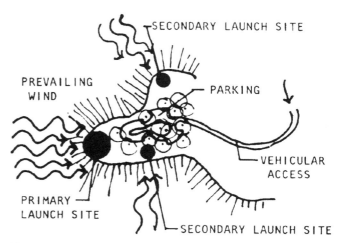

Hang glider launch site.

Minimum slope 20% with a 50' (15 m) wide cleared area extending down slope approximately 200' (60 m).

Maximum slope vertical with a 50' (15 m) wide cleared area extending down slope approximately 100' (30 m).

41

Minimum height 100' (30 m) -- sites below 300' (90 m) are normally considered training slopes.

Maximum height -- unlimited.

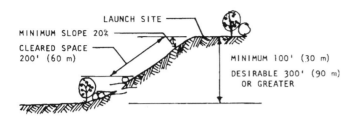

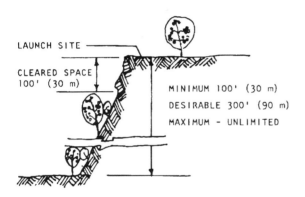

Sloping site.

Vertical site.

Air movement over and around solid objects causes turbulence which leads to accidents. It is necessary, therefore, to have a relatively clear area from abrupt objects, including other hills or mountains for approximately 1 mile (1.6 km) in front (up wind) of the hang glider flying area.

Access and parking by 2-wheel drive vehicles is needed within 300' (90 m) of the launch site; parking for one car per participant is necessary. A shuttle service between launch site and landing area would be a desirable operating feature for any heavily used site.

Sanitary facilities are needed at launch site (vault toilets are OK).

LANDING SITE
A flat site easily seen from the launch area and free of obstructions is needed. It must be free of surrounding power lines, buildings and tall trees. Desired: approx. 200' (60 m) x approx. 500' minimum. Advanced level IV can be as small as 150' (45 m) x 300' (90 m).

Space for spectator viewing is needed. If a road passes nearby, it might cause people to pull off and watch the activity. This must be taken into consideration.

Parking for one car per flyer plus one car per three anticipated spectators.

Sanitary facilities are necessary (flush toilets desirable). Use picnic area standards for determining the number of fixture units.

PARAGLIDING (88)

This sport is very popular in Europe and is rapidly growing in the U.S. It consists of foot launching from a highpoint (or being towed -- see Boating) of an inflatable canopy that can be steered to find lift and maneuver to a landing area. It is lightweight and can be taken along when hiking or mountain climbing. Paragliding in the U.S. is regulated by the American Paragliding Association (APA).

SITE REQUIREMENTS

Basically, the same as for hang gliding. The two activities are compatible and paragliding can use the same facilities as hang gliding.

LAUNCHING
Paragliders require an elevated launch site facing the wind as in hang gliding.

Minimum slope 30% with approximately a 50' (15 m) x 250' (75 m) cleared space. Maximum slope vertical with a 50' (15 m) x 150' (45 m) cleared space.

Minimum height 100' (30 m) for training slopes to unlimited height for experts.

Access to the launching area can be by trail due to the light weight (10 to 15 lbs (4 to 6 kg)) of the equipment.

LANDING AREA
50' (15 m) x 50' (15 m) cleared space, free of nearby power lines and tall obstructions.

Ski lifts can be utilized to move people and equipment between launch and landing sites.

MOTORIZED VEHICLE FACILITIES
GENERAL

Many people like to recreate utilizing motorized vehicles, either as participants or as spectators. Powerboating (see Chapter 17, "Boating"), snowmobiles (see Chapter 20, "Winter Use Areas"), off-road recreation vehicles (ARV's), all terrain vehicles (ATV), motorcycles (track, cross country, and sightseeing), cars (sightseeing, drag racing, track racing and rallying), motorized models of all kinds (direct controlled and remote control) are but some of the activities that utilize mechanical equipment for the primary focus of the recreation activity. Many require site development and support facilities to be able to operate in an enjoyable and safe way without destroying the resources and endangering people.

Most motorized equipment is noisy and many are destructive of the natural resources. Because of these two negative features the majority of park users and park managers object to their presence in park and recreation areas.

Motorcycles, snowmobiles, powerboats, 4-wheel drive vehicles and other motorized recreation vehicles continue to be sold in large numbers, however, and provision for facilities for the type of recreation activities this equipment generates must be considered in any complete recreation system.

USER INTERESTS

All motorized vehicle users are interested in one or more of the following: (1) testing driving skills, (2) testing their equipment, (3) relaxing, and (4) enjoying the scenery.

FACTORS INFLUENCING SITE SELECTION AND DESIGN

- To reiterate, the most important factor in locating a motorized vehicle facility is noise! The location of any motorized vehicle area is first and foremost influenced by noise.

  - Separation from rest of park visually and acoustically to minimize disturbances to other park users.

  - Separation from desirable wildlife habitat.

  - Separation from other surrounding land uses that require quite, i.e., residential areas, library, offices, etc.

- Like most recreation activities, the closer to the potential users the facilities are located, the greater the likelihood for success of the facilities.

- Variation in topography -- some flat, some hilly.

- Access.

- Adequate parking, both participants and spectators.

- Trailhead orientation signs.

- Sanitary facilities.

- Viewing areas.

- Soil stability.

- Utilities: water, electricity, sewage and telephone.

- Winter use by snowmobiles.

- Other items to consider:
  - Children's play area.
  - Swimming.
  - Shade.
  - Picnic facilities.

TRAILS

To be successful motorized vehicle trails must have sufficient length and frequent direction and grade changes. They basically follow the same criteria as hiking or equestrian trails on a conceptual basis. Major differences are as follows:

(1) Much more damage occurs to the ground -- special care must be taken to avoid fragile areas. Special features are not special when destroyed by overuse.

(2) Special features should be bypassed by the main trail with side trails leading to them. This will make them much more special when you get there.

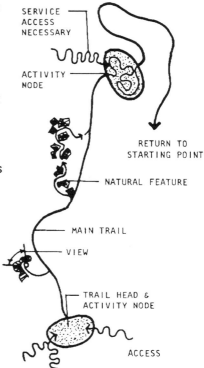

Trail layout.

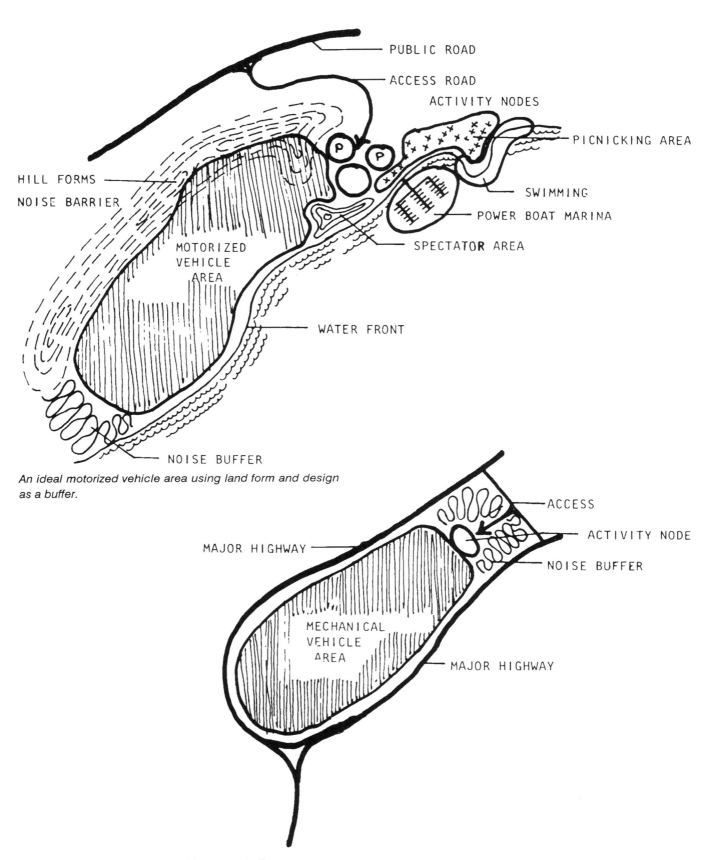

PUBLIC ROAD

ACCESS ROAD

ACTIVITY NODES

PICNICKING AREA

HILL FORMS
NOISE BARRIER

SWIMMING

POWER BOAT MARINA

SPECTATOR AREA

MOTORIZED
VEHICLE
AREA

WATER FRONT

NOISE BUFFER

An ideal motorized vehicle area using land form and design as a buffer.

MAJOR HIGHWAY

ACCESS

ACTIVITY NODE

NOISE BUFFER

MECHANICAL
VEHICLE
AREA

MAJOR HIGHWAY

An alternate location using land form as a buffer.

44

(3) Steep hill runs almost always suffer from severe erosion. Special care must be taken to accommodate this erosion, i.e., sediment ponds, changes in vertical alignment to allow for water removal.

(4) Utility R/W's frequently utilized by trail riders. These are often not -- and frequently cannot be -- legally open to use. Utility companies must be contacted prior to any serious consideration of their use in the trail system.

(5) Activity Nodes -- large tracts of land up to several hundred acres (hectares) in size -- can be a real asset to a motorized trail system with areas for free riding and organized activities as well as designated trail riding. Many riders enjoy competition and the nodes properly designed can accommodate this activity.

ATV

All terrain vehicles can basically go almost anywhere, even across small bodies of water, if necessary. On trails, a one-way loop system is best.

TRAIL REQUIREMENTS

Length -- approximately 20 miles (30 km) or 3 to 6 hours ride.

Surfacing -- varied, including wet areas; rough but as dust-free as possible.

Alignment -- varied and challenging; avoid grades over 75 percent. Curves -- 10 to 12 feet (3 to 4 m) radius.

Width -- Six feet (2 m) one way; ten feet (3 m) two way (not recommended).

Clearing -- Vertical -- 8 feet (2.5 m); Horizontal -- 8 feet (2.5 m).

FOUR-WHEEL DRIVE

KINDS OF TRAILS

(1) Trunk or main trail for all ability levels.

(2) Primitive for the more expert user -- for low volume use and can be extremely difficult.

For both types of trails a one-way system is best, and, in fact, almost a necessity for safety, construction costs and minimizing impacts on the environment.

TRAIL REQUIREMENTS

Length -- depends on terrain; 50 to 100 miles (30 to 160 km) is minimum desirable. Utilize as many miles of existing dirt roads, old logging roads, and utility corridors as possible to keep costs down. A loop road system is not necessary if the designed-for four-wheel drive vehicles are normally licensed to travel on the public highway system.

Signing -- needed for both safety and information on trunk trails. Minimal needed on primitive trails except to warn the novices to stay off.

Surfacing -- rough.

Alignment -- Do not duplicate public road conditions. Make it difficult. Trunk trails -- 40 percent maximum grade desirable; 60 percent and greater grade for short distances on Primitive Trails is permissible.

Width -- Trunk -- 8 feet (2.4 m) minimum; Primitive -- 6 feet (1.8 m) minimum.

Clearing -- 8 to 10 feet (2.4 to 3 m) -- vertical; horizontal -- trail width plus 2 feet (.6 m) on both sides.

TRAIL BIKE
USER INTERESTS

Motorcyclists love the backwoods. It's fun to be there and it is an escape. Most riders want challenge. All types of bikes can and are used.

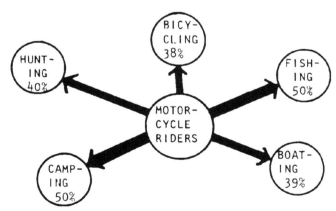

Motorcycle riders who do other activities.

Trail riding is usually physically demanding, especially on rough terrain. Basically similar to "Four-Wheel Drive," and they can, in fact, readily use all four-wheel drive trails. The trail should look unimproved.

TRAIL REQUIREMENTS

Length -- 50 to 100 miles (80 to 160 km) depending on terrain and ability of the likely riders; approximately a 6-hour ride.

Surfacing -- resistant to soil erosion. Mud holes are OK. Watch out for stream sedimentation. Ruts, bumps and small logs are desirable on some segments.

Alignment -- up to 100 percent but have alternate routes for extremely steep runs interspersed with easier segments. Many twists and turns are desirable.

Width -- 3 feet (1 m).

Clearing -- Horizontal -- 3+ feet (1+ m); keep it minimal; vertical -- 8 feet (2.5 m); keep it minimal.

MECHANIZED VEHICLE PARK

All terrain vehicles on a constructed race course. Pennsylvania.

An alternative to utilizing typical park facilities for vehicular use would be to develop recreation areas specially for mechanized vehicles. These could be located on stripmined and other seriously disturbed lands. These lands would, of course, require careful evaluation, and, where necessary, treatment to insure that there is no pollution generated on the site that would harm surrounding lands.

It should be understood that those who use mechanical vehicles for recreation have the same needs as the typical park user. A "mechanized vehicle park" should consider providing space for several types of use, such as ATV's, snowmobiles (in snow country), car racing, four-wheel racing, minibikes, model airplanes, and model rockets, as well as motorcycles. The park, of course, would need special facilities over and above those previously mentioned for motorized trails and those found in typical parks. They might include gas stations, garages, large temporary parking areas for events, visitor viewing areas, fire and ambulance facilities, etc.

A mechanical vehicle park must be located in a sound basin where the noise generated from its many activities **will not** disturb surrounding land uses. Areas between major highways or in industrial areas or in enclosed sound basins are examples of sites which might be suitable for mechanical vehicle parks. (See Factors Influencing Site Selection and Design this chapter.)

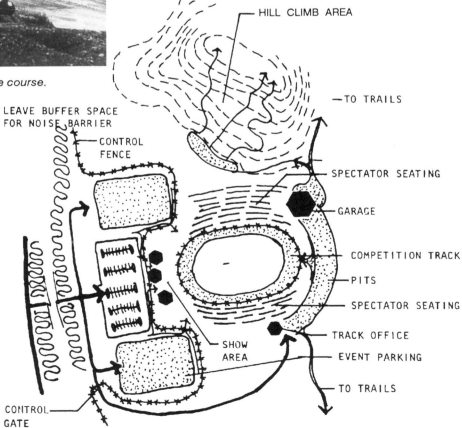

Layout -- Mechanical vehicle park.

MODEL AIRPLANES

CONTROLLED AIRPLANES

Normally located in urban areas in large multi-purpose parks. Could also utilize facilities built for remote controlled planes.

REQUIRED
- Parking.
- Set-up and waiting space.
- Cleared, smooth space for takeoffs and landings. (turf or asphalt); 150' R (45 m) maximum, 75' R (225 m) minimum.
- Safety barriers between flying area and surrounding uses.
- Sanitary facilities within 400 feet (120 m).

DESIRABLE
- Spectator area.
- Clubhouse.

These facilities will also serve for small model rockets, and, if paved, for remote controlled model cars, etc.

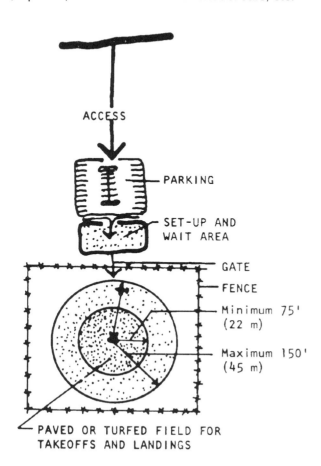

Controlled model plane field.

REMOTE CONTROLLED AIRPLANES

Remote controlled model plane flying field. Hillman State Park, Pennsylvania.

REQUIRED
- Parking.
- Paved set-up, waiting and display space.
- Paved access (taxiway to runway).
- Paved runway of a minimum of 100 feet (30 m) x 100 feet (30 m).
- Spectator viewing area.
- Control tower.
- Electricity.
- Sanitary facilities.
- Safety barriers to separate spectators and participants.
- Cleared area 1000 feet x 1000 feet (300 m x 300 m) with no major obstacles which would damage airplanes when they are forced to crash land.

DESIRABLE
- Clubhouse
- Water supply and sewage disposal.

These facilities will also ideally serve for launching model rockets of all sizes.

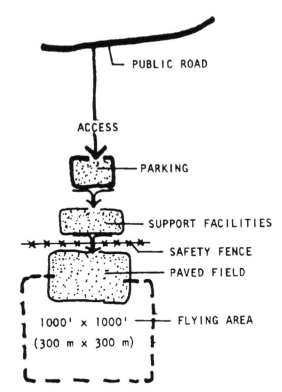

Remote controlled model plane area.

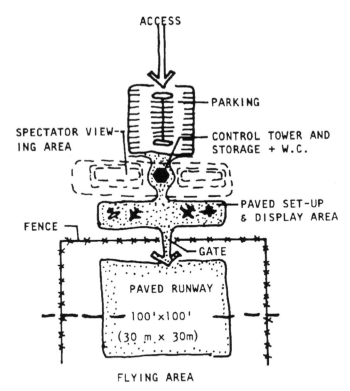

Layout -- Remote controlled model plane field.

Chapter 10
ROADS AND PARKING

The major means of access to most large-scale parks is and will continue to be by automobile. The movement of cars to and through a park and their storage in the park will continue to be a major item in park development. Car sizes and horse-power are varied and likely to continue this way for the next several years. Access by chartered buses, especially by older people, is likely to increase.

Many forms of transportation within a park area are possible, such as tramways, monorails, conveyor systems, buses, trackless trains, helicopters, hydrofoils and hovercrafts. In most instances, roads are probably the most cost-effective means of moving people through the park; however, a thorough and thoughtful determination should be made of the most meaningful way in which people can experience the park before a road system is built. [23] It should be noted that almost all non-conventional (non-car/bus) transportation requires considerable capital investments and, more importantly, incurs on-going operation and maintenance costs. Unless a user fee is charged it is unlikely that any form of transportation other than cars/buses can be considered in any park/leisure time project.

All vehicular access and storage in a park should be handled in the most aesthetically pleasing manner possible. Major cuts and fills and log tangents must be minimized. In effect, the roads and parking should be molded to the terrain.

The various types of circulation systems (vehicular, pedestrian, bicycle, equestrian, etc.) should be kept separated where possible to avoid conflicts. This is particularly necessary for equestrian trails.

ROAD ALIGNMENT [77]

Like all roads, park roads must provide safe, efficient and economical transportation for the park visitors. In addition, however, park roads **must** also provide for the driver's pleasure and enjoyment while fitting closely to the land.

A roadway is a linear element which provides the opportunity for continuous rapidly changing visual experiences. As such, not only is it necessary to make the road safe, efficient and economical, it is imperative that it be designed as a continuous series of visual experiences. This necessitates a thorough visual analysis of what can be seen from the road.

"For pleasing visual quality, there must be good coordination between horizontal and vertical curves." "The best appearing" road alignments occur when horizontal and vertical curves generally coincide, with the horizontal curve beginning slightly before and ending slightly after the vertical curve. From a visual standpoint the roadway should be perceived as a constantly changing three-dimensional curve. Generally (1) long tangents should be avoided, especially in rolling topography, and (2) avoid "short dip" vertical curves on long tangents or horizontal curves.

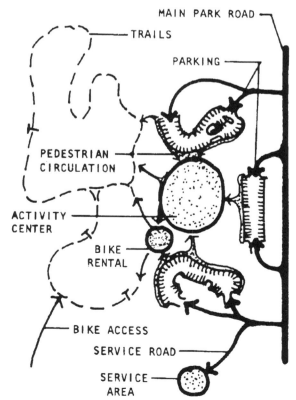

Park circulation system.

Roads are also strong visual elements in the landscape, and their impact must be considered visually from the surrounding land uses.

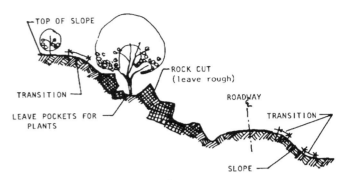

Section of a cut slope through stone.

Parking area. Craters of the Moon National Monument, Utah.

Road alignments should result in a roadway that minimizes its adverse impact on the land. The alignment should:

(1) generally run parallel to bold, linear landscape features such as shorelines, rivers, estuaries, valleys and hills to complement natural spaces and forms;

(2) never cross hills and ridges head-on, but at oblique angles and crossing the top at naturally occurring saddles;

(3) make rock cuts in irregular form and conforming to the geologic characteristics of the rock strata (occasionally some cuts may be cut clean for educational interpretive purposes);

(4) avoid constant slopes in cuts and fills;

(5) provide transitional grading between cuts and fills and at the top and bottom of slopes.

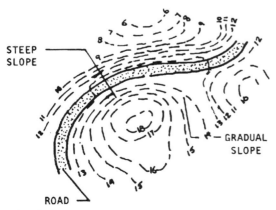

Transitional slopes.

DRAINAGE

The primary reason for road failure is poor drainage. It is of paramount importance that adequate drainage of water off of and away from the road section be done. All water intercepted by the road must be carried under the road in adequate-sized drainage structures; 18 inches (45 cm) is the minimum size necessary to enable the culvert to be easily cleaned.

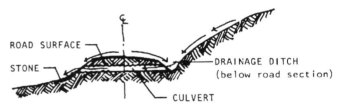

Road drainage.

PARKING

Parking spaces should be located so that they are within 400 feet (120 m) of the activity they are intended to serve. Parking at distances greater than 400 feet will only be used on unusual occasions, such as beach access where no other alternative is possible. If adequate parking cannot be provided within a reasonable distance of the activity, provision of alternative transportation should be seriously considered, especially for handicapped, i.e., trams, buses, etc.

Where possible, parking areas should be screened from roads and activity areas. **Please note** that right angle parking is the most space efficient parking system. It takes 10 percent less space than 60° parking and 20+ percent less than 45° parking. The size of parking lots should be a minimum of 60 feet (18 m) with a minimum of 9 feet (2.7 m)-wide parking bays.

50

VIEW BLOCKED

Parking lot screened with grading.

VIEW BLOCKED

Parking lot screened with plants.

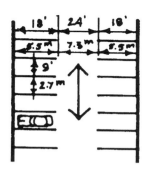

Right angle parking.

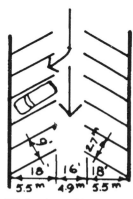

60° Angle parking.

Barrier free, signed, handicapped parking spaces of 8 feet (2.4 m) in width, plus 5 foot (1.5 m)-wide pedestrian aisles must be provided throughout the park in locations adjacent to handicapped use areas.

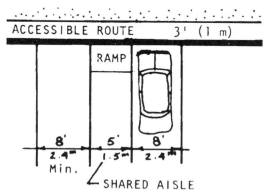

Handicapped parking.

(1) Car: gross area per 90° car space -- 300 square feet (28 sq. m); approx. 140 cars per acre (350 cars per ha).

(2) Car and boat trailer: gross area per space -- 600 square feet (56 sq. m); 70 per acre (175 per ha).

There are two basic car and trailer parking types: (a) pull-through; easiest to use but expensive in land use and construction costs, and (b) pull in-back out at a 45° angle; somewhat more difficult to use but requires less space and less construction costs. [2, 6]

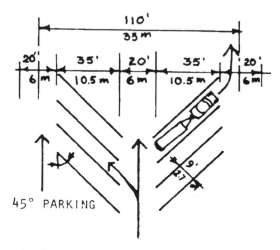

45° PARKING

Car and trailer pull-through parking.

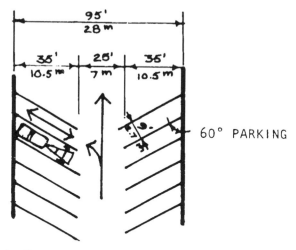

60° PARKING

Car and trailer pull in-back out parking.

(3) Maximum desirable grade is five percent, with lots of ten percent grades possible under careful design. [2] Handicapped parking must be essentially flat; maximum -- two percent grade.

Where practical, it is advisable to provide overflow parking on stabilized turf, i.e., parking needed only for peak holidays and summer weekends. Caution should be taken so that the extra space needed for people on major use days is not filled with cars.

ENVIRONMENTALLY SENSITIVE SURFACING

Traditionally, paved roads and parking areas seal off the land from the environment. This creates 100 percent runoff of all rainfall, increasing stream volumes, reducing aquifer recharge and increasing the likelihood of erosion. Some roads and parking areas are not heavily used throughout the year. Those areas should be considered for alternative surface treatment. There are three currently used approaches.

(1) Construct a standard base, surface with crushed stone and choke with top soil. This is then seeded and maintained as an open field except during heavy use periods. A variation frequently used is to pave the roadway and leave the parking grassed.

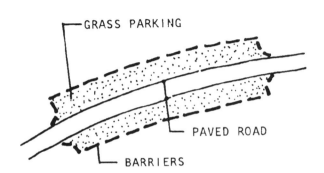

Grass parking with paved road.

Porous paving blocks.
Northeast Coast National Scenic Area, Taiwan.

(2) Install porous paving.

(3) Use of open grid type pavers/topsoil and planting as per (1) above.

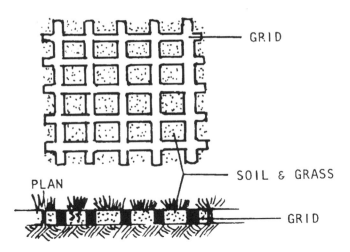

Open grid concrete pavers or other non-corrodable material.

Open grid concrete pavers permit water to go through and grass to grow. Germany.

PROJECT ROADS

Road systems within the recreation area (interior circulatory roads), should be so designed as to protect the safety of patrons using the recreation area while preserving the aesthetic qualities. Interior roads are not meant for high-speed travel, generally not more than 25 mph (45 kmh). A primary consideration in designing and constructing recreation roads is the principle that roads are made to fit the site's natural features and without untoward interference with other recreation pursuits. The types, number and purpose of the potential users should be considered.

Road designs should keep the need for reduced maintenance constantly in mind, i.e., limit mowed areas and ornamental plantings requiring care.

Control gates should be provided for all park access roads.

Park roads are classified as major, minor and special-purpose (including one-way roads). Adequate drainage **must** be included in the design to prevent damage from erosion.

DESIGN STANDARDS

Width (feet)	1-lane*	Minor 2-lane	Major 2-lane	Parking Spur
Roadbed - including shoulders	16' (4.9m)	24' - 26' (7.3m-7.9m)	28' - 30' (8.5m-9.1m)	12' (3.7m)
- w/o shoulders face to face of barriers or curbs	12' (3.7m)	20' (6.1m)	22' (6.7m)	10' (3.0m)
Surfacing	12' (3.7m)	20' (6.1m)	22' (6.7m)	10' (3.0m)
Shoulders	2' (.6m)	2'-3' (.6m-.9m)	3'-5' (.9m-1.5m)	2' (.6m)

*Width of road surface at curves should be increased up to 14 feet radius (4.2 m) or sometimes greater, especially where campers, camp trailers and boat trailers are expected, will be necessary.

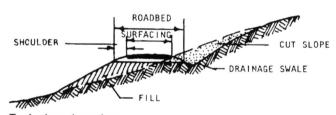

Typical road section.

SIGHT DISTANCES

(1) At park road intersection -- 300 feet (90 m) in either direction.

(2) At intersections with exterior highway system -- 400 feet (120 m) minimum with the distance increasing with the amount of park use.

(3) At places other than intersections -- 175 feet (55 m).

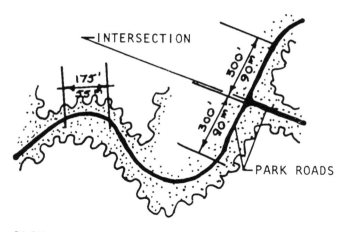

PLAN

SECTION - VERTICAL CURVE
Sight distance.

ALIGNMENT

Minimum radius	- 50 feet (15 m)
Minimum desirable radius	- 80 feet (25 m)
Road intersections	- 50 feet (15 m) radius desirable - 35 feet (10 m) radius minimum
Dead-end circle or Turnaround	- 40 feet (12 m) radius minimum - 50 feet (15 m) radius desirable

GRADIENT

Maximum desirable -- nine percent. Short stretches of road may exceed the maximum desirable grade but careful consideration should be given to types of traffic, e.g., passenger cars, trucks, passenger cars pulling trailers, and service vehicles such as garbage trucks, etc.

SCENIC VIEWS

Locations that are outstanding for visual and for photographic purposes, particularly when separated from designated parking areas, frequently justify the development of pull-over parking.

TURNOUTS

Overall length -- 100 feet (30 m) minimum; 50 feet (15 m) of two-lane width plus 25 feet (7.5 m) of tapered end sections.

Scenic overlook -- Bryce Canyon National Park, Colorado.

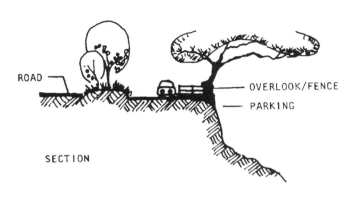

ROAD

OVERLOOK/FENCE

PARKING

SECTION

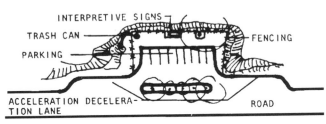

INTERPRETIVE SIGNS

TRASH CAN

PARKING

FENCING

ACCELERATION DECELERA-
TION LANE

ROAD

PLAN

Scenic overlook.

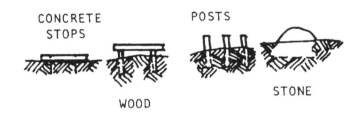

CONCRETE STOPS

POSTS

WOOD

STONE

GRADING

CURBS

Roadside barriers.

SURFACING

Surfacing of roads should be adequate to support the intended use.

The road systems within a recreation area should have, as a minimum requirement, a stabilized surface to control dust. Low use roads can be gravel (requires annual maintenance). Higher use roads can be oil and chip or blacktop. Concrete is not recommended due to cost.

Low use campground road. Ohiopyle State Park, Pennsylvania.

UNDERPASS

A major road or highway passing through a park is a barrier to all types of non-vehicular circulation, including wildlife. This can be partially alleviated by the installation of culverts, sometimes over-sized, which include a pedestrian underpass in addition to transporting water.

BARRIERS

Barriers should be installed where needed to prevent unauthorized vehicular travel within the recreation area. Control of automobile traffic is important from the point of view of safety and also to prevent the deterioration of the terrain and vegetation of the recreation area. The barriers should be as unobtrusive as possible and still provide the necessary control. If wood barriers are used they should be pressure treated with a wood preservative.

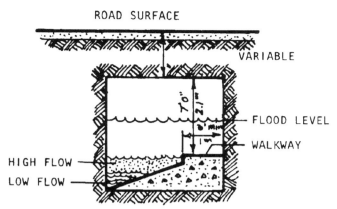

Combination culvert and pedestrian underpass.

Plants can be an effective barrier for snow and sand.

The multi-purpose culvert should have the following standards:

(1) The shape of the channel should maintain sufficient depth for fish during low flows. [39]

(2) The walkway will have a minimum seven foot (2.1 m) clearance and be three feet (1 m) wide for acceptable pedestrian use at other than flood stage. [39] A slightly larger space will be needed if used for part of an equestrian trail.

(3) The depth of the culvert from the road surface varies except for minimum required coverage. [39]

(4) The drainage structure must be wide enough to contain an existing stream-bottom in addition to the walkway. [39]

(5) Construction of the walkway must be integral with the culvert so that washouts will not occur.

Plant material can be used for sand or snow barriers. Saudi Arabia.

ROADSIDE TREATMENT [77]

"The roadside is an integral part of the total" road. "Roadside development is the treatment given to the roadside to conserve, enhance and display natural and cultural beauty." ". . . and features of interest . . . through which the [road] passes."

The conditions on the immediate highway right-of-way are almost always manmade and will usually differ radically from the surrounding natural systems. Within these conditions, however, the addition of plant material should be used to:

(1) stabilize the soil and reduce or prevent erosion;

(2) guide traffic and reduce roadside distractions;

(3) screen objectional views;

(4) snow control (and sand control in deserts);

(5) transition from the rigid geometry of the road to the natural surroundings;

(6) for visual enhancement by enframing vistas, creating selective views, break monotonous stretches of roadway.

Plant material can consist of trees, shrubs, wildflowers and grasses, and should, wherever possible, be associated with the existing vegetation.

Not all areas need to be planted with trees and shrubs. In open grass country or other areas the primary treatment may be to re-establish the native grasses. In some heavily vegetated sites it is necessary to selectively thin or remove vegetation to open views and develop irregular clearing lines and natural transitions between open areas and the dense woods.

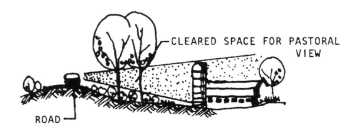

Views are important and may require clearing some road-side vegetation.

ENTRANCE STATION

The prime functions of an entrance station are:

Control
    a. Collect entrance fees
    b. Issue use permits and/or assign campsites
    c. Regulation of visitors
    d. Protection
    e. First aid

Information
    a. Directions
    b. Communications

DESIGN FACTORS

• Adequate vehicle back-up space must be provided commensurate with the expected use.

• The design of an entrance station must be predicted on the need to move people through this potential bottleneck **quickly and efficiently.**

• Electricity, phone and sanitary facilities for the staff must be available. In addition, a public pay phone should be provided.

• Water and sewer connections are desirable.

• Parking for staff is required.

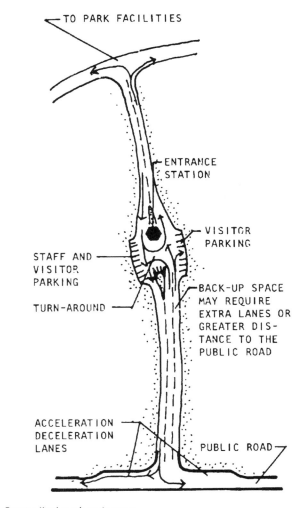

Controlled park entrance.

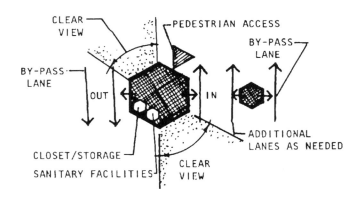

Park entrance station.

Chapter 11 UTILITIES

GENERAL

The significance of utilities as an integral and indispensable part of every park cannot be over-emphasized, especially in light of ecological and environmental consequences. The utility systems' concept development as an integral part of a project at an early stage of planning will save considerable time and money. Inadequate preliminary work as to the location, aesthetic considerations, capacity, arrangement and conditions will be detrimental to all succeeding phases and may endanger the successful completion of a project.

Investigations and surveys for early planning stages of a project are broad in nature, with emphasis on covering all factors relating to utilities as an integral part of the project. Some planning considerations are as follows:

(1) The extent of the area to be served and the pattern of present and future park growth.

(2) The estimated present and future utility needs.

(3) Off-site utility services, if available, and the life-cycle cost of the project to be connected to them, especially in regards to long-term operation and maintenance costs.

(4) General arrangement of the utility system to best serve the needs.

(5) Excavation for utility lines is expensive and should be considered at the earliest planning stages with adequate subsurface investigations.

(6) In arid environments the re-use of treated waste water for non-consumptive uses must be evaluated.

WATER SUPPLY

A complete study of available water sources should be made. Generally, it is most desirable to utilize an existing municipal service. The second most desirable source for a park system is wells, because they generally produce a consistent quality of water at reduced treatment costs. However, this does not preclude the use of lake or creek water. In fact, in certain situations, these might be the only feasible sources and **must** be considered. In the event that alternative water sources are available, they should be considered, and the best system -- on the basis of life-cycle costs including operation and maintenance costs and not merely on initial costs -- chosen. All possible water conservation techniques such as self closing faucets, low volume flushing accessories, reduced pressure showerheads, etc., should be considered during the detail of a project.

The quantity of water storage is dependent upon amount and reliability of water source and variations in use. As a general guide, storage should be provided for a maximum of a three-day weekend period. With good quantity and quality of water, storage might be held to the **maximum** day use. The minimum operating level of water storage and distribution line size should be such that a pressure of 25 p.s.i. exists at each building requiring flush valves. However, in exceptional cases where other factors demand a lowered pressure, an absolute minimum of 15 p.s.i. for flush valve facilities may be accepted. It is generally preferable to use an elevated storage/gravity system over a mechanically maintained pneumatic pressure system.

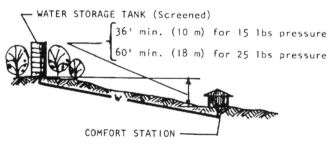

A gravity system is most desirable.

Water storage structures such as gas tanks, standpipes, or elevated storage tanks are usually out of character with the parkscape. Therefore, the location of a storage tank is of extreme importance in a park environment. Wherever the topography permits an underground storage tank, it should be provided; even though it might be more costly, the aesthetic gain will far outweigh this added initial cost. Standpipes should be considered next, and elevated storage tanks should be considered as a last resort.

Through judicious site selection, making maximum use of existing trees and topographic features, balancing structural dimensions and site excavation with landscaping, cutting out the bank and keeping a low storage tank profile, and selection of a color to blend with the surrounding landscape, the criteria for aesthetics and the water utility's functional needs can be satisfactorily met.

Water tank located in trees and painted to blend with surrounding colors. Katherine Gorge National Park, Austrailia.

Use of pumps without storage, a pneumatic system, forcing water directly into the mains with no other outlet than the water actually consumed, could be considered where quantitative demand and pressure allow these methods.

Whenever possible, adequate visual screening and a security gate at the entrance to the site of water storage tanks should be provided. The site should be sufficiently far back from the road as to be out of view, and a minor service road provided. This road should be so laid out with the use of curves that a view of the facilities will not be possible at the intersection with the park road.

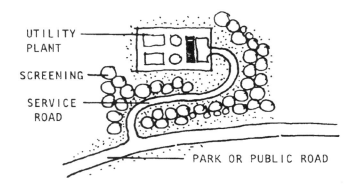

Utility plants should be screened.

In areas of high fire danger or of historic or other valuable structures, provision should be made for adequate water supply, pipe sizes, and outlets for fire suppression.

Wherever winter use of park facilities is planned, suitable means in the water storage tanks to guard against freezing of water should be provided.

SANITARY

A park or recreation area is like a small community, only with a transient population and complicated by severe seasonal sewage flow fluctuations.

Sanitary waste disposal and/or treatment is one of the most crucial aspects of park development to serve this transient population. Adequate disposal and/or treatment of all waste is a necessity and park development and expansion cannot proceed without these facilities. The type and extent of the system should be discussed with the responsible health officials in the area in which the development of the park is to occur.

NOTE: All data available strongly points to a public desire/demand for flush toilets. [21, 28, 34, 51]

All sewer lines should be located for as much gravity flow as possible and, where feasible, they should follow the road system.

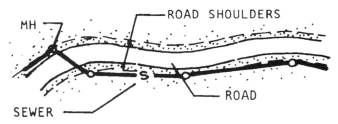

Utility lines should be placed in road shoulders where possible.

Where it is not possible to follow roads, trails can frequently be developed over utility lines.

Trail constructed over sewer line -- man hole should be set lower. Little Buffalo State Park, Pennsylvania.

There are a several methods of sewage disposal available:

• Tying into an area-wide waste system should be considered, even if the initial costs are somewhat higher than other disposal systems, provided it proves economical on a "capitalized costs" basis. For this purpose a 15 to 20-year design life for the treatment plant facility and a 25 to 35-year design life for the collection and conveyance facility should be considered.

• Major park developments may be economically served by constructing a sewage treatment plant. The plant should be located away from, downwind, below any dams, and downstream of use areas. It can be prefabricated and placed in a container and the "package" set in the ground. It is desirable to plan for one properly located treatment plant, even if the initial cost is somewhat higher than having two or more treatment plants in the same park because of the economics of scale and the excessive operational and maintenance demands placed on the park resources, personnel and finances by the latter system.

A wastewater treatment plant or management technique can be designed to treat and dispose of the

"Package" sewage treatment plant set in ground. Ohiopyle State Park, Pennsylvania.

effluent in ways other than discharging into water courses.

AQUACULTURE

In certain park situations, aquaculture, or the production of aquatic organisms (flora and fauna) under controlled conditions, can be utilized. The wastewater flowthrough system, or batch treatment system basin covered by plant material, is utilized. The plants remove nutrient and the pollutants from the wastewater. The plant material is periodically harvested and can be used as fertilizer, soil conditioner after composing, animal feed, and a source of methane when anaerobically digested. The system is most suitable for recreational facilities due to the seasonal nature of these recreational facilities. Water hyacinth (Eichhornia crassipes) is one good plant; however, **extreme** care must be taken to insure that the plants cannot get into the natural waterways due to its prolific growth habits. It grows in about 50°F. (10°C) water temperature and flourishes when the water temperature is approximately 70°F. (21°C). Basin depth should be adequate to maximize plant rooting and plant absorption. A detention time of 4-15 days average and 2-15 acres (1-6 ha)/mgd are required.

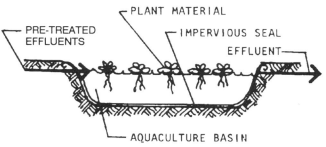

Aquaculture.

LAND APPLICATIONS

Where suitable land is available treatment by land application is an attractive and feasible alternative. The technology has been widely and successfully utilized for more than 100 years. Sewage is applied to land to nourish vegetation and purify the partially treated liquid wastes. Three methods can be utilized:

(1) **IRRIGATION -- Especially good in arid areas** or areas where irrigation is needed for good vegetative growth. Liquid is applied to plantations, crops, golf courses or to forests (silviculture) by sprinkling, flooding or ridge and furrow methods. The liquid is sometimes disinfected before land application. This process is limited by soil type and depth, topography, underlying geology, climate, plant material and land availability. **Slopes should be less than 15 percent to minimize runoff and erosion.** Typical equipment needed are pipe, pump, valves, gates and spray nozzles. Required field area is 56 to 560 acres (20 to 200+ ha) per million gallons per day. Application rates are governed by state requirements--generally 0.5 to 4 inches (1.2 to 10 cm) per week, i.e., 2 - 20 feet (.6 m to 6 m) per year is allowed. A soil depth of 2 - 5 feet (.6 to 1.5 m) and soil permeability of 0.06 to 2 inches (.15 to 5 cm) per hour are desirable. Most states have requirements of preapplication treatment varying from a minimum of primary treatment to secondary degree of treatment.

(2) **OVER-LAND FLOW** -- Liquid flows through vegetation on a graded slope. The runoff is collected at the bottom and reused or discharged to a river or stream. Other considerations and design criteria are the same as for the irrigation system.

(3) **RAPID INFILTRATION** -- Partly treated sewage is applied in controlled doses to sandy soil, i.e., deep and permeable soils. Three to 56 acres (1.2 to 20+ ha) per million gallons per day are needed. Application rate of 20 - 400 feet (6 to 120 m) per year or 4 - 92 inches (10 to 230 cm) per week is allowed. Soil depth of 10 to 15 feet (3 to 4.5 m) or more and soil permeability of 0.6 inches (1.5 cm) per hour or more are desirable.

LAGOONS

Lagoons are large holding reservoirs frequently several acres (hectares) in size with detention periods of several weeks. They are used to biologically treat wastes. Treatment capacity can be increased by oxygenating the ponds. The size depends on the amount and characteristics of the wastes, the location (temperature affects biological activity), adequate site

conditions and effluent discharge requirements. Generally, the effluent is disposed of by spray irrigation of crops, golf courses, or other landscaped areas. Lagoons which consider aesthetics can be a very attractive park feature.

ALTERNATIVE SEWAGE TREATMENT SYSTEMS

There are many other types of sewage treatment systems which might be suitable for serving a specific park or unit within a park. Most alternative systems are small and use less energy, water and materials than the larger central treatment systems. Such systems are almost always more cost-effective than a conventional central sewage treatment system and should be seriously considered where they are technically feasible. The following is a discussion of some of the alternative systems that can be used in park areas.

(1) **SEPTIC TANK SYSTEMS** -- There are several variations of the basic system depending upon the site soil conditions. In all these variations, a septic tank is followed by a distribution box and some type of effluent disposal (dispersal).

(a) **Septic Tank and Soil Absorption Field (Trench)** -- Most common on-site systems are of this nature. It is suitable only for certain soil types. It generally requires level ground to moderate (less than 10 percent) slopes. Most states and many municipalities have design requirements for such systems. In the trench system, liquid from the distribution box flows through perforated pipes in trenches and through the surrounding crushed rocks or gravel and soil to groundwater.

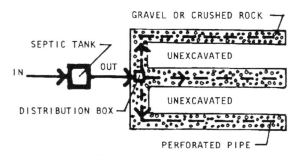

Septic tank and soil absorption field (trench).

(b) **Septic Tank and Soil Absorption Field (Bed)** This system is similar to the trench type. It uses a smaller field. In this system the total field is excavated. This is useful where the space is limited. It requires nearly level ground (2 - 5 percent slopes).

60

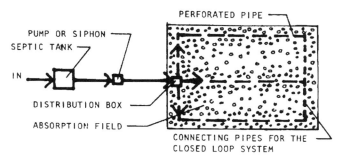

Septic tank and soil absorption field (bed).

Dosing system.

(c) **Alternating Absorption Field** -- Another variation uses alternating absorption fields. One field rests while the other is in use. This alternating pattern allows a field to renew itself, extends life of the field, and provides a standby if one unit (field) fails. Two distribution boxes following the valve box are needed. The valve directs sewage liquid to the proper field. Fields usually are switched every six to twelve months. Such systems are suitable for heavy use areas and could be used together for major use days, i.e., holidays.

(e) **Septic Tank with Sloping Field** -- This type uses the serial distribution technique where the absorption field is sloping (10 to 15 percent). A pump forces liquid through perforated pipes in the contoured absorption field. Drop boxes regulate liquid flow. The highest trench fills up first and lower trenches fill up last. Plastic fittings are sometimes used instead of drop boxes to regulate flow.

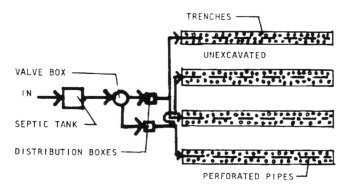

Septic tank with alternating absorption field.

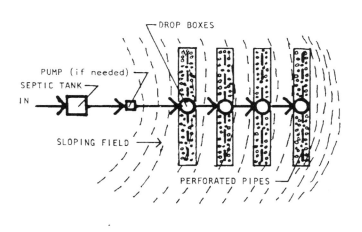

Septic tank with sloping field.

(d) **Dosing System** -- This variation of the septic tank system refinement uses a pump or siphon to force liquid through perforated pipes in controlled doses. All pipes, therefore, discharge liquid almost at the same time (dosing), and the system better utilizes the entire field. This procedure allows a spreading of the liquid evenly over the field and gives the field a chance to dry out between dosings. The absorption field could be an open or closed loop type.

(f) **Septic Tank with Seepage Pit** -- For limited space but good soil conditions, a seepage pit instead of leachfield could be used. Liquid from the septic tank flows to a pit that has open-jointed brick or stone walls surrounded by rocks. The system allows liquid to seep through walls or holes of pre-cast tanks and through rocks to the surround soil. Such pit sites need a periodic cleaning to avoid clogging.

61

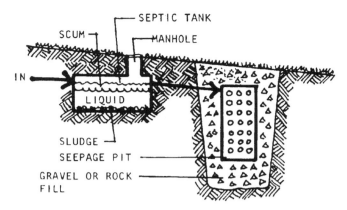

Seepage pit following septic tank.

(2) **AEROBIC SYSTEM AND SOIL ABSORPTION FIELD** (basically replaces a septic tank system) -- In some soil conditions where septic tank/leachfield systems are not suitable an aeration tank instead of septic tank is provided. In this tank air is blown through the wastewater. Such a system, although requiring more attention and periodic maintenance, provides a better degree of treatment than standard septic systems. Water is thus provided a higher degree of treatment before going to absorption fields. Such systems use more energy and require utility connections.

(3) **SEPTIC TANKS/SAND FILTER/DISINFECTION AND DISCHARGE** -- In certain soil conditions treated effluent discharge to surface water is utilized. A septic tank discharges liquid onto sand filters. The filter could be at ground level but usually is a buried sand pit due to use and aesthetic considerations. The liquid enters by perforated pipe at the top of the sand and filters through the sand and gravel to the bottom pipe. The underdrain pipe conveys the liquid to the disinfection unit.

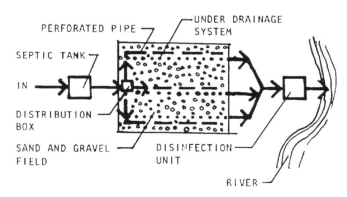

Septic tank / filter field / disinfection / discharge.

Subsurface sand filters should not be installed in areas where bedrock is encountered or the seasonal high-groundwater table is within three feet (1 m) of the surface. Size of sand filter should be determined on the basis of loading rate and the estimated volume of maximum flow per day. The loading rate of 1.15 gallons per day per square foot (900 sq. cm) of filter area is generally utilized. At least two inches (5 cm) of 3/4-inch to 1-1/2 inch (2 to 4 cm) size gravel should surround underdrains and distribution pipes. A six-inch (15 cm) layer of gravel should be placed on top of the two inches (5 cm) of bedding gravel over which 24 inches (60 cm) of clean sand of 0.3 to 0.6 mm effective size should be used.

(4) **MODIFIED SAND-MOUND SYSTEM** -- Where existing soil conditions (rocky or tight soil or high-water table) are not suitable for disposal systems and effluent discharge to surface water (stream or ditch) is not possible, a sand mound or evapotranspiration bed system can sometimes be used. Such systems could be used with septic or aerobic tank units.

(a) In the sand-mound system liquid is transported from the storage tank through perforated plastic pipe in the sand mound that covers **plowed** (scarified) **ground.** Liquid flows through rocks or gravel and then sand to natural soil. Mound vegetation helps evaporate liquid.

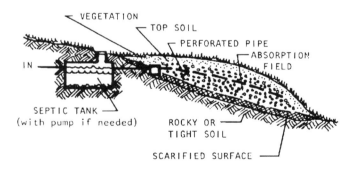

Sand mound.

(b) In the evapotranspiration bed variation, the sand bed is lined with plastic or other waterproof material. The bed can be mounded or level. Liquid evaporates because it is prevented by the liner from filtering through the natural soil. Plants help in the evapotranspiration process. Mounds for such systems can be creatively located where desired to screen use areas.

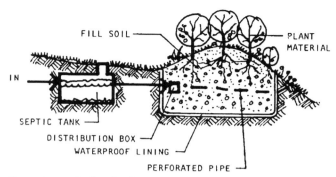

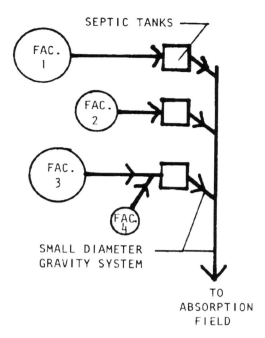

Evapotranspiration bed.

(5) **CLUSTER SYSTEM** -- Where more than one use area or facility lie in proximity of each other, a cluster system approach could be used. Several such facilities could be served by a common treatment and disposal system.

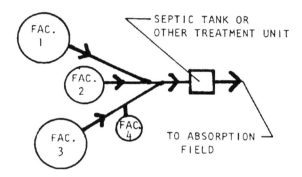

Cluster system.

Several combinations are possible. Each building could be connected to its on-site septic or aerobic tank and treated liquid connected to a common absorption field by a small diameter gravity system. Such clusters could also use other alternative systems such as mounds, pressure sewers and sewage treatment lagoons.

Alternate cluster system.

(6) **PRESSURE SEWERS (Grinder Pumps)** -- Pumps which grind solids in the sewage are installed in the storage tanks at each building and are able to pump wastewater through small diameter pipes to a central or alternate treatment and disposal system. The grinder pump could be installed in the storage tank which collects wastes from multiple buildings. Yet in another modification, multiple buildings, each served by septic tanks, could discharge to a storage tank by gravity from where it is pumped by the grinder pumps to additional treatment and/or disposal.

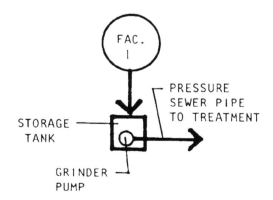

No septic tank.

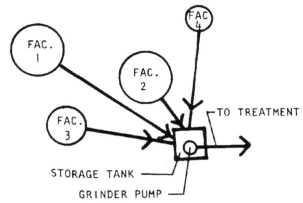

Cluster system -- no septic tank.

(7) **DUAL SYSTEMS** -- Dual systems are the systems that segregate "black water" and "gray water" and handle them separately. The term "black water" is used to describe wastes from toilet fixtures and is usually handled by waterless or low-water toilet systems.

The term "gray water" is used to describe other waste-water from the kitchen, laundry, etc. Such water needs less treatment and can be treated or disposed of by septic or other approved treatment and disposal systems.

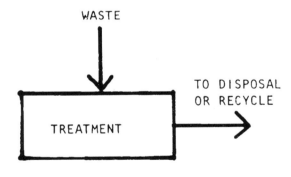

WATERLESS OR LOWWATER TOILET SYSTEM

Black water.

The main advantage of using the dual system is the necessity to handle only a small fraction of wastewater compared to conventional waterborne systems. Because of its inherent water conservation it also reduces the need to provide large amounts of water and is particularly useful in remote areas and sites where there is limited water availability.

(a) **Composting** -- This system does not need any water. It converts toilet wastes and most food wastes to compost. Electric vent, fan and heating element are optional on large waterborne sewage systems but are essential on small systems which will be the case in most small and/or remote park or recreational facilities. The use of solar (photovoltaic) panels is strongly recommended as a means of providing the limited electricity necessary. Proper care of such a system is essential.

(b) **Incineration** -- This system also does not involve any water. Electricity, gas or oil burns solids and evaporates liquid. Ash will need to be removed on a periodic basis depending upon the load on the incinerator. A roof vent and proper care are needed. Not recommended.

(c) **Recycling Oil Flush** -- This system does not use any water. Oil instead of water is used for flushing. It is similar to airline flush toilets. Oil and waste go to a large storage tank where wastes settle to the bottom and oil rises to the top. Oil is filtered and recycled for flushing. Periodically makeup oil is required and after some time the oil needs replacing. This system uses electricity and requires proper care and attention. In remote areas the use of solar panels is recommended.

(d) **Recycling Chemical** -- These systems use small amounts of water. A water-chemical flush mixture is used instead of water in the toilet bowl. Mixture and waste water go to a storage tank and are filtered with the chemicals being recirculated. A water hookup for adding make-up water is needed, chemicals are added periodically. The same care and attention as in the oil flush system are needed.

(7) **VAULT/PUMP-OUT TOILETS** -- Low-use primitive areas and use areas within floodplains can often be served best by vault or portable chemical toilets. Vehicular access is, however, necessary to service the units.

COMFORT STATION REQUIREMENTS

Suggested fixture unit requirements for the various recreation activities are given in their respective sections. Most states have strict requirements in this field and they should be determined very early in the design work. Although most sanitary requirements do not provide for it, the number of fixture units actually needed in the comfort stations is normally greater for women than for men.

A woman takes approximately 2 to 2.5 minutes to use a toilet.

A man takes approximately 1.1 minute to use a urinal and approximately 1.8 minutes to use a toilet.

Men in day use areas use a urinal 3 to 4 times more frequently than they use a toilet. (36)

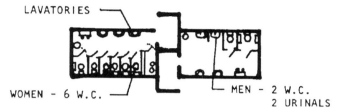

The number of fixture units needed is usually greater for women than men.

All sanitary facilities located on handicapped accessible routes shall have handicapped accessible facilities provided, including doorways, lavatories and W.C.'s. At least one W.C. stall for each sex shall be approximately 60" (150 cm) wide by 60" (150 cm) deep with grab bars and outward opening door.

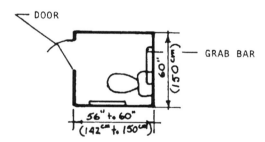

W.C. stall with grab bars.

Hot or tempered water has normally been provided at most comfort stations with running water and at all comfort stations with showers. Because of fuel costs consideration should be given to eliminating hot water in all day-use comfort stations including showers at beaches. Where hot (tempered) water is necessary strong consideration should be given to using solar heat.

MISCELLANEOUS

Lift stations and sewage pumping stations, wherever necessary in the sanitary system, shall be provided with an emergency generator unit or with a suitable outlet for hooking into a portable generator unit at the time of power outage. An audible and visible alarm system should be incorporated outside the lift stations to indicate the breakdown condition.

When budget permits, a central control system located at the treatment plant should be considered.

Security is becoming more important every day and can be enhanced by:

(1) Proper screening of the treatment facilities from public view.

(2) Provision of a gated, fenced barrier.

(3) Night lighting.

SOLID WASTE DISPOSAL

Solid waste disposal is a continual and often overlooked problem of major proportions and should be planned for when developing a park. The best solution is to remove the refuse from the park, either with park forces or by contract. Recent trends are for removal by contract. In either situation, it is necessary to know the kind of equipment to be used in solid waste collection before a system for trash receptacles can be designed. In some instances, it may be necessary to dispose of wastes on site. This should be by whatever method is least disruptive to the park and should be located away from the downwind of public-use areas. Conformance to requirements of the local health department is mandatory. This type of disposal should only be considered as a last resort option and only after all other solutions have been thoroughly investigated.

Adequate solid waste collection facilities should be provided. These can best be located adjacent to walks, roads, and service drives to facilitate mechanical pickup. In recent years more parks have been forced, due to economics, into utilizing a few strategically located "dumpsters" instead of the more familiar and widely dispersed trash cans. It should be noted that walks used by service vehicles must be designed to withstand the intended use. This will usually mean more base material and wider paved surfaces and larger radius horizontal curves.

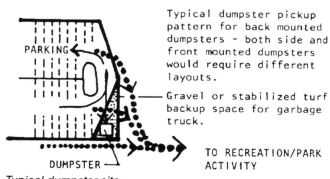

Typical dumpster pickup pattern for back mounted dumpsters - both side and front mounted dumpsters would require different layouts.

Gravel or stabilized turf backup space for garbage truck.

Typical dumpster site.

ELECTRICITY AND TELEPHONE

All major day-use installations and all overnight areas except primitive areas should be serviced by electricity and telephone. Primitive overnight and low-use areas can frequently be served by solar generated electricity thus eliminating the need for expensive electric line installation. Public telephones should be placed where they are easily found -- generally at major comfort stations, bathhouses, visitor information buildings or entrance stations.

All lines should be placed underground unless special conditions make such installation costs prohibitive. Whenever possible, electric and telephone lines should be placed in a common trench and, where feasible, in conjunction with water and/or sanitary lines.

All underground utility lines should be marked with non-decomposing markers. Plastic tape identifying the utility below is the best and least expensive technique. Two-inch thick concrete pavers are an alternative.

Sanitary facilities in day-use areas which are closed at dusk do not require electricity.

When overhead lines become imperative, special care must be taken to break up long views down the right of way. Rights of way and clearings should be kept to a minimum and planted with low vegetation to minimize this undesirable visual intrusion.

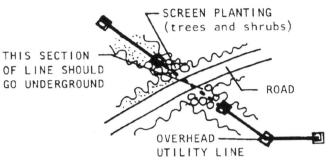

Road/overhead utility line crossing.

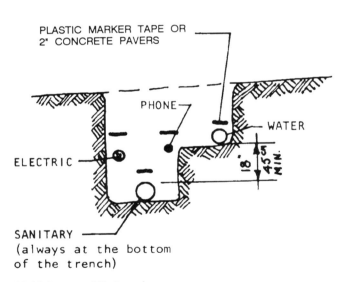

Multiple-use utility trench.

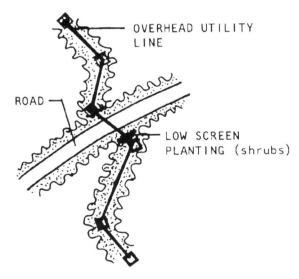

Alternate road/utility line crossing.

66

Chapter **12**
SIGNS

GENERAL

Signs are a necessary part of the total circulation system of any park, and, as such, they should be effective aids to the public in understanding and enjoying their visit. **All signs in a park should be unified in character** and relate to the total design theme of other park facilities. Pay careful attention to the design and placement of signs; they can add significantly to the park aesthetic experience or they can detract from the visit. In addition to park signing, it is necessary to have adequate "trailblazer" signs to direct the visitor to the park. The design of these signs and their placement must be coordinated with the affected highway departments.

The primary sign concept in use in large-scale parks today consists of word messages routed into wood. The wood blanks are usually stained or painted brown with the message in yellows, reds, oranges or white. These signs require repainting at regular intervals.

Many parks have now decided to rely more on graphic symbols and color associations. [29] This type of sign system consists of an arrow and symbol on a color field. It should be basic, functional, and should, in most instances, **not** attempt to decorate the landscape.

The use of graphic directional information on rubbish cans. National Zoo, Washington, D.C.

Park entrance sign. Denali National Park, Alaska.

The signs are frequently made of metal with applied decal-type symbols and lettering as used by highway departments.

The system now being put into effect by the federal government and, in particular, the National Park Service and shown in detail in their publications, is a slight modification of the standard international sign system and is strongly endorsed. [37]

DESIGN

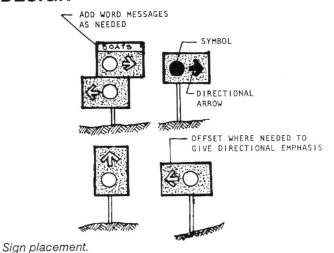

Sign placement.

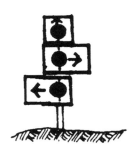

Sign cluster.

All sign components used in the construction of signs should be readily available and long lasting (seven to ten years minimum). Other than the main entrance sign all signs should be easily fabricated (e.g., by park staff or local highway sign shop) and easily maintained by the local park staff.

The design of individual symbols is not recommended, especially for parks which will serve foreign visitors. However, if the design of sign symbols is undertaken, it should produce a clearly understandable message which is rapidly communicated to the reader.

Symbols.

Signs can be two sided with messages on both sides.

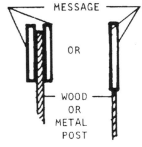

Two-sided sign.

Directional arrows must be clear. Do not try to invent your own. Use the international federal highway standard. It works!! Yours may not!

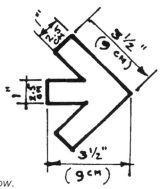

Directional arrow.

LAYOUT

Sign layouts must be planned.

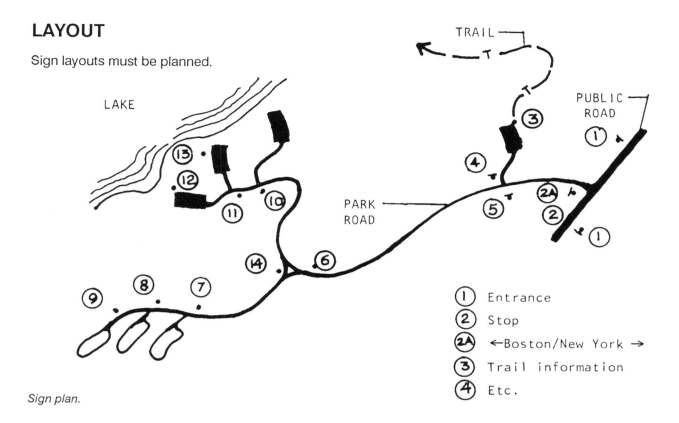

1. Entrance
2. Stop
2A. ←Boston/New York →
3. Trail information
4. Etc.

Sign plan.

In general, a minimum number of signs should be used. Good park planning can help reduce the number and kinds of signs needed.

Factors to be considered in a sign system layout:

- Visual distance and reaction time (number of feet needed between reader and sign increases as speed increases).

- All speed limit, stop, or other motor vehicle regulation and control signs must be legally enforceable to be of real value. Therefore, the signs must meet the specifications and standards of or be acceptable to the local traffic-enforcing authority.

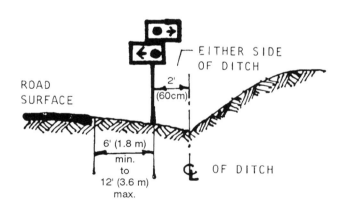

Sign location.

Chapter 13
OVERNIGHT USE

Extended stay desires of the people, relative inexpensiveness, and the nation's mobility have sustained this country's love for "camping." People have demonstrated a continued interest in the out-of-doors and "getting away from it all." To satisfy this need, public and private camping facilities have been developed and some continue to be built almost everywhere. Proper planning and design are particularly important to the preservation of the natural setting (one of the main reasons for most campgrounds being), and for effective, economical campground operation and maintenance. There is some indication that the number of "campers" may be declining, while at the same time overall tourism is increasing.

GENERAL

Before looking for areas suitable for overnight use, a determination must be made as to the need for such facilities. A survey of surrounding overnight facilities should be made which would include kinds of facilities, location, number of overnight units, number of capacity nights and the number of turn-aways. If the survey shows a need for overnight accommodations for the park users, the type of facilities desired should be determined. Most campgrounds having less than 100 sites are questionable; due to high operating costs they frequently operate at a loss. [85]

TYPES OF OVERNIGHT ACCOMMODATIONS

Many types of overnight stay can be provided. These experiences vary from primitive, walk-in camp sites to modern, full-service lodge facilities. A variety of types of overnight facilities are generally desirable in any major park and might include any or all of the following:

- Primitive walk-in sites; few or no amenities -- one of the few areas where there has been sustained growth in overnight use.

- Walk-in sites; water and sanitary facilities provided.

- Trailside shelters; limited water and sanitary facilities. As the name implies these are located along trails. See Chapter 8 Trails, page 31.

- Typical family campground; limited water and sanitary facilities.

- Typical family campground with flush toilets, showers and laundry tubs.

- Typical family campground with complete utility hookups at each camp site (trailer court). Almost exclusively private ownership.

- Housekeeping cabins.

- Lodges, with complete service including restaurant and/or cafeteria.

In addition, there are special types of overnight uses such as:

- Group tent camping -- water and sanitary only.

- Caravan camping areas -- limited sanitary facilities.

- Campventions -- large organized groups, i.e., Boy Scouts, National Recreation Trailer Association.

- Organized group camps -- complete lodging and dining facilities provided.

- Transient camping; usually along major tourist highways -- most frequently privately owned.

- Youth hostels.

The use of private or non governmental capital is normally considered and encouraged for the construction and operation of the more elaborate, financially viable types of overnight facilities such as group camps, lodges, cabins, trailer courts and youth hostels. The reasons for this are to avoid competition with private enterprise and to provide additional complimentary-use facilities to the typical park recreational activities.

GENERAL LOCATION FACTORS

Initial considerations in determining the location of overnight use areas include:

- Relationship of the facility to the park as a whole.

- Location of the site with respect to other internal park recreational facilities.

- Location of the site with regard to related facilities such as access roads, potable water supply and other utilities.

- Terrain that is level or gently rolling, well drained, wooded and/or partial shaded. Certain adverse conditions can often be overcome with good design.

Topography is the most compelling of the characteristics, followed by vegetative cover, soil conditions, drainage and rock outcrops. Visual separation between camp sites is desirable. It is necessary to screen camping areas from other uses.

TOPOGRAPHY

Gently rolling with good drainage, one to five percent is desirable. Fifteen percent maximum slope permitted, one percent minimum -- anything less will

Adverse sites can make exciting campgrounds as this one does in Craters of the Moon National Monument, Idaho.

- Size of campground and potential for expansion should be determined. It is generally not desirable to design campgrounds with less than 150 sites due to more expensive per site construction and operation costs.

GENERAL SITE REQUIREMENTS

The design of a camping area is necessarily dictated by the particular characteristics or natural environment of the site.

require extensive site modifications for drainage. Flat sites can be developed, but it is difficult and expensive.

VEGETATION

Vegetation with canopy for shade and understory for screening is best. Mature timber stands are undesirable because of eventual loss due to age or disease. Thinning of canopy and other forest management practices should be considered, when possible, prior to development to improve vegetative conditions.

SOILS

Soils should be such that water permeates quickly to avoid wet and/or muddy conditions. They should be able to take repeated traffic without adverse compaction or erosion. Depth to high or seasonally high water table should be enough so as not to adversely affect use or construction.

CHARACTERISTICS

Young adult campers without children are the most likely to seek remote camping (backpacking, etc.). As families begin to rear children, they are likely to modify their camping style to the traditional family camping with some backpacking. During the period when their children are between 5 and 14 years old, families are most likely to do only roadside camping.

However, as their children mature and leave home, some parents will again seek out remote-only camping experiences. [43] Most will leave the camping market altogether or utilize recreational vehicles.

ACTIVITIES [42]

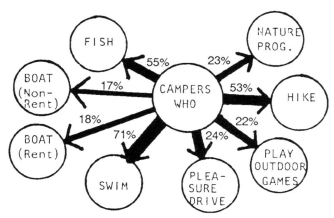

Campers who do other activities.

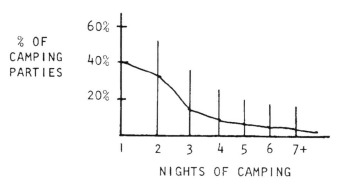

Length of stay.

ATTITUDES [43]

- Camping is . . .

  For 10% a social experience, not a physical one.
  For 27% a physical experience, not social.
  For 28% neither physical nor social.
  For 34% both a social and a physical experience.

- Screening between campsites is considered to be more important than spacing.

- There is a diversity of desires for campground size.

- **Water** -- both the availability of water-oriented activities and of campsites in sight of water are, overall, the most dominant factors in campground attraction.

TRENDS IN CAMPING

- Many people (possibly 40%) during the camping season camp with friends. Consideration should be given to providing accommodations (10% of sites) for more than one family site complex, possibly two to three units together. [7, 13, 33] See page 80.

- Off-season camping use may be declining; it generally averages between 10% to 20% of total attendance.

- Trailer and camper to tent ratio varies according to type of campground and section of the country. Generally in the East it runs about 2 to 1; the figure is stable at this time. [20, 34] Four to thirteen percent of sites had two or more cars. [4, 21]

- Activity peaks at camps: 1:00 p.m., 5:00 p.m. and 9:30 p.m., with 50 percent of the campers never leaving campground. [7]

- Friday and Saturday are, by far, the most heavily used nights; weekdays about one-half capacity. [6, 85] The three major camping weekends are Memorial Day, the Fourth of July and Labor Day. Some parks run at 100 percent capacity for several days at a time; however, recent trends have been for campground occupancy to vary anywhere from 10% to 20% in small, rustic parks to approximately 50% except on holiday weekends. [20, 85] Approximately 85% to 90% of the campers in Pennsylvania stay three nights or less. Off season they stay only one-and-one-half days. [34]

- Fireplaces are seldom used for cooking (hot dogs, coffee, marshmallows are exceptions), and their prime function is for heat and evening atmosphere.

Cooking marshmallows over an open fire. The essence of camping for the young and the young at heart.

- Private campgrounds continue to upgrade their camp site facilities with a greater number of full hookup sites to meet their clientele's demand for full amenities. This includes expanding the amperage from 15 to 30 amps due to more electric appliances in the campers. [85]
- The distance traveled for camping trips is reducing.

TYPES OF CAMPING EQUIPMENT

There are significant regional trends in the use of recreational vehicles, with the west and the plains country having a very high percentage of camper trucks; the remainder of the country using a combination of travel and camping trailers. This regional difference is important when preparing the campground layout, and particularly the individual camp spurs and their living spaces. The size of a vehicle and its functional characteristics dictate how the arrangement of the living area should be developed. [18, 34]

RECREATIONAL VEHICLE OWNER PROFILE

In general, recreational vehicle owners fall into three categories: skilled, professional and retired. Nearly one-half of the owners have no children at home. Of the families with children, one-third have one child, one-third have two children and the remainder three or more. The average camper with children had two children, ages 0 - 17, with 82 percent of the parties having two children, ages 7 - 12. Recreational vehicle owners are generally affluent. Median age of household head is fifty, with 70 percent between 36 and 65, and 11 percent over 65. The median distance traveled by respondents in 1968 was 3,400 miles (5,500 km).

Distance traveled is being reduced due to high gas prices and available time. This information was based on 2500+ replies--divided 80 percent travel trailers, 10 percent truck campers, 5 percent camp trailers and 5 percent miscellaneous [27, 62]

Rental is becoming an alternative to ownership of this expensive equipment and should be recognized as a factor which will influence the kinds of campers and their camping needs.

WATER AND SANITARY FACILITIES

The minimum sanitary facilities provided in the family campground should be sealed-vault latrines. This would include toilets for the women and urinals and toilets for the men. Hand-washing facilities should be provided. A hand pump for potable water supply is necessary; potable water supply from faucets is desirable.

The more modern facilities would be washhouses or a combination of washhouses and comfort stations. The washhouses include tempered water showers, flush toilets, tempered and cold running water in the lavatories, electric receptacles and night lighting, and may be heated for winter use if the campground is to be used in the off seasons.

Night lighting and electrical receptacles in comfort stations are desirable. In remote areas photovoltaic collector panels with storage cells may be a feasible way of providing the necessary minimal electrical requirements.

If extended-stay camping is expected, coin-operated washers and dryers can be provided in the washhouses or a centrally located camp center facility. The comfort station should have flush toilets, tempered and cold running water in the lavatories, and electrical receptacles. A comfort station may be heated depending on need.

A potable water supply should be provided with freeze proof faucets in cold climate areas where camping is permitted during the winter within 150 feet (45 m) of each campsite.

WATER SUPPLY

- With showers and flush toilets: 25 to 30 gallons (95 to 115 l) per camper day. [31] With flush toilets only: 15 to 20 gallons (60 to 75 l) per camper per day. [31] Without showers and flush toilets: 5 gallons (19 l) per camper per day. [31]

- Emergency storage: estimate at double the anticipated average maximum day use for the capacity of the water storage reservoir.

- Distance from drinking water to most distant camp site: 300 feet (90 m), maximum; 150 feet (45 m), optimum.

SANITARY FACILITIES

- Distance from comfort station to farthest unit: 500 feet (150 m), maximum; 300 feet (90 m), desirable.

- Distance from washhouse to farthest unit: 600 feet (180 m), maximum; 400 feet (120 m), desirable.

- In cold climates, at least one washhouse should be heated in campgrounds that are to be used during the off-season.

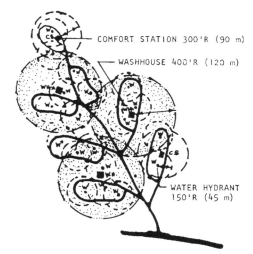

COMFORT STATION 300'R (90 m)

WASHHOUSE 400'R (120 m)

WATER HYDRANT 150'R (45 m)

Location of campground water and sanitary facilities.

Suggested Sanitary Requirements -- Most states have standards which must be followed. [16]

No. of Tent or Trailer Spaces*	No. of Toilet Seats Male/Female**		No. of Lavatories Male/Female		No. of Urinals Male	No. of Showers+ Male/Female		No. of Sanitary Stations
1-15	1	1	1	1	1	1	1	1
16-30	1	2	2	2	1	1	1	1
31-45	2	2	3	3	1	1	1	1
45-60	2	3	3	3	2	2	2	1
61-80	3	4	4	4	2	2	2	1
81-100	3	4	4	4	2	3	3	1

* For recreational areas having more than 100 tent or trailer spaces, there should be provided: one additional toilet seat and lavatory for each sex per each additional 30 tent or trailer spaces; one additional men's urinal per each additional 60 sites; and one additional sanitary station per each additional 100 tent or trailer spaces or fractional part thereof.

** Urinals specifically designed for females may also be provided in lieu of toilet seats, but for not more than one-third of the required number of toilet seats. American women have not readily accepted this type of fixture.

\+ A centrally located washhouse can be substituted for individual bathhouse shower facilities -- this facility can be concession-operated and may be part of a camp center complex.

TRAILER WASTE STATION

The trailer waste station is a necessary service to campers providing for the dumping and cleaning of their sewage holding tanks in a designated location. This station should be located, wherever possible, between the entrance station and the first campsite, and properly screened from the road. One trailer waste station should be provided for each 100 sites or fraction thereof. Proper sewerage inlets to accommodate drain hoses and water facilities for cleaning the trailer tank should be provided. Instructions as to use and health hazards should be displayed. Locate, when possible, so that connection to the campground sanitary system can be made.

Campground dump station. Denali National Park, Alaska.

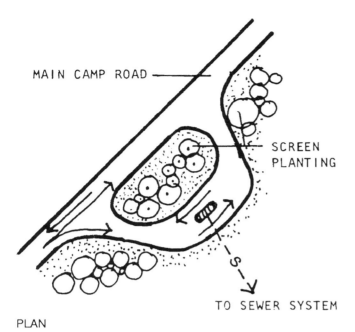

MAIN CAMP ROAD

SCREEN
PLANTING

TO SEWER SYSTEM

PLAN

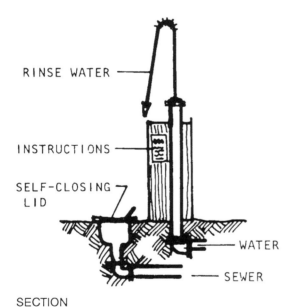

RINSE WATER

INSTRUCTIONS

SELF-CLOSING
LID

WATER

SEWER

SECTION

Trailer waste station.

ELECTRICITY

- Required for all public-use buildings in modern campgrounds.

- All-night lighting is desirable at all comfort stations. In primitive areas consider using solar panels.

- Electrical service to individual campsites is a frequently requested camper amenity -- consider in some highly developed campgrounds and especially in private camp areas. [26, 34, 62]

CAMPING ROADS

The main camping area entrance road should be two-laned and located to permit easy, safe ingress and egress relative to site distance and grade from the public road.

Roads within the developed area should be designed to fit into the landscape with as little disturbance to the surroundings as possible. All roads should receive an appropriate surface treatment to minimize maintenance and dust problems.

Roads should not exceed a 12 percent grade where camp vehicles are permitted. Grades to 18 percent may be possible in tent-only areas under unusual conditions. Road width will depend on unit design, traffic flow, topography and the vehicular circulation pattern. It is necessary to lay these roads out by eye at the site or, at a minimum, field check after a survey to make any desired adjustments that will save trees and other natural features of the area as well as to obtain maximum usage of the site.

One-way loop roads throughout the campsite area, where possible, will provide a minimum intrusion on the landscape, reduce through traffic and improve circulation (see Chapter 10, "Roads and Parking").

ENTRANCE STATION AND SECOND CAR PARKING

The purpose of the entrance station is to organize the operations of the campground. These operations include the collection of fees and the issuing of camping permits, dissemination of campground information, security for the campers and provisions for emergency communications. Experience indicates that contact stations should be so designed as to allow issuance of permits to the camper sitting in his car and also allow space for parking for several car-camper units so campers can stop and walk back to the contact station to obtain additional information. The functions associated with the contact station are as follows:

- The back-up space length should be determined by anticipated use and operational characteristics of each campground. One guide is to provide for ten feet of back-up space for every campsite.

- There should be a by-pass lane around the contact station for campers already admitted to the campground and separate exit lanes.

- There should be turnaround provisions for campers finding the campground full.

- Reception space and counter space, office/storage and employee sanitary facilities should be provided in the contact building.
- Some park operators prefer that a second-car parking lot for the campers and visitors be provided adjacent to but before entering through the contact station. The size of the second car parking lot should equal 10 percent of the campsites and be capable of expansion to 25 percent depending on the demonstrated needs. (See Chapter 10 - "Roads and Parking.")

CAMP FIRE PROGRAMS

Provision of facilities for evening camp fire programs should be considered for all campgrounds of 150 or more units. A high-quality program may attract users from outside the overnight use area and possibly some late staying day-users.

LOCATION
- Within walking distance of the overnight accommodations.
- Adequate visual and sound separation from campsites.
- Within 400' (120 m) of parking. Parking can possibly be combined with other parking. The number of parking spaces needed is determined by the distance the amphitheater is from the overnight units. The greater the distance, the greater the number of parking spaces needed.
- Handicapped accessible.
- Can sometimes utilize visitor center facilities; however, most campers would prefer the outdoors.

DESIGN
- Seating capacity -- maximum - one-half the overnight use capacity; recommended - one-fourth of overnight capacity. Varies with quality of the evening program.
- Orientation -- screen must be put in evening shade, facing east.

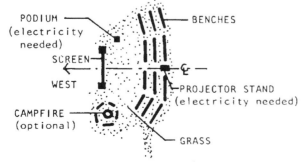

Orientation of campfire program facilities.

- Place on slope for better visual exposure.
- Benches desirable for at least one-half of the design capacity. In areas where there is not much rain the remaining capacity can be lawn and/or bring your own seating.
- Screen -- rear projection nice but not required.
- Desirable items:
  - Lighting -- along walks; flood lighting in seating area.
  - Camp fire circle.
- Utilities -- electricity - required.
- Must be made accessible to handicapped from the parking lot.

See Chapter 7, "Interpretive Facilities" for additional information.

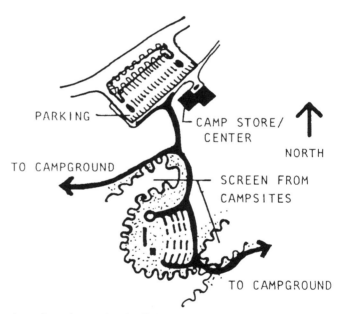

Location of camping facilities.

GENERAL AMENITIES

Laundry facilities (coin-operated) -- desired by most campers staying longer than two days. [34] They can be located in the bathhouse or centrally located in a camp center complex.

Camp Store -- centrally located on the main campground road. All major campgrounds (200+ sites) should have such a facility unless there is a local store where camper supplies can be purchased.

Firewood -- should be made available to campers, possibly on a fee basis by the concessionaire.

Telephone -- All overnight facilities should have access to pay telephone(s). [25, 26] These can be located as needed but, at a minimum, one should be provided at each contact station.

Facilities for Handicapped -- Some campsites should be designed and marked for use by the physically handicapped.

Trails (hiking and bicycling) -- Trails in overnight areas are as much an integral part of the facility as roads. Pedestrian trails should connect all washhouses or comfort stations and be strategically located so they are easily accessible from all campsites. They should also connect to play areas, the central camping complex and to main recreation and day-use areas when feasible. (See Chapter 8 - "Trails.") In addition, bicycle trails should be designed into the basic campground layout.

Play Areas and Play Fields -- Play areas are of importance in family campgrounds. Play fields should be provided in all areas subject to heavy group use. (See Chapter 14 - "Play Areas and Play Fields.")

Boat Launching – Facilities for launching boats should be provided in campgrounds located on navigable water. Generally, these facilities should be much less elaborate than those in day-use boat launching areas. The launching will be for campers only. A mooring rail should be provided for overnight storage of boats. (See Chapter 17 - "Boating" for details.)

FAMILY CAMPGROUND

Family campground layout.

The family campground area basically provides a campsite including a living area, tent pad and parking spur for locating the trailer and car. Water and sanitary facilities are provided for camper convenience. Usually an overnight charge is made for the use of the site and this includes conveniences.

The degree of sophistication -- that is, flush toilets and showers -- is dependent on the type of facility desired, the availability of capital funds for development and the aesthetic and natural character of the area.

It is generally desirable to separate transient campers from long-term campers, especially along major tourist routes. Long-term campers generally like their quiet, while transients may not be so considerate. The designation of one of the segments of the campground which is somewhat separated from the rest of the camp may be an adequate solution.

CAMPING SITE

The basic type of camping unit consists of a cleared and leveled area for table, fireplace, tent, and camping trailer. Other recreational vehicles and automobiles should be located on, and restricted to, the parking spur.

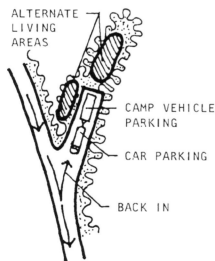

Campsite.

PARKING SPUR

- Level areas adjacent to the living site; two percent maximum grade over the last 25 feet (7.5 m). Total length of spur should be 50 feet (15 m). Space for two (2) vehicles.

- Seventy percent of the spaces should be developed to accommodate one car and trailer.

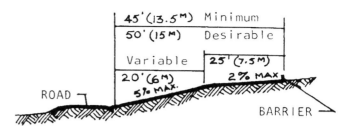

Section -- Campsite parking spur.

THE SITE

- Privacy -- Generally, campers prefer a sense of privacy, while many wish to have all the comforts of home. Approximately 70 percent to 75 percent wish to have flush toilets and hot showers. However, only one-third want on-site water or sewer hook-ups. [34]

- Number of people per site: eight — maximum; four — average.

- Units per acre: Six to ten units spaced about 60 to 70 feet (18 - 21 m) on site centers is optimum. Number of units varies according to results desired, topography, vegetation and general land character. Ten to 14 units spaced 50 feet (15 m) on site centers is maximum developement. [14, 18] Use 50 feet (15 m) spacing only in urban situations or for transient camping. Many campers prefer site spacing of 100 feet (30 m) but development costs per site, especially in the more modern campgrounds, are too high.

- Campsites should be numbered so the numbers can be seen from the cars. A place to display a camp permit (possibly on the number post) is desirable.

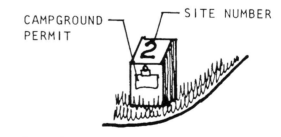

Campsite marker.

RUBBISH

- One trash can per two-to-three campsites depending on the frequency of rubbish pick-up.

- If dumpsters must be used, locate at sanitary facilities on a prepared surface.

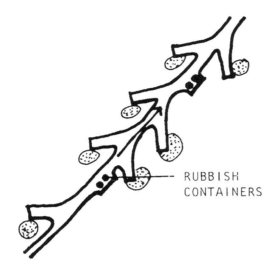

Rubbish container placement.

- **Multiple Family Sites** -- As previously noted, 10 percent or more of the sites should be designed to accommodate two or more families.

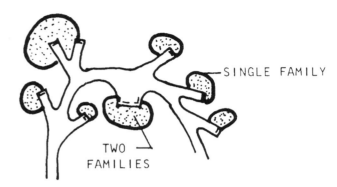

Percentage of sites should be multi-family.

LIVING AREA

- **Location** -- In the East and Midwest it is desirable to locate 90+ percent of the living spaces to the left of the spurs (facing the spur from the road) since the most-used recreational vehicles' doors are located on the right side. However, in the West and the Southwest a significant percentage of the sites should be located in the rear of the spur to accommodate pickup campers. In hilly areas it may be necessary to select an alternative location for the living area. These sites should be reserved for tent campers.

- **Tables** -- They should be secured in a permanent location so the campers cannot move them. This eliminates the problem of compaction and loss of vegetation over the entire camp site. The area around the table should be prepared with stone or other appropriate material to protect the site from deterioration.

- **Living Space** -- 600 square feet (55 sq. m) is desirable. 400 plus square feet (40 sq. m) is minimum for table, stove and tent space of which 300 square feet (30 sq. m) should be leveled (1% ± grade) for tent space.

- **Campsite Surfacing** -- Campsites should be well drained, free of large rocks and have a surface which does not become muddy.

- **Parking Spur** -- Campers prefer their parking spur to be surfaced with gravel - 45%; paved - 35%; grass - 15%. [26]

- **Site Spacing** -- Adequate space, 100 to 150 feet (30 to 45 m), should be left between campsites and bodies of water. This is public-use space for all campers.

- **Buffer Space** -- Area surrounding the campground is necessary, in addition to the pervious requirements, to give a sense of spaciousness and the out-of-doors.

- **Parking** -- A small parking space of two or three cars should be provided at each comfort station and washhouse, one of which must be designated for handicapped use.

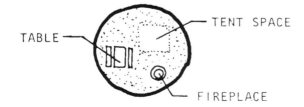

Living area.

80

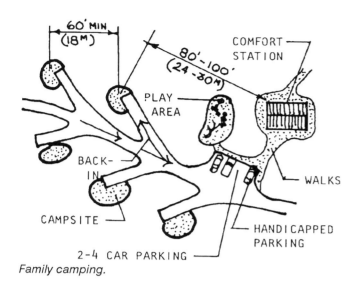

Family camping.

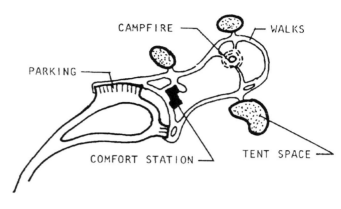

Group tent camping.

GROUP CAMPING

Groups vary in size from 10 to 200 with most groups being less than 30. They are frequently noisy and like privacy. Because of this, group camps should be removed from other public-use facilities and be able to accommodate various numbers of people. It may be desirable to develop several smaller units within an area which could accommodate several small organized groups separately or, by combining units, a large group could utilize the area. The campsites should be for groups of 10 to 80 persons and include tent sites, tables, fireplace rings, campfire circle, parking, sanitary and water facilities, internal roads, trail system, barriers, signs and possible cooking shelters. These units require a minimum of five acres (two hectares). [4]

Suggested Sanitary Requirements* - Most states have standards which must be followed. The following are patterned after those of the State of Pennsylvania. [16]

No. of Persons	No. of Toilet Seats Male/Female		No. of Lavatories Male/Female		No. of Urinals** Male/Female		No. of Showers Male/Female	
1-20	1	2	1	1	1	1	1	1
Each addtional 20 persons	+1	+1***	+1	+1	+1	+1	+1	+1

 * Organized camps which do not provide overnight lodging and serve a maximum of one meal per day are not usually subject to these minimum number of sanitary facilities but should provide toilet and lavatory facilities.

 ** Urinals for males may be provided in lieu of toilet seats but for not more than one-third of the required number of toilets seats.

 *** Urinals specifically designed for females may also be provided in lieu of toilet seats but for not more than one-third of the required number of toilet seats.

Parking - one area for 15 to 20 cars.

CAMPING – BOAT-IN UNIT (ACCESS FROM WATER ONLY)

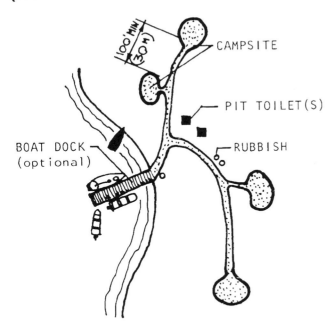

Boat-in camping.

A campsite for family use on land adjoining rivers, reservoirs and lakes, not accessible by car, with cleared shoreline for boat access, tent site, table and stove. The areas are relatively small, accommodate but few camp units, have water-tight pits or chemical toilets and no developed water (except where a source is readily available and may be developed at little cost); some areas should be retained in a primitive nature. A service road to the area is desirable.

REQUIREMENTS

- **Minimum area** is a level space adequate to accommodate a tent and possibly a table and camp fireplace. Ample buffer space between units should be provided.

- **Number of people** -- 8 - maximum; 3.5 - average.

- **Units per acre** (ha) -- variable to fit site with two to four/acre (four to eight/ha) being average.

- **Distance between units** -- 100 feet (30 m) - optimum; generally greater than in a typical campground.

- **Toilet facilities** -- one pit or chemical toilet to four camp units.

- **Rubbish receptacles** should be placed at each boat area; one per four campsites minimum unless a carryout policy is enforced.

- **Boat tie-up** -- Adequate space should be provided – either a boat dock or mooring rail. (See Chapter 17 "Boating.")

CAMPING – PRIMITIVE (NO PUBLIC VEHICULAR ACCESS)

A campsite similar to a boat unit, the difference being that one walks to the area from a central parking space rather than boating to it. At some locations, these campsites may be adjacent to riding and hiking trails and could be utilized by the trail users. See Chapter 8 - "Trails," Trailside Camping, page 34.

Frequently no facilities of any kind are provided under these conditions. Tight control must be maintained on the number of users to prevent site deterioration.

Service vehicle access is desirable to camp areas with several sites. An area with one or two sites might be serviced by horseback or trail bike.

CAMPING – CARAVAN (ORGANIZED ADULT GROUP CAMPING)

An area for groups of self-contained camper units may be desirable in larger destination parks. Make sure there is a demonstrated demand before including space for this activity in the plans.

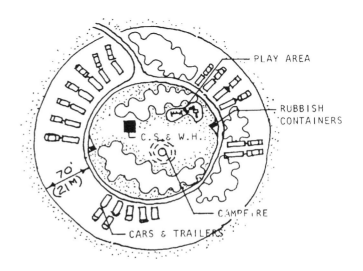

Caravan camping.

REQUIREMENTS

- Large grassed or surfaced level site approximately 160 feet (50 m) in diameter and circular in shape with a minimum of one washhouse per 200 camper units.

- Central showers and sanitary facilities

- Central campfire circle.

- Separated from other campers.

- Rubbish receptacle at a minimum of 200 feet (60 m) on center, or dumpsters at the comfort stations.

- Recreation facilities -- e.g., horseshoe pits, area for badminton, volleyball, softball, etc.

CAMPING — ORGANIZED GROUP

An area set up specifically to handle formal organization camps. They are frequently built and operated by the organization and consist of a sleeping space (cabins, tent platforms or tent areas), washhouses, lodge, dining hall and staff residences and parking.

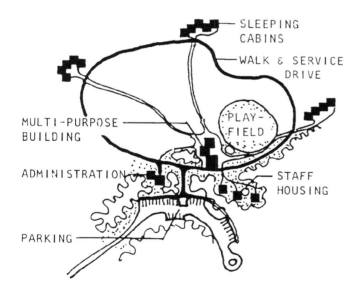

Organized group camp.

REQUIREMENTS

- Maximum distance from sleeping and use areas to sanitary facilities -- 300 feet (90 m); desirable -- 200 feet (60 m) or less.

- Maximum distance to showers -- 1000 feet (300 m); desirable -- 600 feet (180 m) or less.

- Maximum distance to dining hall -- 1000 ´feet (300 m).

- Minimum size -- 5 acres (2 ha).

- Parking space for 20 percent of the number of beds and overflow parking for an additional 10 percent.

TRAILER AREAS — SPECIAL TRAILER FACILITIES

REQUIREMENTS

- Ten units/acre (25 units/ha) calculated as follows: width - 40' (12 m) x length - 70' (21 m) + 25' (8 m) for road = 4000 square feet/unit (360 sq. m/unit).

- Design factors: 8 percent or less slopes, good access, adequate utilities -- picnic tables and stoves (campfire space) not required but desirable. Comfort stations not required to the extent needed in camping areas.

- Complete utility hook-ups required at each site.

- Central showers and washhouse - 600 feet (180 m) desirable maximum distance from trailer units.

- Private capital normally used for the construction and operations.

- A combination recreation room, office and store is usually provided.

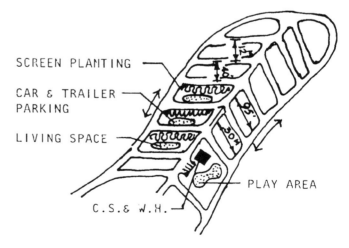

Trailer areas.

LODGES, CABINS, TENT PLATFORMS

The larger, more heavily used parks should consider all types of overnight accommodations, including lodges, cabins and tent platforms. These basically manmade types of facilities should be developed and operated with private funds with adequate using agency controls to insure a quality service at reasonable prices. Long-term leases (30 years or more) are necessary to encourage adequate capital for this type of development. A complete market analysis must be done before undertaking these capital and labor intensive facilities.

TRANSIENT CAMPING

These are campers who stay overnight in a campground while in route to a destination area. Standards for this type of overnight user are typical of family camping with the following exceptions:

(1) Site density may be very high with camp units located as close as 40 feet (12 m) on center and camp roads 150 feet (45 m) on center.

(2) Should be located only when in proximity to a major transportation route and easy access is available to the park from the main highway.

(3) Recreation facilities should be limited to children's play areas (use native material where possible).

(4) Interpretive facilities and programs should be minimized.

Chapter 14
PLAY AREAS AND PLAY FIELDS

Most large-scale parks are intended for use by a variety of age groups. These groups have different needs and interests in addition to the major recreational activities or picnicking, swimming, etc. [33] This is especially true for younger people, although older people's needs must also be considered.

PLAY AREAS

Play areas should be developed for various age levels and designed to meet the ability and the interest of the intended users. Recommended age groups are pre-school (ages 3 to 5), elementary (ages 6 to 13) and teenagers and young adults. Where possible, play areas for the different age groups should be separated since the interests and abilities of the three age groups are NOT compatible. [83] For additional information, refer to one of several excellent books available on the design of these types of facilities. [80, 81, 82]

PRE-SCHOOL AGE

(1) Locate out of general traffic patterns but still close to areas of adult activity and, if possible, adjacent to grass fields.

(2) Design to accommodate little people with minimum supervision.

(3) Few moving parts.

(4) Locate in partial sun in northern climates while shade is necessary in southern areas.

(5) Provide benches for supervising adults.

(6) Should have sand for playing and digging, climbers, slides, and possibly small swing(s). The area should blend into the surroundings and utilize materials and designs not commonly found in the neighborhood parks.

(7) Keep separate from older play areas.

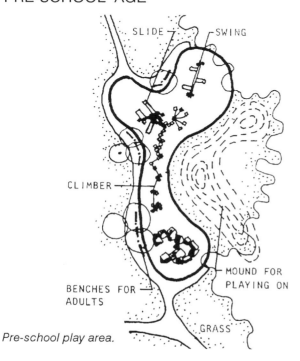

Pre-school play area.

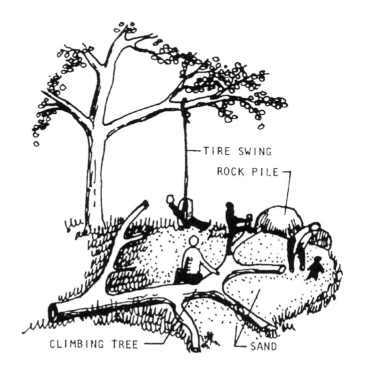

Natural material can be made into a children's playground.

ELEMENTARY SCHOOL AGE

(1) Locate within sight of adult activity areas but some-what away from picnic sites due to noise. Possibly locate in conjunction with a play field.

(2) Design to accommodate active, inquisitive children who, although seeking a challenge, also need to succeed. Make it clearly more challenging and interesting to older children so they will not be tempted to use the pre-school area.

(3) Moving parts "OK" and of major interest to this age group -- separate activities for safety.

(4) Limited seating needed for adults.

(5) Some shade desirable, especially in southern states.

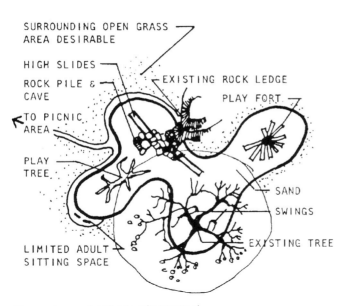

Elementary school-age playground.

TEENAGE AND YOUNG ADULTS

(1) Locate only in parks where there is a desire to have this age group present. Especially desirable in areas of urban concentrations in conjunction with beaches and swimming facilities.

(2) Separate from family activity areas.

(3) Facilities to consider: weight lifting, parallel bars, high bar, horse, rings, adult-size swings and volley ball.

(4) Viewing -- spectator area.

PLAY FIELDS

A large open space, 200' x 200' (60 x 60 m) - minimum; 300'± width x 600'± length (90 x 180 m) - desirable; gently sloping for drainage -- two percent - desirable; five percent - maximum. Locate, where possible, in existing open fields or in poor timber stands where trees can easily be removed without environmental damage. However, if necessary, good trees must be removed. Care should be taken in locating facilities to minimize environmental damage from vegetative removal or grade modifications.

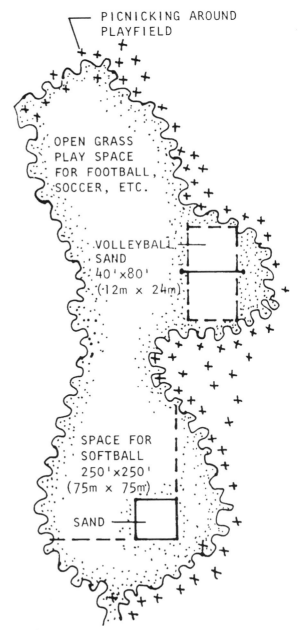

Playfield.

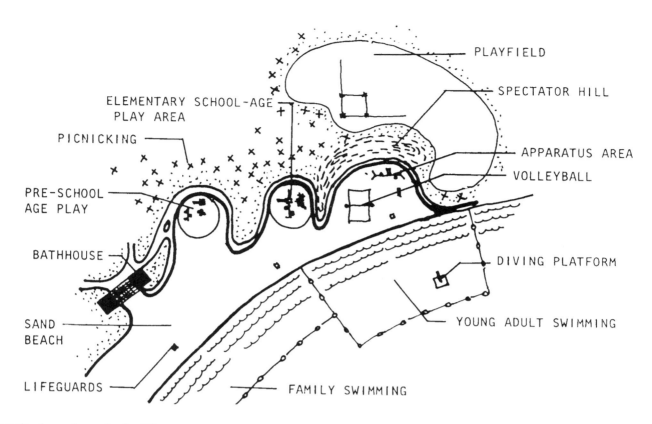

ELEMENTARY SCHOOL-AGE PLAY AREA

PICNICKING

PRE-SCHOOL AGE PLAY

BATHHOUSE

SAND BEACH

LIFEGUARDS

PLAYFIELD

SPECTATOR HILL

APPARATUS AREA

VOLLEYBALL

DIVING PLATFORM

YOUNG ADULT SWIMMING

FAMILY SWIMMING

Location for various play facilities.

Playfields would normally be located in conjunction with picnic area, beach areas and all group-use areas. The space should be designed to allow for softball/ baseball, football (pickup type), frisbee throwing and volleyball. In addition, special use spaces for regionally important activities such as soccer should be considered. Volleyball areas are frequently located on beaches. When they are part of the project see Chapter 21 - "Swimming."

OLDER PEOPLES' SPACE

Provide space for horseshoes, sitting and viewing park activities and possibly, shuffleboard. These facilities should be in close relationship with other activity areas so that the users will be part of the whole recreating scene but separate enough so they can enjoy their activities at their own pace.

Handicapped accessibility standards must be utilized throughout these older people areas.

One or more picnic pavilions with tables should be considered.

Chapter 15
PICNICKING

This type of park use appeals to all ages, with particular appeal to urbanites, and normally originates within 1-1/2 hours' drive of the park. [21, 33, 35] The day-use party participates in an average of 2 to 2.5 activities. About 15 to 20 percent of visitors, **excluding** sightseers/transients, participate in only **one** activity. Sixty-five to 70 percent of use occurs on weekends during the primary use season -- normally summer, except in the mild winter areas of the southern states. [8, 20] For more locally oriented urban parks the use is likely to be slightly more evenly distributed over the week.

ACTIVITIES [42]

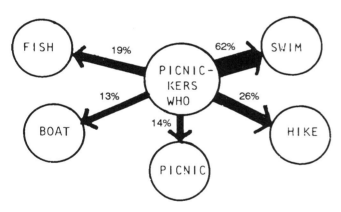

% of Picnickers who do various activities.

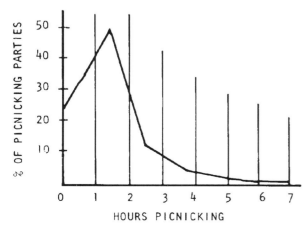

% of parties who picnic for various time periods.

ATTITUDES

• Prefer tables located where there is some shade and, to some extent, a sense of privacy. Open areas with scattered trees are most desirable or under low, coniferous canopy in preference to high, deciduous canopy. [43]

• Definite preference for tables near parking areas. Use drops off greatly over 60 feet (18 m) beyond a parking area (about the length of many back yards) and, given the opportunity, many picnickers will drive right up to the picnic table. [43]

• Picnickers will spread their lunches on the grass rather than walk 400 feet (120 m) to a table. [43]

• All people will picnic as close to a water body as they are allowed or to which they can physically get.

GENERAL

• The typical visitor parks as close to his final destination as possible and then goes to his major objective (beach, picnic table), and then to the comfort station.

• Most prefer to be able to have an opportunity to swim. One in two wants play fields and areas nearby. One in three expresses a desire for hiking trails. [33]

• Most picnickers have a variety of equipment including ice chest, supplies, cooking stove or grill, chairs, blankets, radios, etc.

Typical picnic site.

- Picnic facilities with a view (especially of water) are used more than those without a view. [41] Picnicking adjacent to swimming is usually heavily used.

- Many picnic areas with partially shaded grass areas will have a significant percentage of the users picnicking informally without using tables.

Lawn picnicking.

- Maximum slope -- 20 percent requires terracing; desirable slope -- 2 to 15 percent.

PICNIC SHELTERS

Groups prefer shelters. [21, 22, 28, 35] When provided, these popular facilities should be built to minimize operating and maintenance costs. They should be considered for all heavy-use areas. Size and number of shelters depend on the normal weather conditions and local interest. In all cases, the shelters must be designed to be compatible with the existing or proposed park architecture and the surrounding environment. Most park agencies reserve pavilion space for a fee.

Vehicular access to shelter is required to drop off supplies and equipment and for service. There is also need for a fireplace with wood storage and work counter and picnic tables.

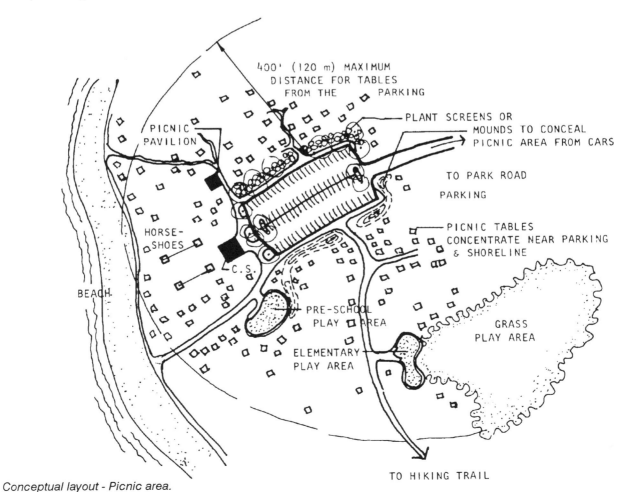

Conceptual layout - Picnic area.

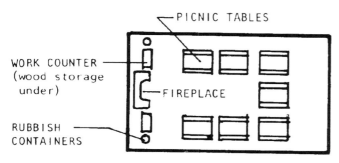

Picnic shelter.

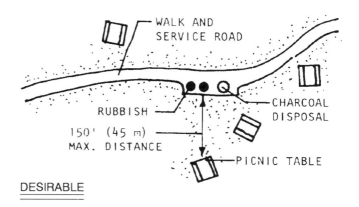

DESIRABLE

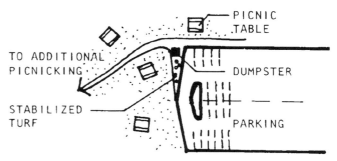

ACCEPTABLE

Location of rubbish disposal receptacles.

SANITARY FACILITIES

- Distance from restroom to picnic tables -- 300 feet (90 m) -- optimum; 400 feet (120 m) -- maximum. Sanitary facilities should be located in relation to the use area, not the parking lots. [14, 28]

SANITARY FIXTURE REQUIREMENTS [16]

No. of Males/Females	No. of Toilet Seats		No. of Lavatories		No. of Urinals*
	Male/Female**		Male/Female		Male/Female**
50/50	1	2	1	1	1
100/100	1	3	1	1	2
250/250	2	4	2	2	2
500/500	3	6	2	3	3
750/750	4	8	3	4	4
1000/1000	5	10	4	5	6
2000/2000	6	14	5	6	7

* Urinals should be provided for men.

** Urinals (bidets) may be provided for women in lieu of toilets but may not exceed one-third the number of required toilet seats (see men's urinals).

RUBBISH DISPOSAL

Desirable: One rubbish can per four units located within 150 feet (45 m) of the picnic tables. They should be easily accessible to motorized equipment for easy pickup. Due to operation costs this type of rubbish disposal has generally been replaced by dumpsters located in parking lots. Rubbish cans are still needed, however, in areas of high use and along major walkways.

Acceptable: Dumpsters located at parking lots. They must be located on a stabilized surface and accessible to a large rubbish disposal truck. They should be painted in a color compatible with the park colors. Location must be visible to all using the picnic area while not becoming a major visual focal point. An enclosure is desirable from an aesthetic standpoint, but may reduce its use for trash disposal if it is difficult to use.

Charcoal disposal facilities located within 150 feet (45 m) of every picnic table. This can be a major safety problem if not properly handled because small children sometimes mistake the coals as sand and have been severely burned by the sometimes still hot coals.

WATER SUPPLY

- Distance from drinking water to farthest unit: 300 feet (90 m) -- maximum; 150 feet (45 m) -- optimum.

- Five gallons (19 l) per person per day (with flush toilets).

- 2.5 gallons (9.5 l) per person per day (without flush toilets).

SOILS

It is extremely important that heavily used recreation facilities be sited on soils that can sustain the intended use and still retain desired vegetation.

PARKING

- Located to minimize visual intrusion on the picnic area.

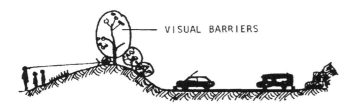

VISUAL BARRIERS

Parking in use area.

- Maximum distance from parking to picnic table -- 400 feet (120 m); 250 to 300 feet (75 to 90 m) -- desirable. [35]

OVERFLOW PARKING

- Usually gravel or turf, frequently called "stabilized turf" and should be considered part of the total design capacity; should be provided in all heavily used areas. This type of parking is inexpensive to build and maintain and minimizes the visual impact on the park when not at maximum use. The amount of over-flow parking can be arrived at by determining the average heavy-use day and then providing the additional holiday and heaviest day parking as overflow. In no circumstances should a park be permitted to exceed its total design capacity.

- Overflow parking must not use open fields normally used for recreational activities. These are most needed for their intended use during heavy attendance.

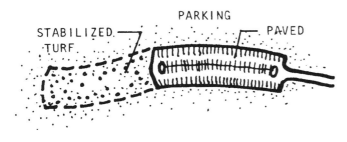

PARKING

STABILIZED TURF

PAVED

Overflow parking.

ACTIVITY AREA

At day-use areas subjected to heavy use, it is desirable to provide facilities and/or space for various recreation activities such as children's play, horseshoes, volleyball, baseball, softball, etc. (these areas to be designed for informal, non-supervised use). Areas should be surfaced according to intended use. Play fields should be a minimum of 200' x 200' (60 x 60 m); desirable - 300' x 600' (90 x 180 m), of clear, nearly level land suitable for playing ball games (see Chapter 14 - "Play Areas and Playfields").

FOOD SALES

All areas of heavy use in parks should be studied for the need to provide for the sale of picnic supplies and/or prepared food. The facilities range from coin-operated vending machines to traditional restaurants. For a profitable operation, sales buildings should be located so as to maximize visitor access while not adversely affecting the resource or park function.

REQUIREMENTS

- Market analysis to determine if there is adequate clientele to support the proposed operation.

- Adequate parking.

- Service access, including delivery trucks.

- Water, sewer, electric and telephone services.

- If year-round operation, facility must be winterized and heated in cooler areas. The size and kind of eating facility is dependent upon the number and kind of clientele.

- Provide an enclosed, screened rubbish area.

FAMILY UNIT

Designed for a typical family group of 3.5 to 8 people.

REQUIREMENTS

- Minimum area: 225 square feet (20 sq. m).

- Minimum table spacing: 20 feet (6 m) on center; 40 feet (12 m) - desirable. Tables should be fixed (non-movable) in heavily used areas and may be fixed or movable in normal developments. At least 10% of tables should be handicapped accessible.

A handicapped accessible picnic table. Earthworks Park, Kent, Washington.

- Units per acre (hectare): 40 (100) -- maximum only in extremely heavily used parks and then only when site conditions will permit; 10 to 15 (25 to 35) -- desirable maximum.

- Water: one hose bib-fountain combination within 150 feet (45 m) of all picnic sites.

- Parking: two cars per picnic unit in urban areas; 1.5 cars per unit in non-urban areas.

- Adequate shade from 11:00 a.m. to 5:00 p.m. In cool areas such as the coastal areas of Central and Northern California, Oregon, Washington and British Columbia, the opposite would be necessary -- adequate sun plus wind protection from 11:00 am to 5:00 pm.

FAMILY LAWN UNIT

Lawn picnicking takes place on portions of lawn or turf areas and consists of turf, shade and parking area. Density may be greater than family units. All other facilities provided for table picnicking will be needed.

GROUP UNIT

A picnic area for groups with a minimum of 25 persons constitutes a group picnicking unit. The maximum number of people which can be accommodated in a group area must be determined by availability of space and demand for group facilities by large organizations. Facilities described here will accommodate 50 persons. For groups of different sizes, these facilities can be adjusted proportionally.

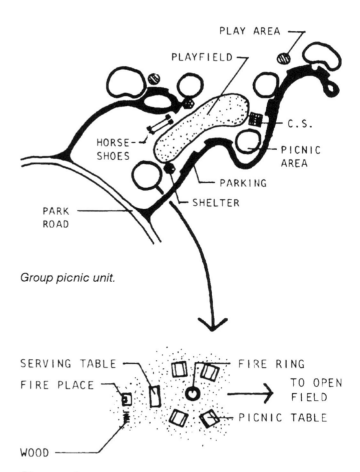

Group picnic unit.

Blow-up of use area.

REQUIREMENTS

- Minimum area: two+ acres (1 ha), usable land.

- Should be located adjacent to a play field (not included in above space needs).

- Barbecue stove and serving table; must have vehicular access.

- Water: hose bibs adjacent to tables and stove area.

- Sanitary facilities.

- Play area (divided into pre-school and elementary school areas).

- Picnic tables: adequate to seat 75 percent of group at one time.

- Fire ring for evening programs.

- Parking: one area for 15 cars.

- Adequate shade.

- Picnic shelters are very desirable.

93

Group picnic area located adjacent to good access and on the shore of a lake. East Bay Regional Park District, California.

BOAT UNIT
(ACCESS BY WATER ONLY)

A picnic site for family use on land adjoining large bodies of water not accessible by car, with cleared shoreline for boat access, table(s) and fire ring. The areas are small, accommodate but few picnic units, have watertight pit or chemical toilets, no developed water (except where a source is readily available and may be developed at little cost), and retain a primitive nature. Service road access should be provided where possible to facilitate maintenance; if not possible, area must then be able to be serviced from the water.

Chapter 16
SWIMMING AREAS

CHARACTERISTICS

Three of every four Americans ages 18 - 24 can swim. This proportion drops as one gets older to only one-third of those over 65 years old able to swim; however, this percentage is increasing. [41] There are three basic types of swimming-related activity areas: (1) fresh-water natural swim areas (lakes and rivers), (2) salt water beaches, (3) swimming pools. Each type has its own kind of users and its own special design needs.

ACTIVITIES [42]

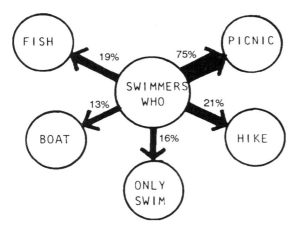

Swimmers who do other activities.

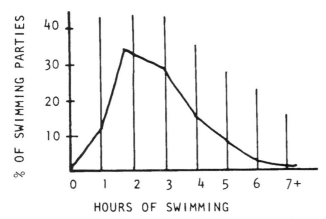

% of parties who swim for various lengths of time.

It should be clearly understood that very few people actually swim. Most swimming in parks is actually water play, and/or just standing around in the water visiting for adults and playing games for children.

ATTITUDES [43]

- There is no evidence that the availability of beach facilities per se attracts certain types of individuals or repels others. Over time certain areas become known for one group or another. This emphasis for group-type segregation can be enhanced or negated by management practices and specialized facility development.

- Natural beauty characteristics of a beach appear to be of more importance to visitors with high socio-economic attributes (e.g., high pay, high education, professionals) than with low socio-economic attributes.

- The availability of food facilities on or immediately adjacent to the beach seems especially conducive to attracting teenagers and older youth; so do beaches with distinct entrances and boundaries and beaches which can be "surveyed" by youths cruising on foot or in cars.

- Teenagers and young adults seem to express a strong positive reaction to crowding on beaches. They also want/need a place to play games such as volleyball, paddle ball, frisbee, etc.

GENERAL

- In natural-type parks there is a strong relationship between picnicking and swimming. [21] Where possible, picnic and swimming areas should be located adjacent to each other with no vehicular separation. For those going to saltwater beaches, picnicking generally occurs on the beach and is much more limited in extent.

- Sixty-five to seventy percent of the bathers in inland waters are likely to be on the beach at any given time. The remainder of the bathers are either in the picnic areas or going to and from other areas of activity or their parked vehicles. Forty-five square feet (4 sq. m) of beach (above water) per person is the minimum. Ninety square feet (8 sq. m) of beach per person is desirable.

- Almost ninety percent or more of the coastal bathers are likely to be on the beach and/or in the water with the remainder to be found going to and from their cars, at concession facilities, on piers or boardwalks, etc.

- Only thirty to forty percent of the bathers at the beach, freshwater or coastal, are in the water at any given time. Of the bathers in the water, only a very small percentage actually swim. Twenty square feet (1.8 sq. m) of water per person is the minimum; forty square feet (3.6 sq. m) is desirable. Minimum desirable water temperature is in the upper 60's F. (above 20° C.).

- Where practical in fresh water areas, diving areas should be provided. [33] These should be separated from the main swimming/wading areas and require a minimum of thirty square feet (2.8 sq. m) of water per person; desirable -- 50 square feet (4.6 sq. m) of water.

FRESHWATER BEACHES AND POOL COMPLEXES

Type of Area	Square Feet (Sq. m) Needed Per Person							
	Water		Beach		Back up & Buffer		Total	
	ft	(m)	ft	(m)	ft	(m)	ft	(m)
High Density	30 (2.8) minimum 20	(1.8)	45	(4.0)	400	(35)	475	(45±)
Median Density	40	(3.6)	60	(5.6)	800	(75)	900	(85±)
Low Density	60	(5.6)	90	(8.0)	1200	(110)	1350	(125±)

Further, the number of people supported by one lineal foot (meter) of beach could be derived from the schematic cross section of the areas as shown below.

Total number of persons/lineal foot (meter) of beach = (x + y + z).

Type of Area	Number of Persons/Lineal Foot (Meter) of Beach							
	In Water		On Beach		In Back up & Buffer		Total/L.F of Beach	
	ft	(m)	ft	(m)	ft	(m)	ft	(m)
High Density	5	(16)	10	(32)	4	(16)	20	(64)
Median Density	3	(10)	6	(20)	3	(10)	12	(40)
Low Density	2	(6)	4	(12)	2	(6)	8	(24)

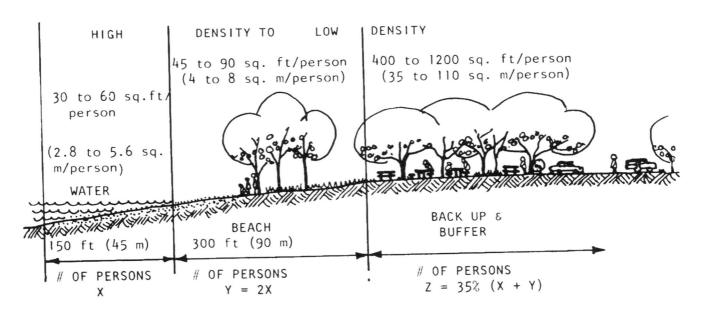

The number of people a lineal foot of beach can accommodate at any given time.

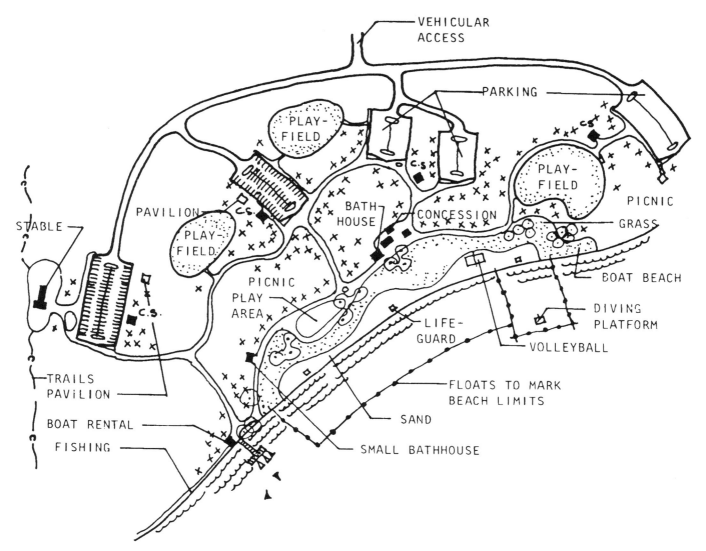

Beach complex -- stable water level.

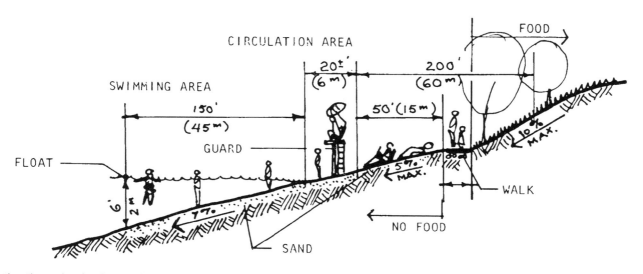

Section through a freshwater beach.

The preceding guidelines are on the conservative side and each particular situation will have to be viewed on its own merit, depending upon its individual topographic and other characteristics. State parks generally use low and median density figures.

- The first 10 to 40 feet (3 to 12m) of beach is an active-use area and is not suited for sunning. This is the main walkway and the location where the people walk to see and to be seen. The majority of beach use will be found within 200 feet (60 m) of the swimming area. [4, 22]

- Water -- turnover of people three to nine times.

- Beach -- turnover of people one and one-half to two times.

- The maximum desirable number of people a swimming complex should serve is 4000, due to distances from various activities and support facilities. If more people are expected, provide additional swimming complexes.

- Site development -- grass area slopes should be ten percent or less.

BEACHES

Above Water: sand surface should be five percent or less; minimum -- two percent. Where local rules prohibit food on "beaches" consider providing a definite visible point such as a walk beyond which no food is allowed.

Below Water: seven percent -- desirable; ten percent -- maximum (sand will not stay on slopes greater than eight to ten percent); five percent -- minimum (slopes less than 5% are too shallow and become too wide for easy guarding). Beaches below water level should have adequate base to prevent the area from becoming muddy. Maximum water depth -- six ± feet (2± m) except in diving areas. Most important, make sure there are no sudden changes in grade -- no unexpected holes or obstructions.

COASTAL BEACHES

Most coastal developments are linear by the very nature of the resource. They vary from the most urban of waterfronts to those almost untouched by man. All are important resources that must be carefully protected while still providing public access to this most desired of resources.

Because of their linear qualities they differ in their design approach from the cluster-style developments at most pools and lakes. Effective utilization requires numerous relatively small access points located at intervals along the beach. This in turn disperses the users and their needed support facilities. Also, unlike most developments discussed in this book, a substantial percentage of the users of resort and urban oriented beaches are people who walk to the beach.

In all beach developments it is necessary to clearly understand and relate to the sometimes violent natural coastal processes. Wind, waves, sand, erosion, littoral drift, flooding, corrosion, saltwater intrusion into fresh water aquifers, and coastal vegetation are all vital parts of the dynamics of the coastal ecosystem.

Man has made many mistakes in trying to tame this system which will not be tamed. We, as users of the coastal resource, must be willing to live with it, not fight it. See Chapter 4, "Environmental Impacts" for some techniques for working with the environment.

The users generally fall into two categories: (1) young people who frequently congregate in one or more areas, and (2) family and family groups utilizing other beach segments. Both groups of users generally bring food, drinks (of all kinds), beach chairs and/or blankets, and frequently some type of flotation device. They, like most park users, "stake out" their piece of territory immediately on arrival.

Most older adult users will walk along the beach or sit and watch other users; from time to time they will take a brief dip to cool off. Family groups (frequently three generations) will stay together and some of the members will be playing in the water (usually the children) during most of their stay. Younger adults and teenagers will spend their time in a number of ways from listening to music (sometimes quite loud), sunning and walking along the beach to see and be seen, to swimming, playing volleyball, frisbee and paddle ball. Although both groups will probably spend some time in the water at water play, they will, however, spend **very** little time, if any, actually swimming.

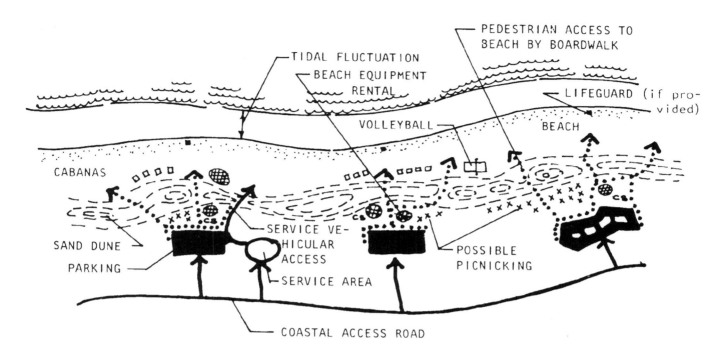

Coastal beach facilities.

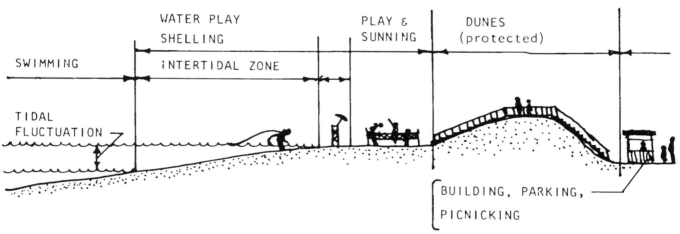

Section through a coastal beach.

SURFBOARDING, SURFSAILING & PARASAILING

Information on these topics is located in Chapter 27, "Boating."

BEACH MAINTENANCE

Most heavily used beaches require cleaning and grooming on a regular basis. This is usually done with a vehicle-drawn rake and/or some kind of debris pick-up device. This type of maintenance will have an effect on the features that might be placed on the beach and/or their design. It also requires vehicular access to the beach.

SANITARY FACILITIES

The number of sanitary fixtures required in a bathhouse complex in a swimming area (beaches or swimming pools) is governed by the prevailing regulations in the area in which it is to be constructed.

Cleaning and grooming beach with a trash picker. Hilton Hotel, Waikiki, Hawaii.

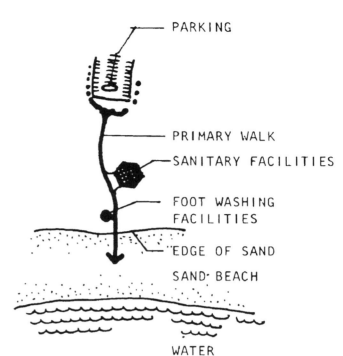

PARKING

PRIMARY WALK

SANITARY FACILITIES

FOOT WASHING FACILITIES

EDGE OF SAND

SAND BEACH

WATER

Location of foot washing facilities.

The following requirements are recommended: [36]

MALE BATHHOUSE [36] *

No. of Males	No. of Toilets	No. of Urinals	No. of Lavatories	No. of Showers	No. of Change Rooms
1-50	1	1	1	1	1
51-100	1	1	1	2	2
101-250	2	2	2	3	4
251-500	2	3	2	4	6
501-750	3	3	3	4	7
751-1000	3	4	3	5	8
1001-1500	4	5	4	6	10
1501-2000	5	6	5	7	12

FEMALE BATHHOUSE [36] *

No. of Females	No. of Toilets	No. of Lavatories	No. of Showers	No. of Change Rooms
1-50	1	1	1	1
51-100	2	1	2	2
101-250	3	2	3	4
251-500	5	2	4	6
501-750	6	3	4	8
751-1000	7	3	5	9
1001-1500	9	5	6	11
1501-2000	11	5	7	13

* Foot washing facilities are necessary at sand beaches, especially at coastal beaches with relatively fine sand. They should be located immediately behind the beach on the walk system leading to the parking lot. Fresh or salt water may be used. Self-closing valves are a necessity.

In picnicking/swimming combination areas, adequate sanitary facilities should be provided on either the beach or in the picnic area. There should be no overlapping of facilities. The number of sanitary fixtures required in comfort stations to serve picnickers' needs can be obtained from the following table. [36]

MALE COMFORT STATION

No. of Males	No. of Toilets	No. of Urinals	No. of Lavatories
1-50	1	1	1
51-100	1	2	1
101-250	2	2	2
251-500	3	3	2
501-750	4	4	3
751-1000	4	5	3
1001-1500	5	6	4
1501-2000	6	7	5

FEMALE COMFORT STATION

No. of Females	No. of Toilets	No. of Lavatories
1-50	2	1
51-100	3	1
101-250	4	2
251-500	6	3
501-750	8	4
751-1000	10	4
1001-1500	12	5
1501-2000	14	6

The figures in the preceding tables could be extrapolated on a straight-line basis to obtain fixture units for more than 2,000 persons.

The distance from the water's edge to the restrooms should be at least 200 feet (60 m) so as not to interfere with the various beach-related activities; 500 feet (150 m) -- maximum. Maximum distance apart -- 1000 feet (300 m).

Dressing Rooms

- Should be located in close proximity to the beach where possible.

- Where picnic and beach combinations are planned, dressing rooms should be located between the picnic area and the beach.

- Wherever possible, dressing rooms should be combined with sanitary facilities and showers.

- Limited coin-operated lockers or other checking facilities should be considered for inclusion in the dressing areas. Most people seem to prefer to keep their clothes with them on the beach or at the pool. Suggest five percent of beach capacity to be considered for calculating the number of lockers.

WATER REQUIREMENTS

- Five gallons (20 l) per person per day without showers; ten gallons (40 l) with showers.

- Drinking fountains should be located at buildings and additional fountains located, as necessary, to provide for 250 feet (75 m) spacing. [33]

PARKING (Often Combined with Picnicking)

Parking areas will be required within 800 feet (250 m) maximum of the beach; 500 feet (150 m) - desirable. The number of cars needed in the parking area should not be greater than the capacity of the beach plus 30 percent. For picnic/beach combinations for coastal beaches it should not exceed the carrying capacity of the beach. (See Chapter 10, "Roads and Parking" for details and Chapter 1, "Methods for Determining Visitor Demand" for number of people per car.)

FOOD SERVICE

These facilities should be provided at all major beach areas. The extent of the facilities can vary from a small vending machine area to a large snack bar, and even to a restaurant complex. They should be located between 250 and 500 feet (75 and 150 m) from the water

and can often be integrated into the dressing room-comfort station complex. It is desirable, if combined with a beach picnic area, that the food service facility be so located that it will serve the picnic area. An eating area should be provided, preferably with a view of the beach, to minimize carrying food onto the beach area.

SAFETY FACILITIES

Adequate safety facilities must be considered for all swimming areas. There are no standards and because of interpretation of liability laws, the safety services provided vary from posting a notice stating there is no protection and swim at your own risk to extensive lifeguard and emergency care facilities.

Lifeguard Chairs -- no existing standards; 400 feet (120 m) on center -- suggested.

Beach Patrol -- Many coastal beaches do not provide lifeguard services. They, instead, may utilize rangers who patrol on all-terrain vehicles. This type of patrol will have an effect on the features that might be placed on the beach and/or their design. It also will require vehicular access to the beach.

Safety Floats -- To demark the swimming area and keep swimmers inside and boaters and fishermen outside 150 feet (45 m) from shoreline and swimming floats or platforms, if possible, at the outer edge of the swimming area. Stable water bodies only.

Lifeguard Room -- In stable water bodies only, many large beach areas and most pool complexes provide a lifeguard room or building. It should have visual control of the beach/pool area. Vehicular access is necessary to the lifeguard building/room for emergency vehicles.

Telephone Service -- Must be provided for safety reasons and should be available for other communications.

Turbidity -- Constructed beaches and beach nourishment projects should be built with sand containing as few "fines" as possible to limit turbidity and thereby enhance safety by making it easier to find people in trouble.

PUBLIC TELEPHONE

Public pay telephones should be provided in all beach areas.

HANDICAPPED ACCESS

A paved walkway meeting handicapped standards must be provided to the water's edge. Ingress and egress to and from the water for handicapped must also be available in all pools.

ACTIVITY AREAS

It is desirable to designate and set aside areas for various recreation activities such as children's play, volleyball and turf fields. They should be located in close proximity to the beach, where possible. In coastal areas they are usually located on the beach, but must be so designed that they can take the adverse conditions or that they can be moved during storms. Where picnic and beach combinations are provided, the activity area should be located between the picnic area and the beach.

Rental facilities, such as bicycle, boats, paddle boats, cabanas, umbrellas, etc., are desirable additions to larger beach areas. They should be located at the periphery of the use areas and along major pedestrian walkways. Vehicular service (walks) access must be provided.

FIRE RINGS

Most heavily used beaches do not permit fires. In places where they are permitted, fire rings should be placed in groups away from the swimming area toward the rear or extreme ends of the beach area. The individual rings should be about 100 feet (30 m) apart. These should be considered only where beaches are open in the evening hours. **Note:** This type of development is likely to attract teenagers and young adults.

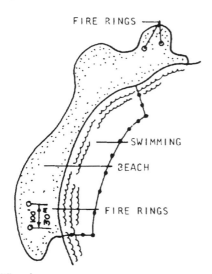

Location of fire rings.

SWIMMING LAGOONS

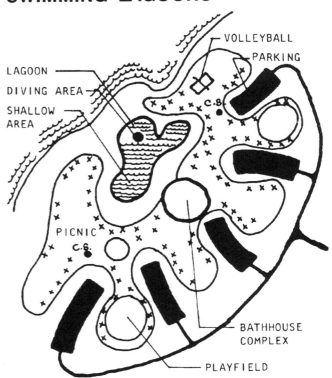

Lagoon concept.

Swimming lagoons should be considered where water quality or water level fluctuations are a problem. Details are the same as for freshwater beach areas plus the following:

(1) Water quality controls including circulation and/or recirculation of the water will probably fall under the same controls as swimming pools and could make lagoons impractical from a cost standpoint.

(2) Water treatment (chlorination) may be necessary as per public health regulations.

SWIMMING POOLS

Swimming pools, when used, should fit the character of the rest of the park development. Pools do not have to be rectangular. Straight lines are easier to build. Corners are more difficult to guard from a safety standpoint.

Swimming pool configurations are limited only by your imagination.

- Because of the limited space around pools, a maximum capacity for the pool and its related uses should be established. Maximum suggested: 1200 car parking or 4000 people.

- Fifteen square feet (1.4 sq. m) of water surface per person -- minimum; twenty-five feet (2.3 sq. m) -- desirable.

- Deck surface minimum -- twice the water surface.

- Sunning area -- equal to the entire pool and deck area.

- A diving or jumping area should be provided when possible, especially in areas subject to heavy use by young people.

- Twenty-five square feet (2.3 sq. m) -- minimum per person, forty square feet (3.7 sq. m) -- desirable for water surface in the diving areas.

- Provisions for the handicapped to enter and to exit the pool, surrounding areas and supporting facilities must be included in all projects.

- Water uses --

  - **Water and water play** -- sixty percent to seventy percent of pool; depth -- one foot to four feet (.3 to 1.2 m). In areas where freezing of the ground occurs, pools with depths less than 3 feet (1 m) will likely experience severe damage due to freezing and thawing. Special construction techniques are required to overcome this problem.

  - **Swimming** -- only twenty to thirty percent of the pool should be at a depth -- five to six feet (1.5 to 2 m).

  - **Diving** - ten to fifteen percent of the surface area and depth as required by height of diving boards and platforms.

- Spray pools -- if a separate area is desired for pre-school children, it is recommended that spray pools be used in lieu of wading pools. Provide benches with shade for parents.

- Water recirculation and filtration should be as simple as possible to minimize operations and maintenance costs. Recommend pipeless, i.e., an integrated water recirculation and scum gutter system with a sand filter system.

- Fencing -- where needed -- should be 42 inches to 48 inches (1.2 - 1.4 m) with adequate gated openings to/from other use areas. This will provide adequate warning to people of a possible danger while still keeping the effect of an open park. Locate the fence to be as unobtrusive as possible and screen with planting where it is visually objectionable.

- Where fees are charged, or may be charged in the future, a six foot (1.8 m) fence with a single controlled entrance will be required. Emergency exits will also be needed for safety purposes.

Swimming pool and bathhouse complex. Codorous State Park, Pennsylvania.

WAVE ACTIVATED POOLS AND AQUATIC COMPLEXES

There are a number of relatively new types of swimming facilities throughout the U. S. and other countries. They consist of a variety of water-related experiences from super slides and wave activated pools to spray pools, tubing areas and waterfalls. They should only be considered for locations where the potential users have undergone a thorough market analysis to make as sure as possible that the facilities will be used. The pool(s)' support equipment and operational requirements are very costly making it imperative to charge sometimes substantial fees for its use.

Chapter 17
BOATING

Boating is a major recreation activity. Most areas have inadequate "boatable" water to meet present demands. All available sources of boating water should be considered for development commensurate with good design. Horsepower limitations should be considered when planning for lakes in natural-type parks, or bodies of water less than 800 surface acres (300 ha), due to noise, pollution and safety problems. The water area required per boat increases as the horsepower increases. Environmental factors are of particular importance in the consideration of building boating facilities in estuarine environments, and sometimes may preclude an otherwise desirable area from being used for boating.

VISITOR CHARACTERISTICS [42]

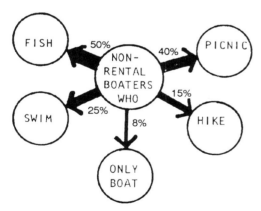

% of non-rental boaters who do other activities.

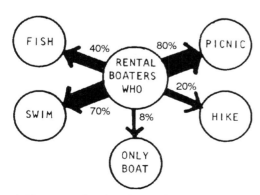

% of rental boaters who do other activities.

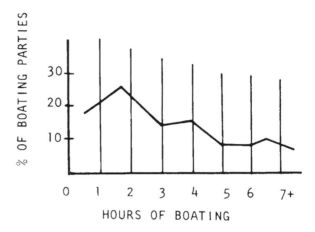

% of boaters who boat for various lengths of time.

Note: These charts and graphs are for inland waters only. No comparable data is available for coastal waters.

- Rental boating is most popular with the younger park visitors; non-rental boating with the older visitors. [42]

- Boaters, like other leisure activity users, prefer to have their boating close to home. In lake reservoir access, the users prefer their boating area to be as large as possible and the water to be clean and weed-free. [43]

- Boaters dislike dirty water, small lakes and lack of activities and facilities. [43]

GENERAL

Where extremely high boat use is experienced, zoning of the water for particular uses will increase the numbers of boaters who can safely be accommodated.

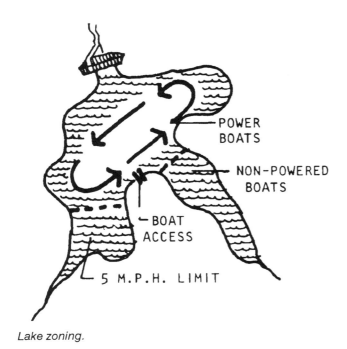

Lake zoning.

Factors to be considered when designing boating facilities include:

- Prevailing wind conditions -- especially important when sailing is being considered and on large bodies of water.

- Open reach of water.

- Sheltering headlands.

- Currents.

- Water maneuvering areas.

- Depth of water in maneuvering areas.

- Silting.

- Special use zones such as fishing, slow zones near the shore, etc.

- Economics -- if by concession operation.

- Winter drawdowns.

- Fluctuating water levels.

- Vehicular access to water.

- Available usable land for onshore support facilities.

- Accessibility to main water bodies, i.e., bridge clearance, tidal mud flats, etc. The closer to the main water surface area the better.

BOAT LAUNCHING

This facility should be considered on all protected coastal areas and on lakes and rivers wherever there is adequate space for boating over and above that required for boat rental facilities.

Vehicular access to boat launching facilities should be located so as to keep vehicles pulling boat trailers from entering into other use areas, i.e., the access to the boat launching area should be one of the first areas to be reached after entering a recreation development.

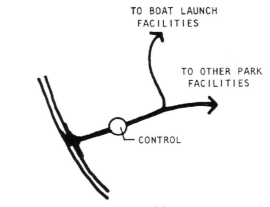

Vehicular access to boat launching.

Adequate parking space must be provided adjacent to the launching facility. Note that many people come to meet friends and/or just to watch the boating activity.

Many boating families have members who do not boat. Where possible, provide picnic facilities near boat ramp area at the rate of at least one table per ten parking spaces.

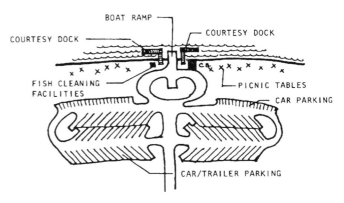

Boat launching area.

106

TYPES OF LAUNCHING

Mechanical (such as hoists, tractors, etc.) can be considered in special areas; usually only in private marinas and concession operations where boats are stored in high density conditions and where income generation is adequate to cover costs.

Mechanical means of boat launching.

LAUNCHING RAMPS

The most commonly used method of launching boats. It takes three to six minutes to launch or retrieve a boat, plus the time to park or retrieve the vehicle and trailer. [4, 5] Ten to fifteen minutes are required to launch a sailboat. [4, 5]

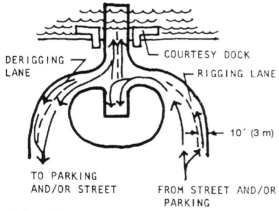

Launching ramp.

A rigging and derigging lane is needed to prevent the boaters from tying up the launching ramps for long time periods. This is especially necessary where sailboating occurs.

- **Slope** - minimum   7 percent
  desirable 13 to 15 percent
  maximum   15 percent

Less than 7% causes the towing vehicle to become submerged. More than 15% causes vehicles to have problems getting the boat and trailer out of the water.

- **Width of launching lane** -- 12 to 15 feet (3.5 to 4.5 m). Multiple-lane launching ramps can be constructed: four-lane -- desirable; ten-lane -- maximum.

- **Parking** -- 40 to 60 car and trailer parking is required for each lane of launching depending on the kind of boats and the distance to the parking lot (see Chapter 10, "Roads and Parking" for details). An additional 10± percent parking is needed for second cars and sightseers in inland waters and up to 50% extra second car parking is needed at coastal waters.

COURTESY DOCKS

Provide at each launching area at the minimum rate of one 40' (10 m) dock per two lanes and preferably one 20' (5 m) dock per lane. They should be located in a manner which will permit continued use of the launch ramp while the boat is being held.

SANITARY FACILITIES

Should be provided as needed to avoid undue wait and/or walk of more than 300 feet (90 m) from the launching ramp. Approximately one fixture per sex per 150 cars should be provided. All launch areas must be provided with a minimum of one fixture per sex.

BOAT SERVICE FACILITIES

Docking, gasoline, supplies and food services should be considered at all reservoirs and launching areas serving more than 300 boats or where there are fewer boats and no alternative areas for service. They should be located so that they are easy to operate from a central control point, preferably located in conjunction with other concession facilities, i.e., a marina or boat rental.

Boat service / Boat dock / Boat rental.
Vacation Village, San Diego, California.

CAR TOP LAUNCHING

Should be considered in addition to the standard trailer pulled boats. Such launching is almost always for non-powered boats. It requires an unloading space adjacent to the shore with gentle slope into the water. On streams, locate at a pool or eddy.

SAILBOATING

Sailboaters are frequently clannish and will often form clubs and indulge in racing. Other factors to be considered are as follows:

- Sailboat facilities need special attention to wind conditions.

- Wherever possible, separate sailboating from power boating, both on shore and in the water.

- Many sailboaters prefer to store their boats on shore, especially those who race, to prevent the build-up of speed-reducing algae growth. [40]

- Design of courtesy docks should consider wind direction and might be hexagonal or some other angle form to allow for different wind directions. [40]

- It is desirable to have a large grass or sand beach with some type of mooring anchor or rail to pull up and secure boats during the day and for launching car top boats. [40]

- Provide extra rigging and derigging space for boat ramps which serve significant numbers of sailboaters.

It takes three times as long to rig a sailboat as a power boat.

- If a club is established or is already in existence, a clubhouse would be a desirable feature. Best located at a higher area than the water to better view the boat racing activities.

- In coastal areas light-weight sailboats are frequently stored at the upper edge of the beach (above high tide) and then pulled or pushed into the water. This is particularly the case for surf sailing and small catamarans.

SURF SAILING

This is an extremely popular activity among teenagers and young adults. It requires little special facility development except a reasonable distance to the parking lot [200 to 400 feet (66 to 132 m)], and needs to be located at the end of the beach for safety reasons. Surf sailing can take place in areas having extremely cold water by the use of wetsuits and has even become popular among the more hearty as far North as Anchorage, Alaska.

JET SKIS

Frequently available for rent at marinas and beach areas, jet skis are very fast and maneuverable and must be kept separate from swimming and other water

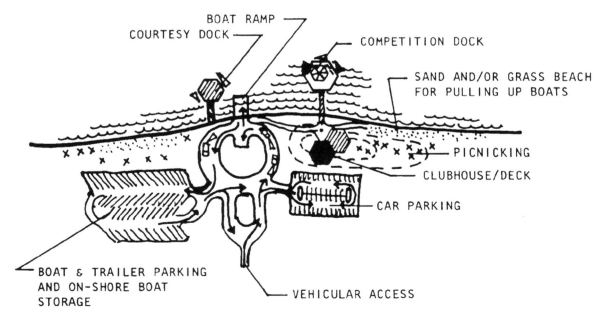

Sailboat facilities.

play areas. They are compatible with other power boating and water ski activities. Very noisy and should be separated from any nature study, interpretive and quiet areas.

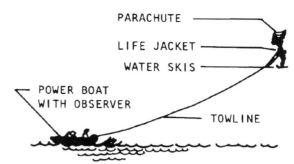

Paragliding.

Jet ski - Done worldwide. Taiwan, R.O.C.

PARAGLIDING - BOAT TOW

Same space requirements as water skiing. See Chapter 9, "Special Use Facilities" for more information on Paragliding.

SURFBOARDING

Yet another popular activity among the teenagers and young adults. Except for competitive events, no special facilities are required for surfboarding other than those normally provided for beach activities. This activity is not compatible with other water-oriented beach uses because of the safety problems with surfboards. An ideal setup would be to reserve the beach segments with the best waves for surfing only. Surfing is dictated by the availability of waves and frequently takes place during periods of inclement weather and the normal off-season for swimming. Surfers winterize with insulated wetsuits and can be found out in almost any weather in any water temperature.

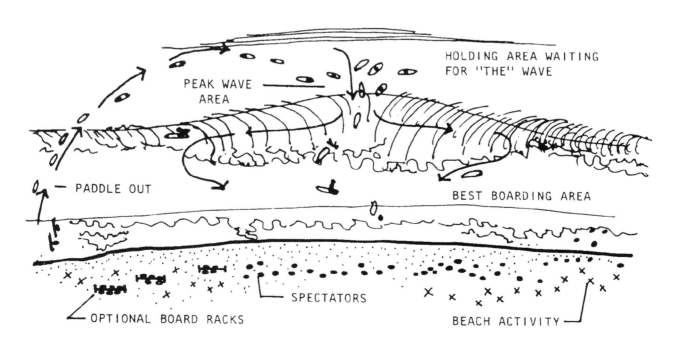

Surfboarding area requires minimum facilities.

Surfboarding -- even minimal waves will bring out the surfers.

REQUIRED

- Area along beach with good waves. If there are no good waves, there is no surfboarding. There is no minimum height; however 2 to 3 foot waves are necessary to provide any kind of ride and preferably larger - 6 to 8 feet. For the very experienced, 10 feet or more.

- Separation from other water activities.

- Close to parking -- 300 feet (90 m) or less desirable -- 500 feet (150 m) maximum.

- Sanitary facilities -- see Swimming Areas.

DESIRABLE

- Surfboard rack(s) as needed.

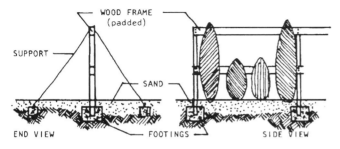

Surfboard racks.

- Spectator viewing area -- ideally from a vantage point above the beach. Normally along the shoreline in front of the surfing area.

RIVER AND STREAM ACCESS

Most rivers and many streams offer tremendous boating potential for small boats. Level of boating difficulty is classified by A, B, C and 1, 2, 3, 4 and 5, with letters being relatively flat water and the numbers designated in ascending order. The more difficult water with a level 5 designation is very dangerous and for experts only. Use frequently starts at one area and ends many miles downstream. To be considered are:

- **Vehicle access** and parking at the beginning and ending points.

- **Launching site** (boat ramps are normally not needed for water courses where power boating is not possible or is not permitted.) (See "Car Top Launching", this chapter.)

- **Water and sanitary facilities** are frequently primitive.

- **Information signs** with data on stream, level of boating difficulty (A, B, C, etc.), including locating and giving the approximate time to take-out points and especially information on dangerous areas, rules and regulations, safety tips, etc.

- **Portage areas** on rough or impossible-to-boat sections of stream including identifying take-out, connector trail and put-in points.

- **Stopover points** on longer stream runs for picnicking and camping.
    - These areas should be located at appropriate distances (which can only be determined by running the water course).
    - These areas should have, where possible, vehicular access for servicing.
    - Where possible, primitive water and sanitary facilities should be provided.

WHITE WATER BOATING

This is an established recreation activity with many regular frequent participants. The participants are usually young (teenagers to the 40's), tend to be in the upper income category and often are going to college or are college educated. They are interested in the challenge, skill, comraderie, excitement and, to a lesser extent, their surroundings. Whitewater tubing has become popular, especially in urban areas. It is dangerous and should be carefully controlled to minimize the number of injuries and deaths.

There are three basic types of whitewater boating -- inflatable rafting, hardboats (kayaks and special white-

White water rafting in a 4-man inflatable raft usually far less experienced boaters. Ohiopyle State Park, Pennsylvania.

Kayaking -- these are normally privately owned boats with skilled boaters.

water canoes), and recently inflatable kayaks. Because of the skills needed and the expensive equipment, whitewater boating is frequently involved with private enterprise (outfitters and equipment renters). There is sometimes a great deal of rivalry between private hardboaters, outfitters and rental boaters.

Most whitewater streams are at their best in the early spring (snow melt and spring rains) and, for a short while, after any heavy rainfall. Frequently many streams have good fall water due to fall drawdowns of upstream reservoirs in preparation for necessary flood storage needs in the spring. Also scheduled dam releases for electrical generation and navigational purposes, etc. can make some rivers very boatable during normally dry periods, i.e., the Youghigany River in Maryland and Pennsylvania. Almost all streams have a maximum boat capacity which, if exceeded, will almost certainly cause a major reduction in user enjoy-

ment and make it very likely that severe injury, and possibly death, will occur.

The best way to determine the river capacity is to verify by observation the number of boats that can go through a given point (the most likely bottleneck) during any specific time period, i.e., 50 boats per hour. In addition, certain prime whitewater locations are favored by hardboaters and these areas can become congested, requiring on-site management. The number of boats per hour is then multiplied by the number of hours available to run the river. Four-hour run -- start at 7 a.m., off at 11 a.m.; start 3 p.m., off at 7 p.m. (at dark latest) or 8 hours. Fifty boats times 8 hours = 400 boats per day.

boats/hour x # of hours (total hours available) = number of boats/day

If the number of boats anticipated is greater than the resource capacity, scheduling and reservations will be needed. The boaters must be evenly distributed over the available time.

Whitewater enthusiasts will travel great distances to participate in their activity on quality whitewater. Therefore, overnight accommodations are needed. Boaters frequently come in groups, are noisy and should, if possible, be separated from other overnight visitors, especially family campers.

All whitewater boating areas must be kept free of submerged logs, sharp metal from bridges and especially from the frequently paralleling railroad embankments.

Another area where whitewater boating takes place is in big surf areas. See Surfboarding in this chapter for guidelines.

REQUIREMENTS

- **Length**
  - A typical one-day run would be 9 to 12 miles (15 to 20 km) and longer for hard boats. Approximate on-river time of 5 to 6 hours.
- **Equipment and supplies**
  - Rafts and inflatable kayaks (at least 2 separate inflatable chambers) or hard boats/flotation devices.
  - Wetsuits, and more recently drysuits (a waterproof suit) in cold weather to prevent hypothermia.
  - Life jackets (an absolute necessity).
  - Safety equipment -- including ropes and first aid kit.
  - Food -- where appropriate.

- **Information** sign or display at river -- includes information on class water, danger, etc.
- **Desirable facilities**
  - Control point -- reservation desk/starter's shack.
  - Phone service.
  - Shuttle service to/from takeout point.
  - River gauge -- to determine water safety and floatability.
- **Boat put-in**
  - Private boaters
    * Equipment drop-off point.
    * Set-up space free of obstructions; 20 rafts and 20 hardboats use 2000+ square feet (200 sq. m).
    * Put-in access to water.
    * Parking -- one car/raft (4 people); one car/2 hardboats (2 people).
    * Sanitary facilities including change house and hot showers.
  - Commercial boaters
    * Preferably separate from private boaters.
    * Equipment set-up space.
    * Electricity for pumps to inflate rafts.
    * Shaded inflated raft storage space -- 5 ft. x 15 ft. (1.8 m x 4.5 m) x number of boats. If space is limited they can be stacked 4 or 5 high.
    * Talk-up area -- to instruct boaters on what to expect and how to use equipment.
    * Truck parking -- two trucks (stake body) per 50 to 60 four-man rafts.
    * Bus drop-off, pick-up points.
    * Sanitary facilities (includes change house and hot showers).
    * Telephone service.
    * Reservation desk.
    * Parking -- one car/two people.
    * Put-in access to water with the greater the number of rafts and the larger their size requiring greater amounts of space.
- **Spectator viewing areas** are a desirable extra if terrain and parking space permit.
- **Concession facilities** -- food (snack) service, photo service of river trips, equipment rental and sales, souvenirs, shuttle service for private boaters. (See "Private" below.)
- **Take-out**
  - General
    * Vehicular access to within 300± feet (100 m) of the river desirable and closer if possible and no steep gradients from river.
    * At the first accessible slack water at end of best whitewater - no long stretches of flat (slow moving) water between end of the whitewater and take-out point. One mile (1.6 km) - is maximum desirable; less is better.

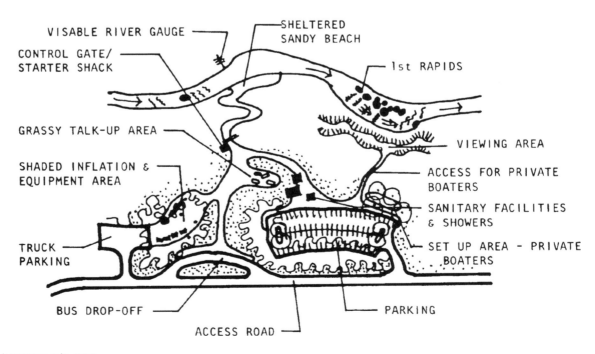

Whitewater boater put-in area.

* Sanitary facilities (vault toilets OK).
* Trash receptacles (dumpsters).
* Changing facilities and warming hut and/or hot showers are desirable, especially when cold water and cold weather conditions are encountered during the use season.
- Private
  * Parking for shuttle cars -- 1 per 8 people in rafts and 1 per 4 people in hard boats.
  * Equipment pick-up within 300 feet (100 m) of river and closer if possible. No steep gradients from river to pick-up point(s). Boaters are usually tired and the equipment is heavy.
  * Bus pick-up (shuttle service back to starting point) is desirable and requires space (trailer or special bus design) for rafts and hard boats.
- Commercial
  * Truck parking -- 2 trucks per 50 to 60 four-man rafts.
  * Bus pick-up (shuttle service back to starting point).

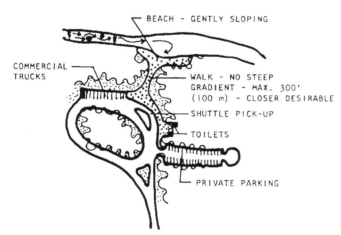

Whitewater boater take out.

• **Stops** -- most whitewater boating includes stops along the way. Areas suitable for the following activities should be identified, especially for group users:
  - Eating -- locate within the normal high water area and preferably on ledges or rocky ground to minimize boater impact.
  - Swimming -- in pools or chutes. In heavy use streams it cannot be in constricted spaces where the swimming would interfere with boating.
  - Sightseeing -- side trips to special views, falls, vegetation, geologic features, etc.

If service access is easily available, vault toilets should be provided at popular stopping spots. If not possible, portable toilets can be carried in by the rafters. Normally the boaters just go behind the nearest tree or bush and, if it is a large group, men go one direction and the women another. This can and does cause pollution problems on heavy use streams and rivers.

Access to whitewater rivers is frequently difficult and expensive. Innovative approaches must be considered for both ingress and egress. Parking may be especially difficult near the river and shuttle buses to the river may be necessary from satellite parking.

WATER TRAILS

Non-powered boating -- especially canoeing and recently tubing, rafts and kayaks -- is continuing its rapid increase in popularity. As the users increase, more pressure is put on known boating areas. Water trails can be easily and economically provided for diversification of activity for some of this non-powered boating demand.

Water trails must be identified, accessible (ingress and egress available to public) and boatable. They can be established on streams, rivers, lakes and lagoons and may be seasonal in nature. (See Chapter 7, "Interpretive Facilities" for additional information on how to interpret the trail and its surroundings.)

Many, if not most water trails will, at least, partially traverse private lands. Although most waterways that can be boated are legally available for "navigational" use, this privilege does not normally extend to the shoreline. In other words, stay off the shore in private ownership areas.

REQUIREMENTS

• **Adequate water depth** - one foot (.3 m) is necessary, preferably year-round to float a canoe/2 people and gear.

• **Length per day**
  fast moving water -- 13 to 18 miles (20 to 30 km);
  medium moving water -- 11 to 12 miles (17 to 19 km);
  slow moving water -- 8 to 10 miles (13 to 16 km).

• **Limit conflicts** between boating and fishing, especially on heavy fishing days - i.e., opening day of trout season.

• **Safe passage** -- includes removal of dangerous logs and sharp metal from bridges and railroad embankments.

Clearing height   6 feet (2 m);
Clearing width   12 feet (4 m) desirable.

Use discretion on the amount of clearing -- too much vegetative removal can cause degradation of the natural environment.

Canoe trail clearance.

- **Portage** -- where water is too dangerous, shallow or obstructions prohibit safe passage, space must be provided -- preferably on public land -- for taking the boat out of the water, a trail around the obstacle and putting the boat safely back in the water.

- **Put-in Area**
  - Parking -- 1 car/boat.
  - Access to slow water.
  - Sanitary facilities - desirable; vault toilets ok.

- **Stopping places** -- rest areas, eating places, overnight camping (see boat-in camp sites) and swim areas are all desirable features which should be considered depending on the length of the trip and the streamside conditions. If special stop places are provided (or develop on their own) vault toilets may be desirable but only if access for service vehicles is easily possible. Rubbish should be brought out by boaters!

- **Take-out**
  - Easily recognized -- i.e., a bridge, dam, etc.
  - Easy egress from water.
  - Parking -- 1 car/2 boats; usually worked on a shuttle basis with one car left at take-out point before trip and the rest of the cars at the put-in point.
  - Sanitary facilities -- hot showers desirable but not necessary. Try to locate out of flood plain or make floodable.
  - Rubbish containers.
  - Shelter/fireplace -- desirable for use by those waiting to be picked up by car shuttle.

- **Information**
  - Signs or information at put-in point describing the water trail are necessary.
  - Warning markers or signs must be placed at dangerous points so that boaters may get to shore and scout and/or portage the danger.
  - Identify take-out point.

WATER USE DENSITY

BOATING

- **High speed boating** -- water skiing: one boat per three acres (1.2 ha) -- desirable, one boat per two acres (.8 ha) -- maximum density.

- **Low speed boating** -- ten horsepower or less: one boat per acre (2.5 ha) -- maximum density.

- **Non-powered boating** -- four boats per acre (10/ha) -- maximum density; two boats per acre (5/ha) -- desirable.

FISHING

One boat per acre (2.5/ha) -- optimum density. One boat per two acres (1.2/ha) when trolling. From four to six boats per acre (10 to 15/ha) for anchored fishing.

SAILBOATING

Four boats per acre (10/ha) -- maximum; one per acre (2.5/ha) - desirable.

Chapter 18
MARINAS

Most large water bodies have need for boat storage. They may vary in size and the kinds of service they provide from several boats to a thousand or more. A marina may include any or all of the following: in-water boat storage, on-land boat storage, boat ramps, fuel sales, boat rental, boat sales, boat equipment sales, comfort station, shower facilities, club house, restaurant, snack bar, boat repair, marina office, harbormaster, transient boat docks, fish cleaning, ice, bait, picnicking, overnight housing, marina maintenance building, Coast Guard, etc.

The location and design of a marina is dependent on water depth, wind direction, access (land and water), need, and amount of usable land on shore for the necessary support facilities. Boating facilities are expensive to build and operate and, therefore, almost always charge user fees. Marinas frequently are built with private capital, and those built with public funds are normally operated by private enterprise. Because of the high costs involved a thorough market analysis should be conducted prior to beginning any development.

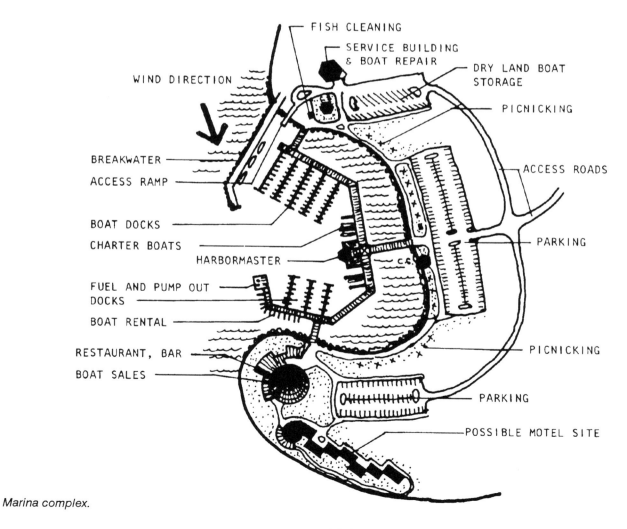

Marina complex.

Marina complex (boat docks, boat rental, food service, boat and fishing supplies). Codorus State Park, Pennsylvania.

GENERAL

SIZE

250 slips usually is large enough for a profitable operation where power boats are involved (American Society of Planning Officials, 1961); 100± slips for small boat docking is a marginally profitable operation.

FOOD SERVICE

Should be considered in larger marinas. A study of surrounding eating facilities is necessary before deciding what level of service, if any, is to be provided. Types of service are vending machine, fast service snack bar, sit-down short order or full service restaurant. In addition, cocktail lounges and bars are sometimes provided. Additional car parking will be required to serve non-marina patrons.

ON-SHORE BOAT STORAGE

Should be considered where water fluctuations or other adverse conditions prohibit the construction of floating docks. In addition, many sailboaters, especially if they participate in racing, prefer to store their boats on shore due to algae build-up. On-shore boat storage can be designed the same as car and trailer parking and must have easy access to boat launching ramp(s). Separate these areas from day-use boat launch parking. Provision of security is a necessity for on-shore boat storage due to the expense of the boats. As a minimum, fencing and security lighting is needed.

LONG-TERM USERS

Owners of larger boats frequently desire to stay on board on weekends and may even make use of the boat as a second home during the recreation season.

If this type of use is permitted, additional on-shore support facilities will be required. Showers in the comfort station, water and electrical hookups and all-night ingress and egress to the marina are minimal considerations.

BOAT DOCKS

Basically an in-water boat parking lot. Approximately equivalent in arrangement and circulation requirements to a typical car parking lot. The only difference for all except the smallest boats is that more space is needed.

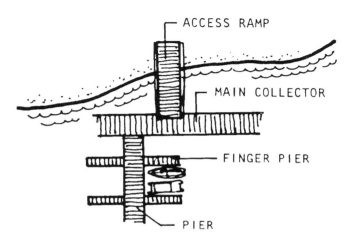

Boat dock terminology.

Sufficient dock anchorage is necessary to resist the various forces acting on the docks **and boats** when all berths are filled -- wind, current, wave, ice (vertical and horizontal) action and water level fluctuations must be included in the calculations. It is necessary to carefully determine the type of boats to be berthed in the marina before any calculations are made, i.e., houseboats have a great deal more wind resistance than small motor boats.

PARKING

Most marinas have less than fifty percent and generally less than forty percent of the boats in use at any given time. Many boating parties arrive in more than one car. Therefore, parking capacity is determined by multiplying 1-1/2 cars (the number of cars per boat in use) x 40% of the marina capacity, or 0.6 cars per boat berth (the maximum number of boats in use at any given time).

Additional parking is needed to store boat trailers. The amount of space varies with the type of marina operation. Boat trailers require the same amount of space as car parking. Additional parking will be required, if a boat rental service is provided, at the rate of one space per rental boat. Also, parking will be necessary for patrons of food services provided in excess of the marina users.

SANITATION
ON-SHORE COMFORT STATIONS

There are no standards available. Suggest one fixture unit per 150± people. Additional fixture units will be needed if eating facilities are provided (refer to local health standards for food service facilities).

SHOWERS (if needed)

Determine the number of people normally staying overnight and then use the chart in Chapter 13, "Overnight Use."

BOAT SANITARY DUMP STATION

Many states require these facilities. Check state and local standards to see if they are required. Suggest one per marina with provision for expansion if use warrants. A dockside sanitary dumping station should be provided wherever large-size boats with sanitary holding tanks are permitted. Locate at service dock.

Need water to rinse out holding tanks and portable toilets.

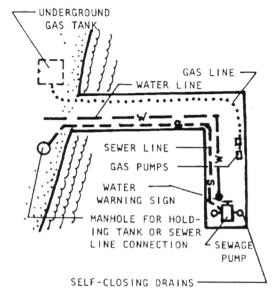

Service dock.

BOAT FUEL

Easy-access by boats and near a manned marina facility for joint use of staff. Fuel storage tank must be underground and accessible to delivery trucks. Installation of fuel tanks frequently requires special permits.

RENTALS AND SUPPLIES

Most marinas provide boat rentals and sale of fishing supplies and miscellaneous minor boating gear sale and rentals. These services should be located in the vicinity of the major pedestrian traffic pattern. Additional parking will be required for boat rental customers. See "Parking" this chapter.

SERVICE AREA AND LAUNCHING

A boat repair and service facility is needed for each 300 boats or more and could also handle fuel and other boater services.

REQUIRED

- Service ramp for use only by marina patrons (see Chapter 17, "Boating" for ramp details).
- Locate away from the main pedestrian circulation.
- Must have vehicular access.
- Visually screened from other boating activities.
- Utilities -- water and electricity.

ADDITIONAL FACILITIES TO BE CONSIDERED

BOAT CHARTERS

The rental of a boat with crew and usually all the necessary equipment to carry out the rental activity. The boats are usually larger than most private boats and are used most days of the use season, sometimes for more than one trip per day.

GENERAL

Required
- Boat dock with easy access to shore.
- Sales area - usually a small booth of 3' to 4' (90 to 120 cm) square.
- Water and electrical hookups.
- Access to sewage pump station for toilet pumpout.
- Phone service to sales area.

Desired
- Phone connection to boat when tied up.
- Small sitting space for early arrivals for trip.
- Place to weigh fish.

Charter boat with 830 lb. tuna. Public Pier, Provincetown, Massachusetts.

TYPES OF CHARTER BOATING

Sailing
- Deep water needed -- over 5' (1.5 m) usually needed at low water levels.

Sightseeing
- Waiting space for next group.

Fishing
- Two kinds (1) party boat -- usually 10 or more people and frequently 20 or 30 or more -- usually for bottom fishing and normally 8 hours or less; (2) charter -- small groups of 2 to 6 or more, usually to go sport fishing. Desirable for the charter area to have a large scale for weighing large fish.

  Access to live bait and other supplies is needed.

  Fish cleaning is usually done on the boat by the crew so fish cleaning facilities are not needed.

Diving
- Same as fishing only normally a scale is not needed.

Shelling
- Same as fishing only normally a scale is not needed.

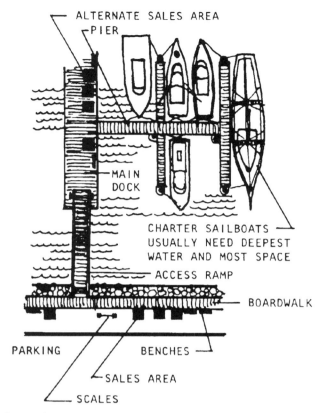

Charter/party boat facilities.

MOTELS
Standard or with boat docks (especially in coastal waters).

SALES
Boat and boating equipment sales.

COVERED MOORING SPACE
Both on shore and in water.

Covered marina spaces. Kentucky Lake, Kentucky.

UTILITIES

• Marina de-icing equipment in areas with winter ice problems is needed to prevent damage to permanent dock facilities. An alternative is to have removable floating facilities which are stored on shore during the winter.

• Water and electricity on docks with large boats, especially where overnight use is permitted.

• Utility (water, sanitary, electricity and telephone) service must be considered in the early study stages since these facilities can be extremely costly to provide.

• Underground electric and telephone services are desirable in all marinas.

• A beacon light is desirable at marinas located in larger bodies of water -- 1000+ acres (400+ ha) to help boaters find their facility at night.

FISH CLEANING FACILITIES

Where productive fishing is anticipated, it is desirable to install fish cleaning facilities near the boat docking and/or launching areas. [33] These facilities are essential to control odor, insects, and pollution which would result from indiscriminate cleaning of fish and the disposal of waste material into reservoirs, streams and along shorelines. The following elements should be considered in planning for fish cleaning facilities:

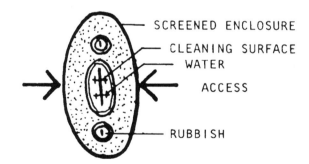

Fish cleaning facility.

• Preferably, fish cleaning facilities should be located in a screened enclosure.

• Lighting should be provided whenever night use is anticipated.

• Water under pressure should be provided to facilitate the cleaning of fish and for general cleanup.

- Disposal of waste: metal rubbish containers, garbage disposal in salt water areas could dispose directly into the water body if health rules permit.

BOAT WASHING

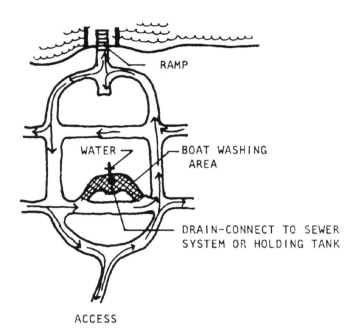

Boat washing location.

Where water quality causes the boats to become dirty, it is necessary to provide a place near the launching ramp or in the mooring service area to wash the boats. It must be located so that it does not impede launching or traffic flow.

MOORING RAIL

A mooring rail should be provided for limited (up to 50) overnight storage of small boats where desirable. This is particularly needed in urban coastal beach areas. Day mooring near picnicking-swimming areas should also be considered.

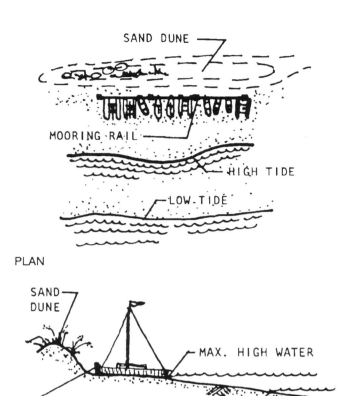

Mooring rail -- coastal beaches.

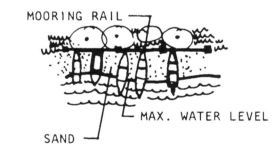

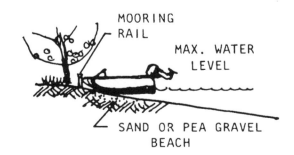

Mooring rail -- stable water areas.

Chapter 19
GOLF COURSES

Many larger parks and recently planned housing developments have adequate space suitable for golf courses. Before deciding on including a golf course in any project, however, a survey of the surrounding region should be undertaken to determine the need. The study should provide information on the number and type of courses in the service area -- existing and proposed -- and include information on the extent and success of the kinds of auxiliary features to be included in the proposed course. [48]

USER CHARACTERISTICS

Golf is a game of power, skill and judgment -- power to hit the ball as far as possible, skill to hit it where it is needed to go, and judgment to decide where to hit the ball and what club to use to accomplish it. Of equal importance for most golfers, it is a place to meet and socialize.

It takes approximately four hours for four players to play 18 holes of golf and about two hours to play 9 holes. [68] The time is not materially affected by the use of golf carts. The time needed per hole is approximately 12 minutes. A maximum of two foursomes can be on each hole at one time. During peak use periods starting times for foursomes must be a minimum of 6 minutes apart. This means a maximum of ten foursomes per hour or 40 people per hour can be accommodated. The total number of golf rounds that can be accommodated by an 18-hole golf course then is 40 times the number of daylight hours minus four hours (the time to play a round). Therefore, in winter in southern states (the prime season in the south) approximately 240 people maximum (10 hours sun light -- 4 hrs. or 6 hrs. x 40 people/hr), while in northern states during the summer (the prime season in the north) over 360 (13 + hrs. - 4 x 40) could be accommodated. Normally private clubs and resorts schedule only 200 rounds [68, 75] per day, while public courses will schedule 250 to 300 rounds. [75]

According to the National Golf Foundation, 21.7 million people played golf in 1987 with preliminary figures for 1988 at 23.4 million or a 7.8% increase. [74] The number of rounds of golf played per year was:

    1985 - 415,000,000
    1986 - 421,000,000
    1987 - 434,000,000.

This was an increase of approximately 6 to 7 million rounds per year. [74] Approximately 90% of golfers play all 18 holes.

Figuring only a 6-1/2% increase in rounds per year, it would require over 400 new 18-hole courses per year to satisfy the growing golfing needs with each course satisfying approximately 17,000 rounds (75 capacity days) per year. If the number of capacity days were increased to 100 or even 150 days per year, a minimum of over 200 courses per year would be needed.

The demographics of golfers are as follows: [74]

By household income:

3.8% of golfers -	less than 10,000
12.9% -	10,000 to 19,999
17.7% -	20,000 to 29,999
20.5% -	30,000 to 39,999
44.9% -	40,000 per year.

By age:

4.0%	5 to 14 years old	11% of golfers and they play 6.7% of rounds played
7.2%	15 to 19	
27.3%	20 to 29	73% of golfers and they play 62% of rounds played
22.2%	30 to 39	
14.1%	40 to 49	
10.2%	50 to 59	15% of golfers and they play 31% of rounds played
5.4%	60 to 65	
9.6%	over 65	

By sex:

77.4% men
22.6% women - however, 41% of the new golfers in 1987 were women which could, if the trend continues, have a major long-term impact of increasing the percentage of women playing golf.

Another way of looking at who the users are is to determine the frequency of play:

20.2% of the golfers play 1 to 2 rounds per year and account for 1.5% of the rounds played:

29.5% of the golfers play 3 to 7 rounds per year and account for 6.5% of the rounds played;

27.8% of the golfers play 8 to 24 rounds per year and account for 19% of the rounds played;

22.5% of the golfers play over 25 rounds per year and account for 73% of the rounds played.

From this information, it is apparent that a very few golfers play most of the golf. These golfers are likely to be mostly mature men who are comfortable financially. [74]

In addition to golf, golfers like to eat, drink and **socialize** while at the course. Golfing for exercise is not a primary goal of most golfers. [75]

SPACE REQUIREMENTS

	Minimum Acres (Hectares)	Desirable Acres (Hectares)	# of people per day**
Driving Range	10 (4)		
Chip and Putt Course	20 (8)	30 (12)	
Executive Course Nine Hole	50 (20)	70 (30)	250 to 300
Regulation Course Eighteen Hole	50 (20)	85 (35)	200 to 250
Regulation Course	120* (50)	170* (70)	200 to 300

* The amount of land required for a golf course is being reduced because of the high cost of land acquisition.
** Weather permitting.

CHIP AND PUTT GOLF COURSE

These courses usually include eighteen holes. The length of holes is from 25 yards to 120 yards (23 to 100 m) long; all holes are par three. Tees usually include rubber mats with rubber tees in place for the hitting area. The greens are usually 2000 to 3000 square feet (185 to 280 sq. m) in size. Sand traps are used very sparingly because of the shot difficulty involved with sand. These golf courses are usually lighted for night play. A limited number of natural and man-made hazards are included in this type of course because of the slow play that results. Irrigation systems should be included, especially for the greens.

THE EXECUTIVE GOLF COURSE

This course is usually similar to the regulation course except as many as eight to ten par three holes are included and one par five, making the par for the course about 60 to 62. This type of golf course provides late afternoon and evening rounds of golf of about 2 1/2 to 3 hours duration. It requires the same demands and talents necessary to score well as on a regulation golf course but the acres of land needed are much less. All in all, the lesser time to play and the resultant lower scores because of the reduced par for eighteen holes interests the golfing crowd. Most executive golf courses are eighteen holes and require the same thought and planning effort as a regulation eighteen hole golf course. Depending on the demand for evening play, night lighting should be considered.

THE REGULATION GOLF COURSE

These provide the ultimate challenge and variety for the golfer. A majority of the regulation golf courses built today are eighteen holes. Each nine should be from 3200 yards to 3600 yards (2900 to 3300 m), depending on the intention planned for the golf course -- championship or regular length. Usually total yardage for championship courses is about 7000 yards to 7200 yards (6400 to 6600 m); regular courses from 6400 yards to 6900 (5800 to 6300 m).

High costs of maintenance and availability of water for irrigation are causing some courses to reconsider the amount of the course to be maintained outside the fairway. Often the roughs are allowed to become rough and native non-maintenance plants allowed to grow. [75]

SITE SELECTION

In the selection of a golf course site, the land should ideally be gently rolling with a variety of tree stands and open areas. Land which is too hilly is tiring for the golfer and it is difficult to maintain in turf. Vehicular accessibility to the site should be easy. Major thoroughfares adjacent to the golf course provide the opportunity for good advertising. The soil condition of the site is important because good soil leads to good turf on the fairway which will increase the popularity of the golf course. A soil analysis, therefore, is a necessity to first determine the need for modifying the soil for tee and green construction and secondly, how to modify the soil. Electric power supply, water availability for irrigating and sewage disposal are all necessary for a golf course and its accompanying amenities. Any site selection must therefore take them into careful consideration.

A continuing trend in golf course development is combining of golf courses with housing developments, both single family and condominiums and resort developments. These courses are normally operated as private courses with limited membership of 350± people.

CLUBHOUSE COMPLEX

The location of the entrance drive, clubhouse and/or pro shop-locker room, practice area, practice putting green, first tee and auxiliary features are important items to consider. The clubhouse is generally located away from the highway but convenient to it, with adequate site features to permit the development of a functional complex. It is desirable to locate the first tee, ninth green, tenth tee and eighteenth green near the clubhouse/pro shop and parking area. Lighting is necessary for parking lots, access roads and walkways and desirable for "highlighting" special features.

Auxiliary features which should be considered are:

TENNIS

Four lighted courts desirable minimum with some limited shaded viewing space located near parking lot. In addition, drinking water, benches, umpire's chair and other standard amenities normally associated with tennis courts are needed. Lighting may be by coin-activated metering. This facility is normally used by non golfers and is frequently a money loser. In private clubs, however, it is a necessary extra for the convenience of non golfing family and guests for prestige purposes.

SWIMMING POOLS

Frequently provided for the interests of the golfer's family. Size is dependent on the intended use. Best located so the pool can be used by non golfers without interfering with golfing activities. Night lighting is required. Separate shower and change rooms from golfing may be desirable.

BAR/SNACK BAR

Minimum food service must be provided. View of the golf course is a necessity. This should be a convenient place to sit and visit. A major revenue generator.

DINING

Desirable and needed in major complexes. Access to parking and a view of the course is a necessity. Golf clubs are sometimes utilized for receptions, parties and meetings. A decision must be made prior to design on whether to provide for these activities.

PARKING

Minimum 100 cars for private clubs, 120 cars for public facilities; desirable 120+ for private, 140+ for public.

GOLF CARTS

Most golf courses provide golf cart rental. This is a **major** revenue generator. Storage facilities, including battery recharging capability, are needed at the clubhouse. For courses with mandatory use, space is needed for approximately 80 to 90 carts. In addition, separate screened space must be provided for their upkeep -- generally in the service yard. Paved walks/drives must be provided at the tees/greens. For courses with heavy use of golf carts, walks/drives should be considered for the entire length of the course.

PRACTICE GREENS

A basic requirement for any good course. Used for putting practice, especially while waiting to start your round. Several holes (cups) are provided. Minimum 10,000 square feet (930 sq. m); desirable 12,000 to 15,000 square feet (1100 to 1400 sq. m).

PRO SHOP/STARTERS SHACK

This is the traffic control point for the golf course. All golf rounds start at the pro shop (normally for private courses) or starters shack (sometimes used in public courses). It is necessary to have vehicular access to this point to drop off the golf clubs.

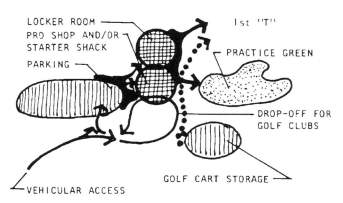

Location of pro shop, starter shack/locker room.

A smooth easy flow of pedestrian traffic should be the result of a well laid-out start to the golf round. The pro shop will, in addition to providing a convenient starting place, provide the normal golf supplies, equipment and repair service and, of course, advice and golf lessons.

DRIVING RANGE

A desirable "extra" feature which, space permitting, can be a valuable addition to any golf course. Minimum space 300 feet x 900 feet (90 m x 280 m), lighted.

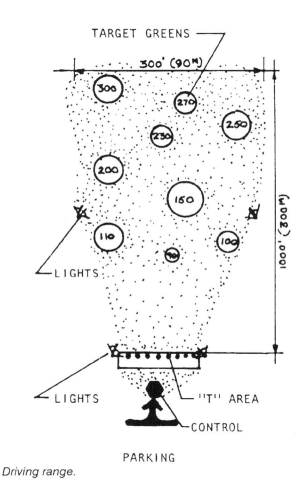

Driving range.

DESIGN

When laying out the route plan for the golf course it is important to consider the natural golf features and hazards, but they should not be overweighed with respect to the character of the soil and the site location. Plan to remove only the trees and other obstacles which will be in the way. Trees are one of the best natural hazards and are an extremely important natural resource.

Most golfers are right handed and up to 90 percent slice the ball to the right. [75] This factor must be taken into consideration in design, especially when the course is surrounded by housing and/or other developments. Proper hole design, screening (plants or man-made features) and locations of hazards can minimize this problem.

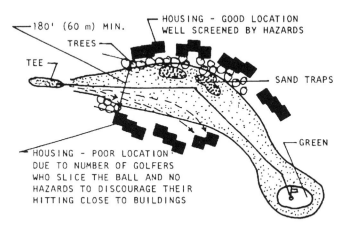

Location of buildings adjacent to golf course.

If at all possible, no golf hole should be laid out in an east-to-west direction because of the evening sun. If unavoidable, plan the first several golf holes in that direction. The northwest direction is extremely bad in northern states.

The distance between the green and the next tee should not exceed 75 yards (70 m); the ideal distance is 20 to 30 yards (18 to 27 m). The first hole should be relatively easy, a par 4 and about 360 to 380 yards (330 to 350 m) in length.

It should be comparatively free of hazards and of heavy rough where the ball may be lost. The first hole should have no features that will delay players. Holes should grow increasingly difficult to play as the round proceeds because of the golfers warming up.

Each nine on a regulation course should also have two par three holes, two par five holes and five par four holes. Par for each nine should be 35, 36 or 37. Total par for the golf course should be 71, 72, or 73 (an executive course would be reduced accordingly). Par six holes should be avoided. Consideration should be given to par three holes first. The first one should be about 130 to 160 yards (120 to 150 m) long. The second one should be between 180 to 240 yards (165 to 210 m) long. Par five holes should also vary in length. The first one being on the short side, about

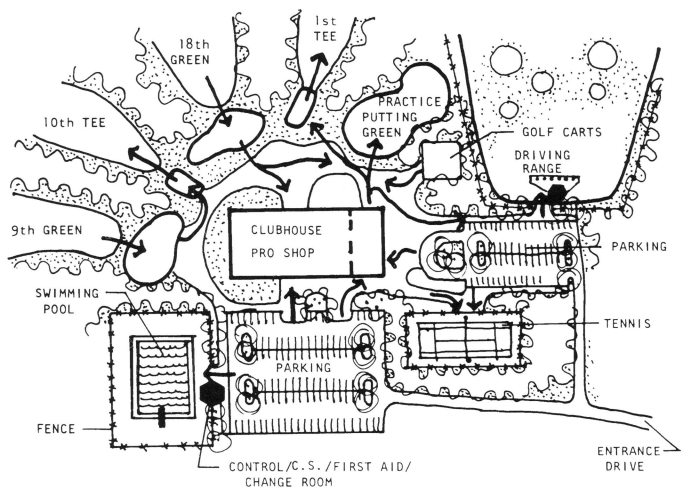

Clubhouse complex.

480 yards (430 m) long. The others range from 520 to 600 yards (475 to 550 m) long. The length of the hole determines the par for that hole.

	Yards	
	Men	Women
4 Par three hole	100 to 250	up to 210
10 Par four hole	350 to 470	211 to 400
4 Par five hole	471 to 625	401 to 575

	(Meters)	
	Men	Women
4 Par three hole	(90 to 230)	(up to 190)
10 Par four hole	(320 to 430)	(290 to 390)
4 Par five hole	(430 to 570)	(390 to 520)

The yardage between 250 yards and 350 yards (230 m and 320 m) should not be used for the length of a golf hole. This is considered "no man's land." This yardage is too long for a par three hole and too short for a par four; **avoid** this length if at all possible.

The mixture of pars on each nine is an important consideration. One good arrangement for a regulation course is as follows with an executive course being reduced appropriately:

Front Nine Holes	Par	Yards	(Meters)
Number one	4	380	(350)
Number two	5	485	(445)
Number three	4	400	(365)
Number four	3	160	(145)
Number five	4	410	(375)
Number six	5	580	(530)
Number seven	4	420	(385)
Number eight	3	180	(165)
Number nine	4	440	(400)
Front Nine Total	36	3450	(3160)

Back Nine Holes	Par	Yards	(Meters)
Number ten	4	390	(360)
Number eleven	5	550	(500)
Number twelve	4	370	(340)
Number thirteen	3	200	(180)
Number fourteen	4	430	(395)
Number fifteen	5	520	(475)
Number sixteen	4	370	(340)
Number seventeen	3	220	(200)
Number eighteen	4	450	(410)
Back Nine Total	36	3500	(3200)
Total Eighteen Holes	72	7150	(6360)

Variety in length of each hole provides different golf shots and the use of each club in the golf bag.

Maintained fairway width generally is approximately 35 to 40 yards (30 to 35 m). Additional space is desirable on the fairway to accommodate inaccurate shots and spectators during competitions. Approximate distance between areas to be built (housing or other built uses) should be a minimum of 60 yards (55 m) width with 70 to 75 yards (65 to 70 m) desirable. By keeping the heavily maintained fairways to a minimum width, the amount of land under intensive maintenance can be reduced to approximately 70 acres (28 hectares) substantially reducing lawn maintenance costs.

There should be no feeling of repetition throughout the round; that is, different types, lengths and characters should be incorporated into the design of the golf holes, creating interest and challenge for the golfer.

Whenever practical, greens should be plainly visible. Sand traps and other hazards should be obviously apparent from the approach area. Generally speaking, fairways sloping directly up or down a hillside are bad for several reasons:

(1) Steep sloping fairways make the playing of the golf shot by the majority of players a matter of luck rather than skill.

(2) The up-down climb is fatiguing to the golfer.

(3) Turf is difficult to maintain on such an area.

It is desirable to mark the distance to the green on the fairway to enable the player who cannot judge distances to better choose his shot and club.

In golf course architecture there are three types of golf holes: (1) Penal, (2) Strategic, and (3) Heroic.

PENAL

The sand traps guard in bottleneck or island fashion. The average golfer must either hit an accurate shot to the green or play short of the green in order to avoid trouble. One or two such holes are usually sufficient in an eighteen hole golf course.

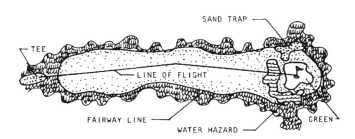

Penal -- approach shot to green requires accuracy to avoid hazards.

STRATEGIC

This type of golf hole uses hazards in designated places so that the golfer must place his shots in a particular location to obtain the best results. About 50 percent of golf holes are of this type.

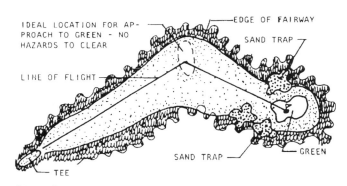

Strategic.

HEROIC

This type of golf hole is a combination of penal and strategic design. The use of natural hazards and sand traps placed on the diagonal set the stage for the golfer to gamble and bite off as much as he can chew. The more hazards he can clear, the easier his next shot will be. Thirty to fifty percent of the golf holes are of this type.

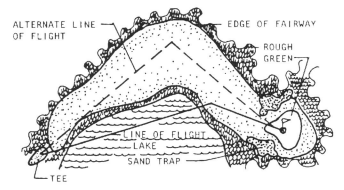

ALTERNATE LINE OF FLIGHT
EDGE OF FAIRWAY
ROUGH
GREEN
LINE OF FLIGHT
LAKE
SAND TRAP
TEE

Heroic -- gambling by cutting across edge of lake results in shorter approach shot to green.

GREENS AND TEES

Before starting the routing of the golf course, all areas which could naturally accommodate greens and tees on the site should be examined. Green sizes will vary from 5000 square feet to 8000 square feet (465 to 745 sq. m) depending on the length of the hole; tees should be 2500 square feet to 5000 square feet (220 to 465 sq. m) in size and designed to accommodate the various golfing capabilities of the expected users. This will make most tees long and relatively narrow, and sometimes result in more than one "T".

Where the pitch of the green is from front to back, the slope should not be over five percent. The slope on the approach of a plateau green can run as high as 20 percent. Mounds and slopes running from the surface of the greens to the sides or back can run up to 20 percent.

A golf player service area should be included in the vicinity of each green/"T" pair and should include information on the hole, a golf ball cleaner (every second hole) . . .

Service area / information on the hole, ball washer and trash container.

. . . and drinking water a minimum of every third hole.

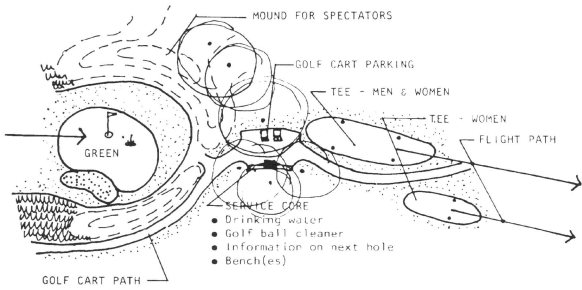

MOUND FOR SPECTATORS
GOLF CART PARKING
TEE - MEN & WOMEN
TEE - WOMEN
FLIGHT PATH
GREEN
SERVICE CORE
• Drinking water
• Golf ball cleaner
• Information on next hole
• Bench(es)
GOLF CART PATH

Player service core at greens/tees.

A toilet facility is necessary at one or more points on the course most distant from the clubhouse, especially on the "back 9".

HAZARDS

There are three basic types of hazards -- vegetation, water and sand. The number, size, location and kind of each is dependent on the availability of existing vegetation, surface water supply and the technical difficulty desired.

VEGETATION

Trees, shrubs and other plant material can be formidable hazards. The retention of plant material in strategic locations is very desirable. The need for reducing heavily maintained areas is expanding this type of hazard.

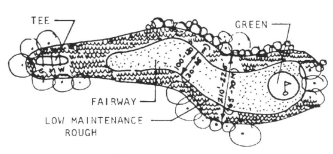

Vegetation as hazards.

Vegetation defines the limits of the course. Kona Coast Resort, Hawaii.

WATER

These features normally occur on coastal golf courses like Pebble Beach in California, and in areas with plen-

tiful rainfall and/or high water tables such as in many of the Florida courses. Where water is available, it should be utilized for hazards as well as for its inherent aesthetic values.

SAND

The slope of the traps in front of or on the side playing toward the green will run from 30 to 40 percent. At the entrance of traps the slope should not be over 25 percent so that the golfer's backswing can be taken with a full, clean stroke.

Sand trap as built in U.S.

Sand trap as built in Australia -- much more of a hazard.

IRRIGATION

In planning a golf course it is important to include a good irrigation system. Golf is dependent on the use of turf, and without water it is very likely there will not be thick and healthy turf year round.

The intent of an irrigation system is to provide the needed amount of water, approximately one inch of water per week, including natural precipitation, on the main playing areas. A watering system for an eighteen hole golf course must cover a minimum of approximately 45 acres (18 ha) of fairway, generally 90± acres (36 ha) where the roughs are irrigated, and about 5 acres (2 ha) for the greens and tees. A properly planned and designed watering system utilizes the most economical pipe sizes and produces an irrigated course with a minimum of labor for operation.

"T"s and greens have special water requirements and should be zoned separately from the fairways. Irrigation in roughs should be minimized and, where possible, eliminated. All irrigation systems must be designed to complete watering during slow or non use periods on the course. They should be capable of being easily reprogrammed to conserve water. Moisture sensors tied into the irrigation controls should be seriously considered to reduce unnecessary watering.

Where available, use should be made of recycled water.

The two major types of irrigation designs are:

(1) **Tree system** -- this system utilizes a trunk line from the pump and has smaller lines branching from this trunk line.

(2) **Loop system** -- the "loop" system, although generally more expensive, should be considered when water pressure or other design considerations such as adequate fire protection dictate.

DRAINAGE

All playing areas on the golf course must have adequate drainage to permit play soon after the rain stops falling. Very special care must be taken to insure excellent drainage on the greens.

MAINTENANCE AREA

The golf course maintenance facilities should be so located that access is available directly from a public road/highway for vendor deliveries. It must also have easy direct access to the course. In addition, it **must** be screened from public view.

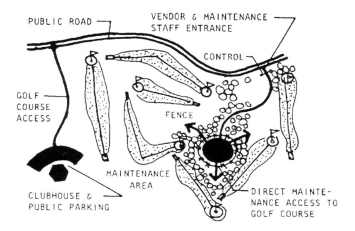

Location of golf course maintenance area.

The maintenance area must be fenced and lighted. It must have adequate covered and climate-controlled work space to permit staff to work on equipment maintenance and repair during adverse weather conditions. Car parking spaces for the anticipated number of employees is needed. In addition, adequate "storage" space, both open and undercover, is needed for extra materials and equipment.

Chapter 20
WINTER USE AREAS

All parks in the cold weather states should be studied for possible winter use areas. Sledding, tobogganing, ice skating, ice fishing, cross-country skiing, snow-shoeing, downhill skiing and snowmobiling should all be considered.

GENERAL

Factors to consider in locating winter use facilities include:

- Snow season (number of days of usable snow without the use of snow making equipment.)

- Ice season (number of days ice is usable, 4" or thicker).

- Suitable slopes for skiing, coasting and tobogganing.

- Access during winter (maintenance, snow removal, cindering, no steep grades).

- Parking -- level area with space for snow disposal.

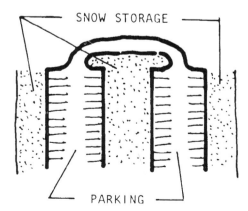

Space is required for snow disposal.

- Buildings -- warming hut, hot food service, rental of supplies and equipment, heated sanitary facilities, ticket sales, ski instruction, ski patrol, lodges, housing, etc.

- Summer use of winter sports area to expand the use season and maximize the return on investment, e.g., install a long water slide to utilize the lifts during the summer.

Summer use of ski slope -- a super-super slide. Laural Mountain, Pennsylvania.

- Urban areas -- possible night activities (outside lighting).

- Utilities -- winterized.

- Slope orientation -- north to northeast with tree cover (evergreens preferably) to provide shade. If tree cover is not existing, it should be established (evergreens preferably).

- Slopes used for skiing, sledding, etc., should be graded and seeded for safety, better performance and ease of maintenance.

- Snow making weather (number of days snow can be made).

- If snowmaking is included in project, then an adequate winter water supply will be required, i.e., non frozen stream, reservoir or underground source. In many cases snowmaking can make or break a commercial winter use project.

131

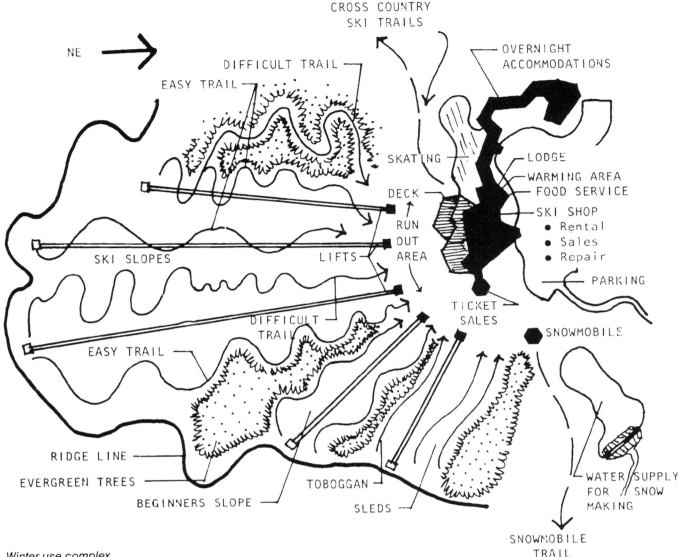

Winter use complex.

DOWNHILL SKIING

This traditional type of skiing continues to have strong support. Twenty percent of the skiers account for 60 percent of the total participation, skiing 20 days or more per year. Infrequent skiers account for 12 percent of the use and amount to 45 percent of the skiers. The remaining, moderate skiers, 35 percent, ski between 5 and 20 days and account for 28 percent of the use.

USER CHARACTERISTICS

Young, under 30, 60 percent male, 40 percent female; they tend to have high incomes, be well educated and the average skier has skied for over six years. [61] Recent trends are for people to continue their skiing habits into their maturity. Downhill skiers travel an average of 200 miles to get to the slopes and frequently will stay two or three days. [43, 61]

ATTITUDES

Single-day skiers prefer:

• Ski areas close to their residence.

• Good physical quality of slope.

• Low price of tow and lift tickets.

• The presence of good lift facilities.

Weekend or vacation skiers prefer:

• Good physical quality of slopes.

- Presence of good lift facilities.

- Good reputation with skiers.

- No crowds.

REQUIREMENTS

- One hundred inches of snowfall (without snowmaking equipment), 80-85 skiing days, N-NE exposure.

- Areas within one hour's drive from major centers of population should consider facilities for night skiing.

- With 3000 people on 1500 acres (600 hectares) of slopes, trails are in relatively crowded condition.

- Trail width -- 40 feet (12 m) -- minimum (larger area should be developed at top of steeper slopes). Trail development only on natural snow.

- There should always be for the beginners and inexperienced an easy way to ski from the top of any slope.

- Rope tow -- 1300 lineal feet (400 m) -- maximum; 25 percent slope.

- Chair lift should be considered in all areas with vertical drop of 200 feet (60 m) or more.

- Gondolas are also available for major ski areas and can be used in summer for sightseeing rides.

- Waiting space must be provided at the base of ski lifts.

- Vertical drop minimum -- 180 feet (55 m); vertical drop desirable minimum -- 350 feet (110 m).

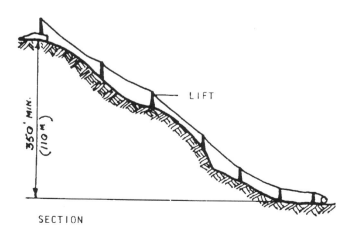

SECTION

Minimum ski slope height.

- Percent of slopes needed: [30]

Beginners	5% to 20%
Intermediates	20% to 35%
Experts	35% and up

- Avoid large open areas at top of mountain.

- Avoid large open areas exposed to the prevailing wind direction.

- Snowmaking equipment is almost a necessity for profitable ski operations and requires a substantial supply of water during the winter months.

- Ticket sales booths should be located between the parking lot and the slopes, preferably outside of the main ski building.

- Support facilities are a necessity for an effective ski operation. [61]

  Food service ⎫
  Liquor (Bar)   ⎬ 21% of all skiing
  Entertainment area ⎭ money is spent on
  Lodging   these activities
  Equipment rental
  Teaching

Other winter activities such as skating, snowmobiling, cross-country skiing should also be considered.

CROSS-COUNTRY SKIING (NORDIC)

This type of skiing has become very popular and its popularity continues to increase.

USER CHARACTERISTICS [55]

Usually cross-country skiers have had some downhill skiing experience. They are looking for solitude, are frequently summer joggers and have had approximately three years of experience. [61] They love the out-of-doors and seek natural settings. A short afternoon or evening trip nearby is preferred to the weekend outing. Many older people are participating in cross-country skiing.

REQUIREMENTS [55]

- Location -- in close proximity (30 minutes drive) of the users.

- Access -- ideally accessible without use of cars, however, parking which can be easily plowed is normally a necessity. The parking can be combined with that needed for other winter activities.

Cross-country skiing in open space along a stream in a suburban area. Pennsylvania.

TRAILS

GENERAL

Provide solitude with scenic diversity and varied terrain and vegetative cover. Skiing and snowmobiling are **NOT** compatible -- not even in the same sound basin. Use existing summer trails where possible. Bicycle, hiking and equestrian trails are generally well suited for cross-country skiing. Please note, however, that back country hiking trails frequently have much narrower clearing widths than that needed for ski trails. Like all winter activities, trails should be located, wherever possible, to the north side of hills and in shaded areas. This is particularly important in marginal snow areas, and will prolong the snow cover and subsequently the trail's usability. Loop trails are strongly recommended with side trails adequately signed and of varying degrees of difficulty offered for the more advanced skiers.

LENGTH

1 to 2 hours	for beginning trails
1/2 day	3 miles (5 km) - Intermediate 6 miles (10 km) - Advanced
All day	6 miles (10 km) - Intermediate 10 miles (15 km) - Advanced

LAYOUT

Essentially the same as all trails except that short quick turns should be avoided. Out runs at the base of slopes must be provided before encountering obstacles (bridges, dropoffs, roads). There should be a variety of grades with approximately 1/3 uphill, 1/3 downhill and 1/3 flat.

GRADIENTS

Beginners	-	as level as possible (under 8%) with some downhill slopes.
Intermediate	-	8%, with some slopes to 10%.
Advanced	-	17% with some slopes to 20%.

Most of the trail should be much less grade-wise than noted, and the steeper slopes should be downhill.

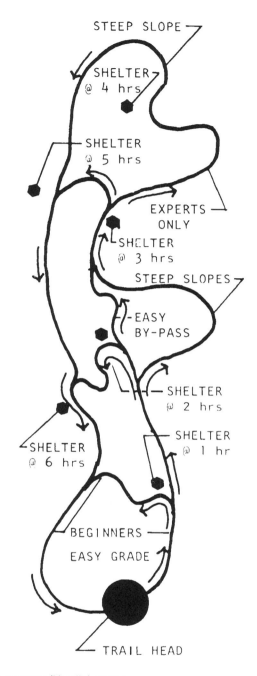

Cross-country (Nordic) skiing.

CLEARING WIDTH

Intermediate — 8 feet (2.5 m) on grades under 8%; 13 feet (4.1 m) on grades over 8%.

Advanced — 6 feet (1.8 m) on grades under 10%; 13 feet (4.1 m) on grades over 10%.

Vertical clearing — 8 feet (2.5 m) above average snow depth.

The increased clearing width is to allow for downhill maneuvering and various uphill steps.

SURFACING

Under the snow cover, ski trails should be free of obstructions, especially rocks. If trail is not used during summer for other activities it should be seeded with grass.

SIGNING

Adequate trail markers above snow line are important especially on longer trails in more remote areas. Interpretive signs can be added for the trail user's enjoyment.

SHELTER AREAS

At the trailheads it is desirable to have a shelter(s) for warming and ski waxing. On longer trails, over 1-1/2 hours, it is desirable to have shelters at approximately one- hour intervals for resting and rewaxing skis.

ICE SKATING

Ice skating should be considered wherever water is available and safe ice conditions can be expected with reasonable regularity.

REQUIREMENTS

- Lighting for night activities in urban areas and major winter-use complexes only.

- Area for warming fires with shelter from wind desirable. Benches for resting and/or skate changing and a firewood supply are needed.

A lighted skating facility with warmup area, Codorous State Park, Pennsylvania.

- Shaded areas directly north of evergreens or a hill or mountain are most desirable.

- Toilet facilities -- winterized.

- Artificial ice skating rinks can be considered.

- Four-inch (10 cm) depth of smooth ice is required.

- Adequate level parking which can be easily plowed for snow removal.

- Use shallow water areas, 3 feet (90 cm) or less deep if possible, for safety reasons. Where the water is deeper, accessible safety equipment must be provided (minimum of a flotation ring and a lightweight wood ladder).

- Designate skating area limits and keep skaters separate from ice fishing.

- Parking lot and level fields can be designed for flooding and can make very desirable skating areas. If asphalt (black) parking lots are used they should be treated with some type of surfacing to minimize the heat absorption, i.e., paint, sand, brushed in cement during construction.

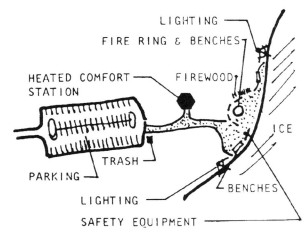

Ice skating area.

ICE BOATING

Large water bodies, 250± acres (100± ha), in areas with good smooth ice coverage are sometimes used for ice boating. This is not a major activity.

REQUIREMENTS

- Vehicular access and a plowable parking area near the ice.

- Toilet facility -- winterized.

- Ice depth -- minimum four inches (10 cm) for several days each year.

- Consider using existing boating facilities for this off-season function.

- Combine support facilities if possible with winter activities such as skating, coasting and ice fishing.

- Provide area for warming fires -- a fire ring -- minimum; a warming shelter -- desirable.

TOBOGGANING
REQUIREMENTS

- Slope free of obstacles, especially rocks; 10 percent to 45 percent -- 30 percent recommended, with a level runout space at the bottom.

- N-NE exposure.

- Planting -- evergreen shade.

- Toilet facilities -- winterized.

- Warming area desired.

- Plowable parking.

COASTING

Should be included in all parks within one hour's drive of urban centers.

REQUIREMENTS

- N-NE exposure.

- Five percent to 40 percent slope with level runout space.

- Planting -- evergreen shade.

- Toilet facilities -- winterized.

- Warming area desirable.

- Plowable parking.

- Night lighting in heavily used urban accessible areas.

SNOWMOBILING
USER CHARACTERISTICS

Riders tend to be married with two or more children, middle-income and often blue-collar occupations and 80% live in rural areas. They frequently have access, without driving, to areas where they can ride, i.e., open fields, logging roads, etc. [43, 64]

ACTIVITIES [43, 64]

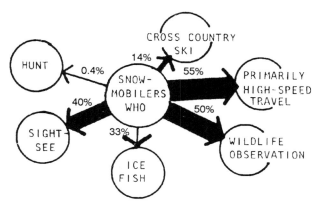

% of snowmobilers who do other activities.

ATTITUDES [43]

General snowmobiler preferences:

- 73% prefer trails between 15 to 25 miles (25 to 40 km) long.

- 90% prefer trail width of 6 to 10 feet (1.5 to 3 m).

- 69% prefer marking danger areas.

- 57% prefer direction arrows (helps prevent accidents).

- 93% prefer loop trails which end up at the starting point.

Trail character:

- 39% prefer rolling terrain.

- 30% prefer woods and timber area.

GENERAL

There are two types of snowmobiling: trails and open fields. It is desirable, where possible, to have a combination of the two. User safety should be kept in mind at all times. Snowmobiling is not compatible with other types of winter activities and must be separated physically, visually and soundwise from other uses. **Note:** Serious damage can be done to the environment if snow depths are less than four inches. Heavily used areas will require grooming similar to that done on downhill ski slopes.

REQUIREMENTS [24]

Major departure point.

For control or operation, designate an area within the park limits as the "Trailhead" from which all activities originate.

The "Trailhead" location should be supported with:

- Adequate plowable level parking facilities to accommodate car-trailer combinations (see Chapter 10, "Roads and Parking" for parking details).

- Heated sanitary facilities.

- Heated warming shed or hut, or facilities for an outdoor fire.

- Orientation sign structure.

- Refuse disposal containers.

- Winterized potable drinking water is desirable but not necessarily required.

- For purposes of "warming up" and/or equipment check, it is desirable to have a large cleared area adjacent to or within a reasonable distance from the departure point. This area can also be designated for groups or clubs that participate in meets and/or for fun and games.

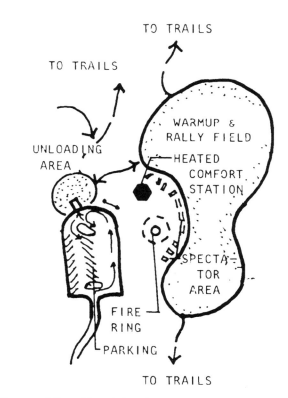

Snowmobile trailhead development.

Trail Layout.

- Trails should be functional and interesting.

- Locate with provision for maximum beauty, i.e., scenic overlooks and vistas, winter landscapes and natural attractions.

- Locate on north facing slopes, through woods and especially evergreens to extend season of use. Avoid southern slopes, especially those without trees.

- Existing summer-use trails may be used for this activity; however, where heavy snowmobiling use occurs, significant damage to the environment is likely. It is better to use abandoned railroad grades, logging trails and non-plowed park roads to avoid conflicts.

- A major one-way loop trail ending at the departure point with various secondary one-way trails leaving and returning to the major trail is the preferred trail alignment.

- Avoid potential avalanche-hazard areas.

- Avoid lake and stream crossings -- where crossings are necessary provide an unobtrusive bridge with a minimum eight-foot (2.5 m) width and a maximum of 12 feet (3.5 m) width with easily seen railings.

- Avoid major park road cross-overs if the road is used during the winter.

- Provide combinations of straight and winding stretches, level and rolling topography, and heavy cover and open areas.

- In the location of trails, wildlife habitat areas, and young forests plantings must be avoided.

- Trail marking above the snow line is necessary for safety, guidance and operations.

- Hazards such as fences, guy wires, banks and cliffs **MUST** be avoided.

Length -- Major and secondary trails should be of various lengths.

	Miles	(Kilometers)
Minimum	5 to 10	(8 to 16)
Desirable	15 to 30	(25 to 50)
Maximum	40 to 50	(65 to 80)

A short loop of one or two miles (1.6 to 3.2 km) is recommended for the novice and for use where several persons are taking turns operating one machine.

Surfacing -- the surface below the snow should be free of rocks and other obstructions. Trails used strictly for snowmobiling use should have a grass or other surface treatment for erosion control.

Alignment

- Maximum sustained grade should not exceed eight percent; a 25-percent grade, 100 feet (30 m) in length, is permissible.

- Curve radius should not be less than 25 feet (8 m) -- minimum; 50 feet (15 m) -- desirable.

- Avoid curves on hills.

- Avoid hillside open field location if at all possible due to tipping of machines.

Trail Width

One-way	Feet	(Meters)
Minimum (low use areas)	4	(1.2)
Desirable (minimum for use of grooming equipment)	8	(2.4)
Maximum	12	(3.6)
Two-way	12	(3.6)

Clearing for trails should be 10 feet (3 m) **above normal snow height,** allowing for snow-bent branches and two feet (.6 m) on either side of the trail.

ICE FISHING

Should be included for all parks with good fishing and where ice conditions permit.

REQUIREMENTS

- Four-inch (10 cm) depth of ice.

- Separate from other ice-use activities, especially skating.

- Parking -- level and plowable.

- Safety equipment. As a minimum, a life preserver ring/rope and light-weight wooden ladder located at the parking area.

- Sanitary facilities.

Desired

- Fire facilities as per ice skating.

- Shelter.

- Combine parking, safety, sanitary facilities, shelter and warming fire with other winter-use facilities where possible.

Ice fishing -- wind shelters are sometimes brought by the fisherman.

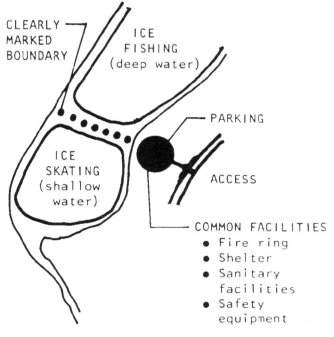

Separation of ice skating and ice fishing.

Chapter 21 FISHING

All parks with relatively unpolluted water can support some type of fishing, many on a year-round basis. There are many types of possibilities for this desirable activity.

USER CHARACTERISTICS [42, 76]

In 1985 58.6 million people over the age of six went fishing a total of over 976 million days for an average of over 20 days per person per year where fishing was the primary activity. Of these, 13.7 million fishermen went saltwater fishing an average of 11 days per year, while the remainder went freshwater fishing. Fishing is done more days by men (68% of the days) than women (32% of the days). Thirty-seven percent of the male population fish at some time as do 16% of the female population. Age is not a significant factor until the 65 and older group which participates only one-half that of the other age groups. Fishing is somewhat income sensitive, somewhat positively educationally sensitive, and percentage-wise twice as many caucasians than others fish. Twenty-seven percent of the caucasian population fish, 13% of the black and 18% of all other groups fish. [76]

Fishing is increasing in popularity with a 32% increase in the percentage of people fishing from 17.6% in 1955 to 23.2% in 1985. [76]

Like non-rental boating, fishing in parks tends to be most popular among older park visitors. However, over one-quarter of the fishing in Pennsylvania state parks was by children under 13 and that primarily from the shoreline. [42]

ACTIVITIES [42]

% of fishermen (on an annual basis) who hunt and do non-consumptive wildlife recreation. [76]

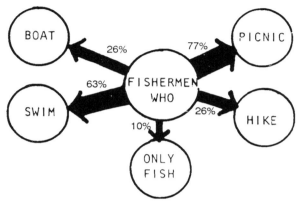

% of summer fishermen who do other activities. [42]

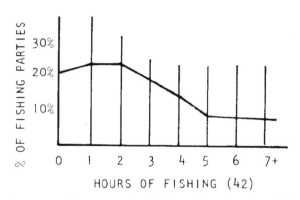

% of summer fishermen who fish for various lengths of time.

USER ATTITUDES [43]

Fishermen want fishing to be available and attractive, and they want clear water.

PRODUCTIVITY

Waters vary in productivity, depending on physical and chemical characteristics. Productivity can be increased by a number of methods, including habitat improvement and fertilization. Both may conflict with other water uses. Supplemental stocking is effective in temporarily increasing fish populations, but increased fishing pressure and availability of food and cover will reduce the population back to the carrying capacity of the body of water within a short time.

METHODS OF FISHING

Fishing methods differ depending on the classification of the body of water, type of fish present, time of year and fishing pressure. [47] The following methods are used:

(1) Still fishing from banks or shoreline.

(2) Moving along banks.

(3) Wading.

Fly fishing -- Pennsylvania.

(4) Anchored boat.

(5) Moving boat.

(6) Ice fishing.

ACCESS

Access is required to make an area usable. For pedestrians, trails along the shore are necessary, or for vehicles, road access.

Many fisherman prefer using facilities in early morning and late evening hours, often necessitating special-access areas in controlled-access parks.

Boat launching sites should be located within reasonable distance (depending on type of boating permitted) of the better fishing areas.

An accessible route for physically handicapped people must be provided, if possible, to at least some of the good fishing areas. Special fishing piers with suitable safety rails and surfaced access ways may be required. See Chapter 6, "Handicapped Accessibility."

GENERAL CONSIDERATIONS

- It is desirable, where possible, for some fishing areas to be developed near areas of other park activity so that the entire family can enjoy the park outing together.

- Heavy fishing pressure is usually sporadic, i.e., opening day of trout season, after stocking, during various fish runs. To make use of the parking areas, sanitary facilities, etc., other **non-water related** recreation facilities could be located in the area.

- Fishing may not be as successful in heavy-use portions of water bodies as in the more remote areas.

- Public sanitary facilities are required at any on-shore locations supporting areas of fishing concentrations. Ample rubbish cans must be located at parking areas in places of heavy fishing concentrations.

- Ice fishing is very popular in areas having adequate ice coverage -- 4 inches (10 cm). See Chapter 20, "Winter Use Areas."

- Provide fish-cleaning facilities in major fish-producing areas. Refer to fish-cleaning facility (see Chapter 18, "Marinas").

- Small streams with heavy fishing pressure -- may need to prohibit wading. Wading creates a disturbance to other fishermen. [47] It also disrupts banks and stream bottom, thus causing damage to aquatic life.

- Fly fishing only, artificial lures only, catch and release areas can be located in more remote areas. The great majority of fishermen who fish this way do not mind walking considerable distances. Trails to such areas could be part of a comprehensive park trail system. The exception might be catch and release areas, which can also be established in certain easily accessible areas.

- Set aside easily accessibile areas with reasonably good fishing water for children under 12 and for handicapped persons.

- On larger streams and rivers, float fishing is very popular. Boats are launched at an upstream location and taken out downstream at the completion of the trip. Camping facilities, areas for preparing meals, etc., are desirable at selected points along the way. [47]

PIERS AND DOCKS

Piers and docks should be provided in areas where the shoreline is inadequate to serve the fishing needs, i.e., shallow lakes, ocean shores, and lakes with difficult shoreline fishing access. All piers and docks should be made accessible to the handicapped.

The length of pier required can be calculated by using 3 lin. ft. of pier per user day of anticipated use.

Consideration must be given to the following:

PARKING

The parking required can be calculated by dividing the lin. ft. of fishable pier by 1.5 and again by 2 people per car for a factor of .75 cars/lin. ft. of pier and sightseers' parking which could be as much as 1/2 the total fisherman parking.

PIER/DOCK

Size

- 6' (180 cm) minimum for a low use area.
- 9' (270 cm) minimum for normal areas with few sightseers.
- 12' to 15' (360 cm to 450 cm) for areas with large numbers of non fishermen. This is usually the situation in coastal resorts.

Fish cleaning area -- with running water and adequate disposal facilities.

Bait sales -- major areas only.

Fishing supplies -- Bait, lures, fishing line and fishing tackle are desirable sales items on larger, heavily used piers.

Enclosed areas -- In some lakes in cold weather areas floating, enclosed, all-weather fishing areas are built.

Lighting -- for night use.

Food sales -- desirable on larger piers with heavy use.

Sightseers -- can account for the majority of the total number of users on a pier if they are permitted access. At any given time (except at night) they may be equivalent to the number of fishermen, and over a day's time could amount to several times the number of fishermen.

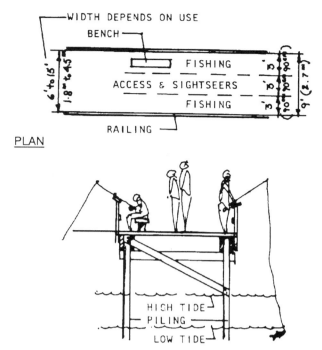

PLAN

SECTION

Pier fishing.

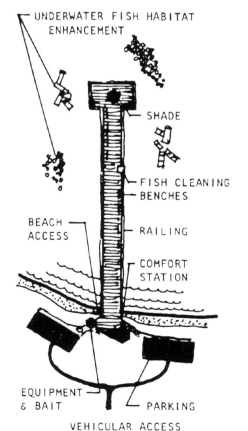

Public fishing pier.

HABITAT MANAGEMENT

It is important that fish management experts and aquatic biologists be consulted to assure proper use of fishing waters. Modification of shoreline habitats for swimming, boating, and other uses can have major adverse impacts on the fisheries.

A careful assessment of fishing as opposed to other water-based recreation is essential to prevent conflicts among users. Stumps, sunken brush and other desirable fish cover may conflict with boating or scuba diving, for example. Aquatic growth necessary for fish cover and to sustain the aquatic food chain can conflict with boating and swimming.

Underwater habitat improvement should be considered wherever heavy use is likely to occur. Properly designed and placed improvements can significantly enhance fishing success in both fresh and saltwater habitats.

Construction of artificial reefs is frequently desirable in coastal areas with sandy bottoms and little fish habitat.

In many areas the environment can be modified by placing clean, void-producing material on the ocean floor. Such things as old ships, junk cars, stones and clean construction debris can be utilized.

STREAM-RIVER FISHING

The support facilities shown for other types of fishing should be provided as appropriate, considering the waterway's size, productivity and location.

Consider installation of stream-improvement devices if justified by the waterway's present or potential ability to sustain natural fish populations. Care must be exercised to insure that the improvements do not degrade the visual environment, especially in park areas.

It may be desirable to establish specific waterway segments for fly fishing or artificial lures only. It is important, however, to recognize that a proper balance must be achieved or young or infrequent fishermen and the underprivileged may be inhibited as these groups usually use natural bait. Fish for fun projects with a one-fish creel limit daily, permitting either bait or lure and requiring barbless hooks, may be appropriate in some areas.

CONFLICTS / FISHING

Fishing is not compatible with most other recreation activities. Fish need their special habitats which are frequently not compatible with people needs. Fishing can be dangerous (hooking people instead of fish). This is especially true between swimmers and fishermen. Zoning and/or special design considerations may be required.

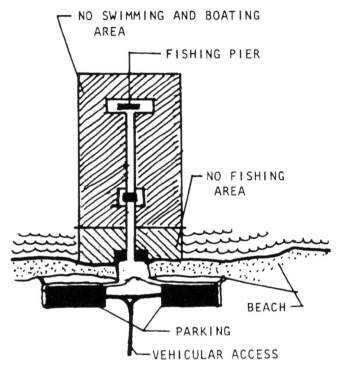

Restricted zoning for fishing pier.

In confined water areas zoning may be necessary if unlimited-horsepower motorboating is to be permitted, as the resulting wake can disrupt the fishing experience.

Chapter 22
HUNTING AND WILDLIFE MANAGEMENT

HUNTING

Parks with 400 acres (160 hectares) or more of undeveloped land and/or water areas that are presently or potentially capable of sustaining hunting within their boundaries should be considered for hunting. it should be noted that this is a very controversial area and one that should be thoroughly explored with conservationists and sportsmen before making a decision.

Hunting requires extensive acreage free of or with minimal conflicting activity. The average desirable density of hunters-per-acre is extremely variable, depending on game species and capability of the natural resources involved. It is important to work closely with game experts to properly develop this particular activity.

Consider the types and volumes of day or overnight uses occurring or anticipated in the park during the hunting season(s) in relationship to the park areas' hunting opportunities, game species, and weapons to be used. It probably will not be desirable in densely populated areas to permit hunting at all, and especially not in late spring, summer and early fall use seasons.

USER CHARACTERISTICS

In 1985 16.7 million people went hunting as their primary activity. They spent an average of 20 days in the field for a total of 334 million days of hunting. The activity can be further broken down into:

Big Game	-	12.5 million hunters
	-	106 million days
Small Game	-	10.8 million hunters
	-	123 million days
Migratory Birds	-	5.0 million hunters
	-	38 million days
Other	-	2.8 million hunters
	-	46 million days

The percentage of population by age who hunted in 1985 was ages 16-17, 14%; 17-24, 11%; 25-44, 11%; 45-64, 8%; 65 and over, 3%. Ninety-six percent of hunters are caucasian and over half are from non metropolitan areas. The rate of participation was not significantly affected by education or annual income variables over $10,000. Eighteen percent of all men hunt, and two percent of all women hunt. Additionally, ten percent of all caucasians hunt, two percent of all blacks and three percent of all others hunt.

Hunting is decreasing in popularity with a 16% decrease in the percentage of people hunting from 10% of the population in 1955 to 8.4% of the population in 1985.

Most types of hunting have the hunters on site ready to hunt at dawn before the sun rises. This affects access and parking.

% of hunters (on an annual basis) who fish and do non-consumptive wildlife recreation.

REQUIREMENTS
LAND REQUIREMENTS

An extensive acreage of land, wetlands and/or water that by reason of its established or establishable habitat and game populations is conducive to hunting.

FACILITIES

- Access (gravel and dirt roads OK) -- must be easily negotiated at night.

- Parking -- small (3 to 10 cars) dispersed parking with gravel or stabilized turf. Must be identifiable at night during the hunting season. These areas could also be used by non-hunters during the non-hunting season as starting points for wildlife observation and hiking.

- Refuse disposal.

- The need for picnic or overnight use is contingent on hunter origins and local customs. Hunting is generally permitted only during the low-use park season and park facilities can frequently be used especially the campgrounds.

- Sanitary facilities, if any are provided, should be located in areas of concentrated hunting, i.e., on game preserves. They must be findable at night. Lighting is not a necessity and pit and portable toilets are acceptable.

MANAGEMENT

Clearly visible and well-defined boundaries between hunting and non-hunting activities must be established, with adequate safety zones (buffer space) provided. Type of game, terrain and weapons used must, of course, be considered in establishing the extent of the buffer zone.

ALTERNATIVES TO HUNTING

Analysis of the site may determine that game harvesting is not practical. As an alternative means of accommodating the hunting public the following should be considered for development:

- Skeet, trap, rifle or archery ranges (see Chapter 24 "Fire Arm Ranges" and Chapter 13, "Archery Ranges").

- Hunting dog training and/or field trial events.

GAME MANAGEMENT

Manipulation of the parks' natural resources to improve game habitat may be necessary. This may include:

- Management of existing vegetative cover.

- Planting of trees and shrubs suitable for game food and may include crops such as domesticated grains.

- Establishment of additional impoundments or wetlands.

- Opening spaces in woods.

Resource improvements to sustain game animal and bird wildlife population is of equal importance to improving the non-hunting visitors' wildlife observation opportunities. In addition to the cultural practices noted for hunting, it is desirable to consider closing certain habitat areas to public use during breeding or other sensitive biological seasons. Keep in mind that good game habitat is generally good for the overall wildlife population. Managing areas for hunting will increase the number of non-gamebirds and animals which are of interest to many people.

Trails, photography and observation blinds should be considered in hunting areas with significant wildlife concentrations. They should be designed to keep man's intrusion into the wildlife habitat at an absolute minimum while permitting him to observe and/or photograph the birds and animals during non-hunting seasons. (See Chapter 25, "Non Consumptive Wildlife Recreation.")

Chapter 23 ARCHERY

There are two types of archery -- target ranges (open fields) and field courses. Both can be used for competitive shooting. Field courses are frequently used for skill sharpening by bow hunters.

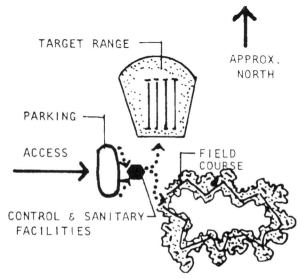

Conceptual layout for an archery complex.

TARGET RANGE
MINIMUM REQUIREMENTS

An open field and surrounding buffer area of approximately 5 acres (2 hectares) for 25 shooting stations.

- Turfed field to protect arrows.
- A marked fenced safety fan of 300 yards (250 m) is necessary.
- Safety embankments and/or arrow stops may be necessary, especially in multi-use park areas where space is limited and possible conflicts could occur with other park use.
- Targets at various distances.
- Electrical supply and communications.
- Sanitary facilities - vault/compost - type toilets "OK".
- Parking - minimum 1 space per station.

DESIRABLE

- Spectator area(s).
- Support structure to have as a minimum a meeting room/registration room, equipment storage and sanitary facilities.
- Flush toilets.
- Potable water supply.
- Spectator parking (could be overflow turfed area equal to 100% of required parking).
- Night lighting.

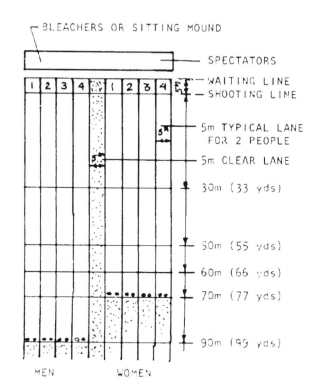

Target range.

RANGE DETAILS

- Open grass field to be approximately 120 m (133 yds.) long oriented on north/south axis.

- Men maximum 90 m (100 yds.) shooting distance plus overflight 20 m (22 yds.).

- Women maximum 70 m (77 yds.) shooting distance plus overflight of 20 m (22 yds.).

- If space is critical a backstop can be installed.

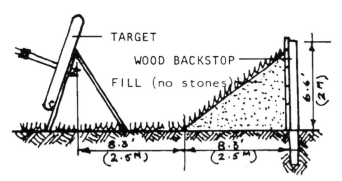

Archery backstop.

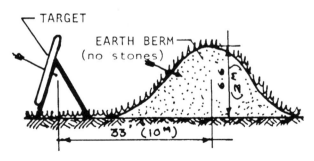

Alternate archery backstop.

- 5 m lane width is normally sufficient for two shooters at one time; however, major competitions may restrict the lane to one shooter only.

- Targets or shooting lines can be moved to accommodate the varying target distances.

Targets are of two sizes -- 122 cm ϕ for 60, 70 and 90 m; 80 cm ϕ for 30 and 50 m.

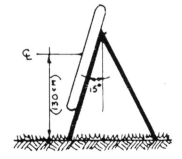

Typical target. [71]

FIELD COURSE

Generally constructed in a manner that will keep an area looking as natural as possible.

MINIMUM SPACE REQUIREMENTS

Approximately 16 hectares (40 ac).

- Trail frequently of compacted gravel or crushed stone and wood chips, especially in wooded areas.

- Targets -- minimum 48 positions required for competition with a total length of 1480 m (5000').

Field courses are of two types -- field courses and hunter's courses.

Field Course

A typical competition field course would have the following: [71]

# of Arrows/ Targets	Distance	# of Targets	ϕ of Target Face	# of Arrows
4	15 m/20 m/25 m/30 m	4	40 cm	16
4	35 m/40 m/45 m	3	45 cm	12
4	50 m/55 m/60 m	3	60 cm	12
4	85 m	1	45 cm	4
1	6 m/8 m/10 m/12 m	1	15 cm	4
1	30 m/35 m/40 m/45 m	1	45 cm	4
1	45 m/50 m/55 m/60 m	1	60 cm	4

Hunters Course

A typical competition hunter's course would have the following: [71]

# of Arrows/ Targets	Distance	# of Targets	Total Distance of arrow flight	ϕ of Target Face	# of Arrows
4	5-15 m	2	80 m	15 cm	8
4	10 to 30 m	4	320 m	30 cm	16
4	20 to 40 m	5	600 m	45 cm	20
4	30 to 50 m	3	480 m	60 cm	12
		Total	1480 m		

REQUIRED FEATURES

- Safety barrier especially in wooded areas to protect park users and others who are unaware of the range and its safety hazards.

- Communications for emergency purposes.*

- Sanitary facilities -- vault or composting type.*

- Parking for users -- minimum 10 cars.*

*Can be shared facilities with Target Range.

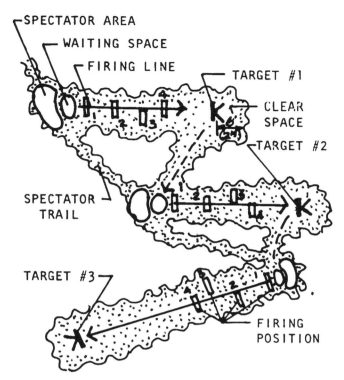

SPECTATOR AREA
WAITING SPACE
FIRING LINE
TARGET #1
CLEAR SPACE
TARGET #2
SPECTATOR TRAIL
TARGET #3
FIRING POSITION

Hunter's course layout. [71]

DESIRABLE ADDITIONAL FEATURES

- Spectator areas.
- Spectator parking.*
- Support structure.*
- Flush toilets.*
- Electricity.*
- Potable water supply.*

*Can be shared facilities with Target Range.

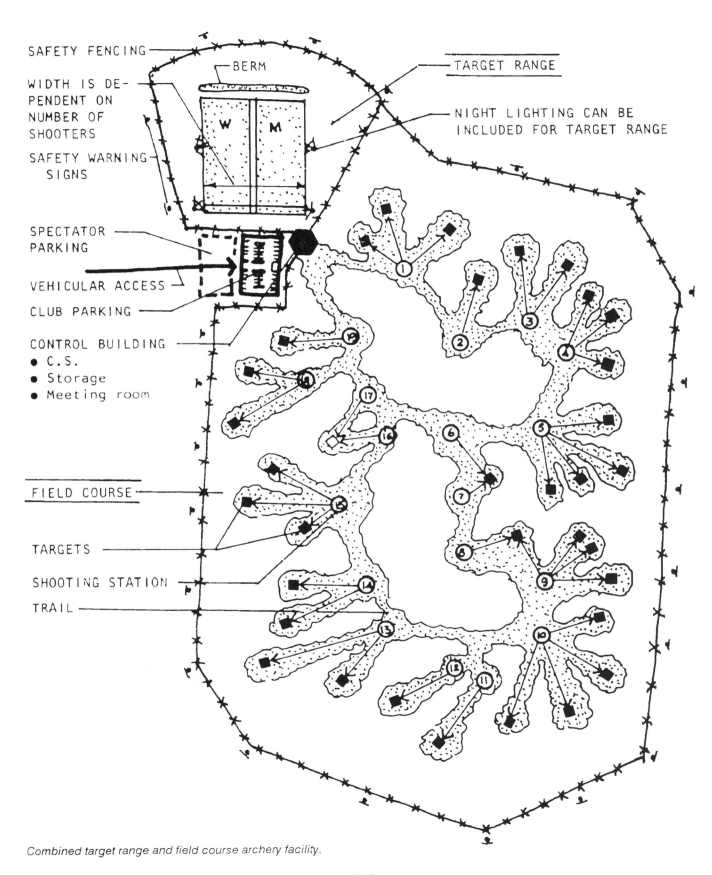

SAFETY FENCING

BERM

TARGET RANGE

WIDTH IS DE-
PENDENT ON
NUMBER OF
SHOOTERS

NIGHT LIGHTING CAN BE
INCLUDED FOR TARGET RANGE

SAFETY WARNING
SIGNS

W   M

SPECTATOR
PARKING

VEHICULAR ACCESS

CLUB PARKING

CONTROL BUILDING
• C.S.
• Storage
• Meeting room

FIELD COURSE

TARGETS

SHOOTING STATION

TRAIL

Combined target range and field course archery facility.

Chapter 24
FIREARM RANGES

The number of hunters has remained fairly constant over the last several years but has decreased as a percentage of the total population. [76] It is assumed that the numbers of target shooters is directly related to the number of hunters. If this assumption is true, it would indicate that the need for new rifle ranges will be minimal, and they will probably be needed only in areas of increasing population. Older established ranges will, however, need renovations, additions, and possibly they will need to be relocated. The National Rifle Association has extensive detailed information on the development and operations of all types of firearm ranges and should be contacted for additional information and advice in this area of recreation facility development. [73]

Firearm ranges can be used for a variety of shooting activities for a wide range of equipment.

Activities	Equipment
Target shooting	Pistols - still and rapid fire Rifles Air rifles Big bore rifles Muzzle loading rifles Shotguns Bows (See Chapter 23 "Archery") Cross bows
Trap & skeet shooting	— Shotguns

Practical shooting
   (hunting, simulation
   combat situations)
	Pistol
	Rifles
	Shotguns
	Assault guns
	(72, 73)

All these activities can be done for either (1) skill enhancement or (2) competition. The ranges can be for a single activity or for the entire list and can include archery and dog training areas as well. They may be indoor and/or outdoor and vary from 10± firing points to a hundred or more.

Many, if not most, ranges are operated by a sportsman's club. These clubs provide the opportunity for fellowship which is the third major aspect of shooting activities.

Many sportsman's clubs have their own facilities while others cooperate with and/or lease land from government agencies. This chapter will only cover large-scale facilities requiring open air range(s) for both public and private developments.

LOCATION CRITERIA

SOUND

Separate from other land use activities due to safety needs and noise from the firearms -- 1/2 mile for rifle noise; 3/4 mile for shotgun noise. The sound distance (unless baffled) can often make the location of the clubhouse and ranges quite distant from the nearest public access. In addition, there is the problem of long utility runs to any available utility tie-ins.

SAFETY ZONES

Rifle, up to 3 miles (5 km); shotgun, 900 feet (270 m).

SIZE

Approximate acreage needed without barriers:

Rifle & Pistol	large bore -- 1260 acres (510 ha) small bore -- 660 acres (270 ha) & pistol
Shotgun	— 370 acres (150 ha)

The needed acreage can be drastically reduced for all ranges by constructing berms and baffles.

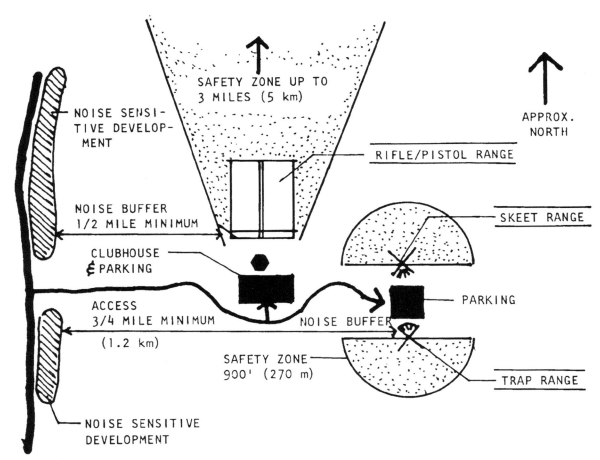

NOISE SENSITIVE DEVELOPMENT

SAFETY ZONE UP TO 3 MILES (5 km)

APPROX. NORTH

RIFLE/PISTOL RANGE

NOISE BUFFER 1/2 MILE MINIMUM

SKEET RANGE

CLUBHOUSE & PARKING

PARKING

ACCESS 3/4 MILE MINIMUM (1.2 km)

NOISE BUFFER

SAFETY ZONE 900' (270 m)

TRAP RANGE

NOISE SENSITIVE DEVELOPMENT

Rifle range complex.

DESIGN

REQUIRED

- Orientation of all ranges (safety permitting) should be on a N/S axis.

- Parking -- 1.5 spaces per firing point + anticipated spectator parking; paved for normal use although well-drained gravel lots OK; gravel and/or stabilized turf is OK for competitions and spectators. All parking must be located outside the safety fan. Handicapped parking facilities and an accessible route to accessible facilities must be provided.

- Clubhouse --
  - Storage ⎰ targets / ⎱ ammunition must be tightly secured
  - Work room for loading, etc.
  - Meeting room
  - Sanitary facilities ⎰ vault type OK / flush system very desirable / -- especially if there are / many women users.

- Target scoring space table(s).
- Electricity ⎰ clubhouse / ⎱ range towers
- Phone service required for emergency; desired for general use.

- Water -- potable
  - Municipal where economical connection can be made
  - Well water satisfactory
  - Can be bottled water.

- Sewage -- can be septic system.

- Vending machines -- beverages and snack -- also provides good income.

- Access road -- controlled for security purposes.

- Range tower -- needs loudspeaker system and electricity.

- Firing line – paved and preferably covered and baffled.

152

- Gun racks -- space for 2 guns per firing point and benches for pistol ranges of 3' (90 cm) per firing point.

- Targets -- frequently have pulley systems for shorter distances -- up to 50 meters.

- Pits for high power rifles only for ranges of 600 feet (180 m) or longer.

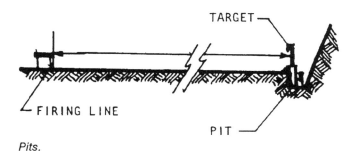

Pits.

- Backstops.

- Side berms -- where unlimited space is not available.

- Safety baffles -- where unlimited space is not available.

- Maintenance building/storage building -- only on large complexes, and then only where other (park) maintenance facilities are not available.

- Solid waste disposal system -- usually a combination of dumpsters and trash cans.

- Walks -- constructed for light service vehicle access to pick up trash and for maintenance purposes.

- Internal communication -- required for all large complexes and for those with target pits [600 feet (180 m) range distances or greater].

- Topography -- must be such that the firing line and targets are at the same elevation.

DESIRABLE

- Waterline tie-in to a municipal system.

- Sewage tie-in to a municipal system.

- Night lighting on ranges.

- Covered firing line -- usually needs artificial lighting. May be constructed in a manner to permit cold weather heating.

- Spectator seating -- needs to be separated from participants but still close enough to see what is going on; shading desirable.

A large rifle range with club house, safety berms, range tower, gun racks. East Bay Regional Park District, California.

SAFETY FACTORS

There are three zones to be considered; direct fire, safety and ricochet.

DIRECT FIRE ZONE

The distance that a bullet will travel from the firing line. This distance can be in miles (kilometers) for high-powered rifles unless baffled by hills and/or constructed barriers.

- High power --
16500' (5,000 m) approx. 3 miles (5 kilometers)

- Small bore --
9,000' (2,700 m) approx. 1.7 miles (2.7 kilometers)

- Pistol --
9,000' (2,700 m) approx. 1.7 miles (2.7 kilometers)

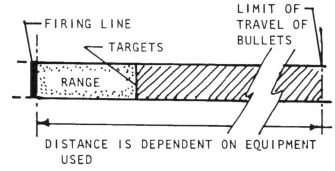

Direct fire zone.

SAFETY ZONE

An area 10° or more angled from either end of the firing line.

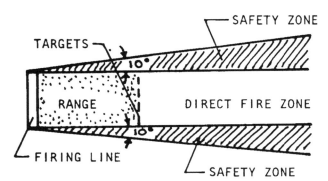

Safety zone.

RICOCHET ZONE

An area of approximately 45° angle from the targets and extending.

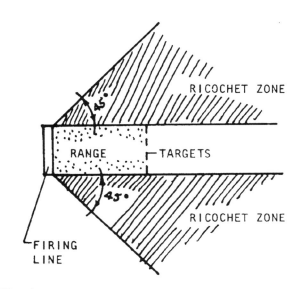

Ricochet zone.

BARRIERS

Because of the vast amount of land that would be required for ranges without barriers, it is imperative to either locate them in areas with hilly terrain or to install baffles and barriers. These barriers will also help in reducing noise problems. Basically sound travels in line of sight; therefore, if the area of noise concern cannot be seen from the firing line (excluding vegetation), then there will be little noise.

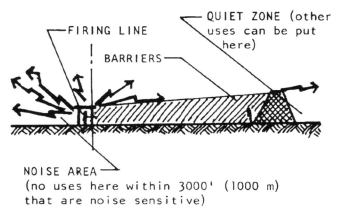

The effects of firearm noises.

Safety Baffles: A structure or series of structures that will restrict the bullets/arrows to a confined space. Basically to be constructed such that you can't see the sky from the firing line. They should be maintenance free if possible, i.e., earth berms on the ground and wood for overhead structures. Most easily done by constructing an overhead shelter at the firing line with tall side berms and backstop. The backstop would preferably be a natural hill. Side baffles of mounded

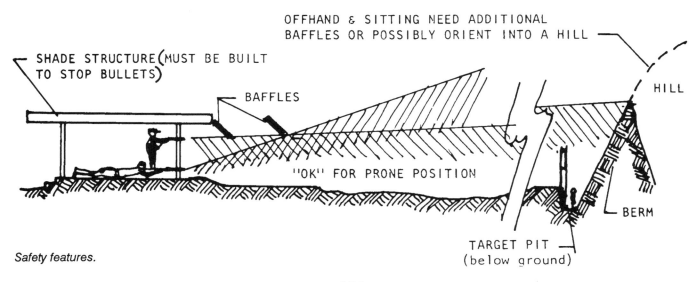

Safety features.

154

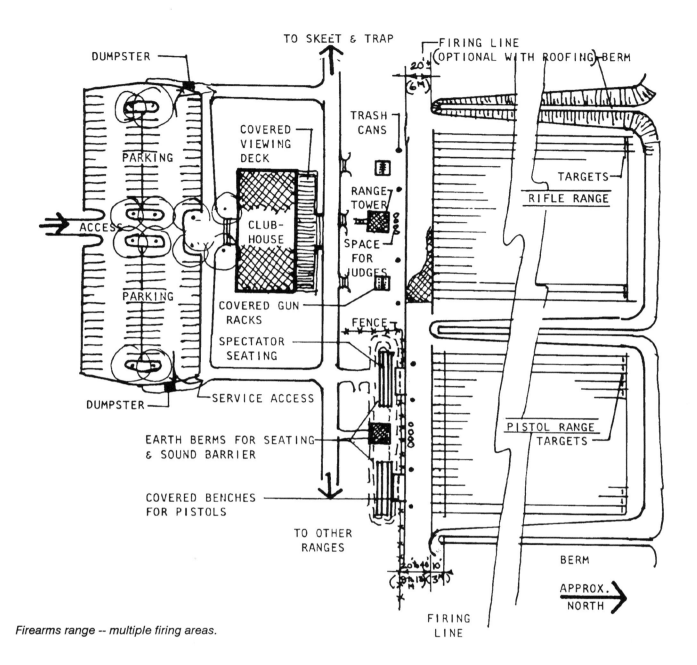

Firearms range -- multiple firing areas.

vegetated earth are recommended, although other types of construction are possible and, where space is at a premium, should be seriously considered. Approximate height 8 feet (2.4 m).

RANGE LENGTHS

Distance on ranges from firing line to targets is variable.

Small Bore -- 7.5 m up to 100 m.

Rifle Ranges -- up to 200 m to 300 m; in long-range target shooting up to 1000 yards (900 m) is sometimes desired.

Pistol -- 75 feet and 150 feet (25 m and 50 m).

Air Guns -- 5 to 40 m (maximum safety zone 300 m).

Muzzle Loading Pistols -- to 50 m (maximum safety zone 1.5 miles)

Muzzle Loading Round Ball -- to 100 m.

Muzzle Loading Mini Ball -- 25 m to 1000 m with 100 m or less normal maximum (safety same as large bore rifle).

155

SKEET AND TRAP

Skeet and trap shooting were originally started to improve hunter skills and, like many sports activities, quickly became competitive events in their own right. Trap shooting is one of the most active parts of the shooting sports and must be seriously considered in any firearms range complex. It is strictly an outdoors event and, other than the problem of noise, takes relatively little space. Approximately 2 1/2 acres (1000' x 1000'), 1 hectare (300 m x 300 m) for skeet and somewhat less for trap.

Trap houses for both trap and skeet competition are required to meet certain specifications. See NRA Range Manual 1988 for specifics.

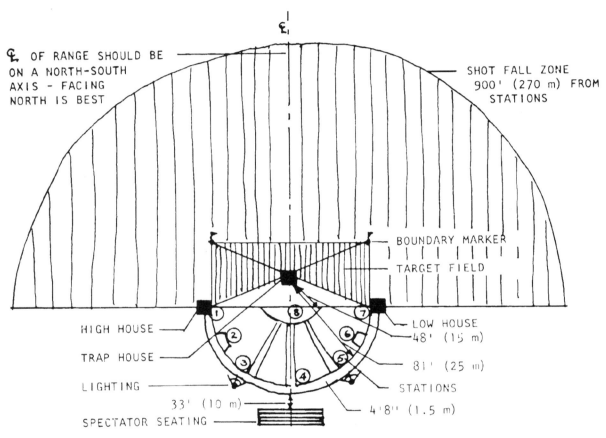

Skeet range. [73]

The Olympic and international competition ranges may vary slightly from the configuration shown. [86] If the ranges are to be used for international competition or for practice for these competitions, then they should be made to conform to the latest standards by the governing body under which the competition is to be held.

There are a variety of other types of ranges and competitions which are practiced in various places such as turkey shoots, crazy quail, running deer, etc. These guidelines will not attempt to provide guidance on these and other variations. For further assistance, please refer to the National Rifle Association.

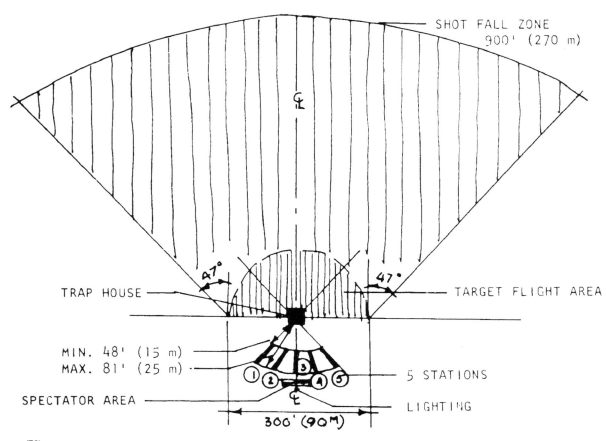

Trap range. [73]

Chapter 25
NON-CONSUMPTIVE WILDLIFE RECREATION

Many people in the United States participate in some form of non-consumptive wildlife recreation as a primary activity consisting of feeding wildlife (especially birds), observing wildlife and nature photography. In 1985 16 percent of the population participated a total of 134.7 million activity days. Approximately 25 percent of these activity days were for trips of over one mile from home to do the activity, while the remaining 75 percent of the activity was done around the home. In addition, 127 million activity days of participation of non-consumptive recreation was done as a secondary activity while doing other primary activities. Such a

primary activity as going swimming might be combined with the secondary activity of going shelling, or a family might primarily be going for a typical park outing and also do bird watching while at the park or while in transit to the park. [76]

A significant number, perhaps as much as 30 percent, of non-consumptive wildlife users are also hunters and/or fishermen.

The participation rate as a primary activity in 1985 was 18 percent for caucasians, 4 percent for blacks and 7 percent for all other ethnic groups.

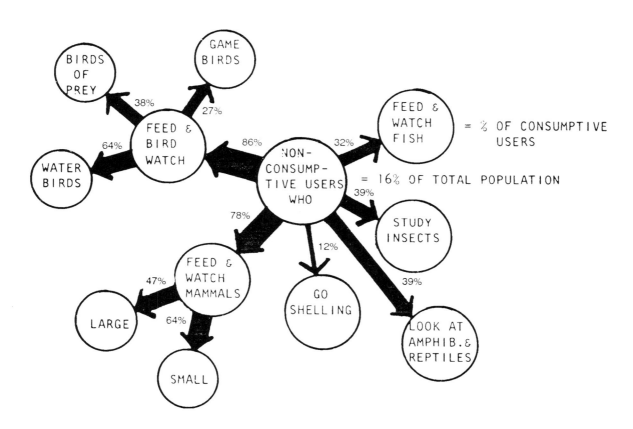

% of non-consumptive wildlife users who are likely to do various kinds of activities at leisure time facilities.

CHARACTERISTICS

The users come from all areas of the country. They are more likely to be from families whose 1985 income was $20,000 and higher. This activity is strongly influenced by education, with almost three times as greater a percentage of college educated (25% of population) as non high school graduates (9% of population) participating. There is also a very strong bias toward caucasian participation (96% of participants). [76]

WHERE ACTIVITIES TAKE PLACE

The away-from-home non consumptive activities currently take place primarily on public lands. The activities were generally distributed in 1985 as follows:

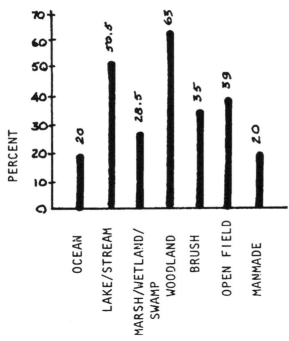

% of primary non-consumptive users utilizing various habitats.

WHAT THEY DO*

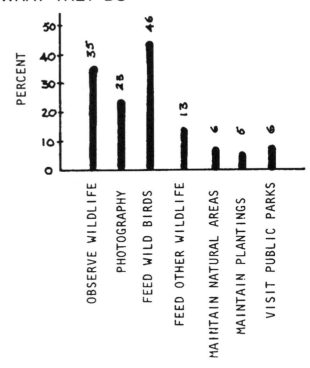

% of the population 16 years old and older who participated in various non-consumptive wildlife related recreation activities at or within one mile of their homes.

*Additional information on primary residential users can be secured from the 1985 National Survey of Fishing, Hunting and Wildlife Associated Recreation published by the U.S. Department of the Interior, Fish and Wildlife Service in 1988.

There is no historical base data to determine trends in this activity.

GENERAL

All existing park, recreation, conservation and preservation areas, and those areas being considered for some form of leisure activity or preservation status, should be inventoried for possible areas to observe and photograph wildlife and plant life. Consideration should also be given to establishing and/or enhancing habitats that will encourage wildlife to come to and/or stay in the areas.

Wildlife viewing.
Yellowstone National Park, Wyoming.

BIRDING

Controlled access and trails should be established that will go through a variety of habitats which are likely to have bird life. In general, the edge or interface between fields and woods, swamp and woods and shoreline areas (especially coastal and estuarine areas) are the most productive locations for birding.

MINIMUM REQUIRED

- Suitable habitat either natural and/or manmade.

- Vehicular access to the vicinity of the site.

- Parking - carefully designed to fit into the natural surroundings.

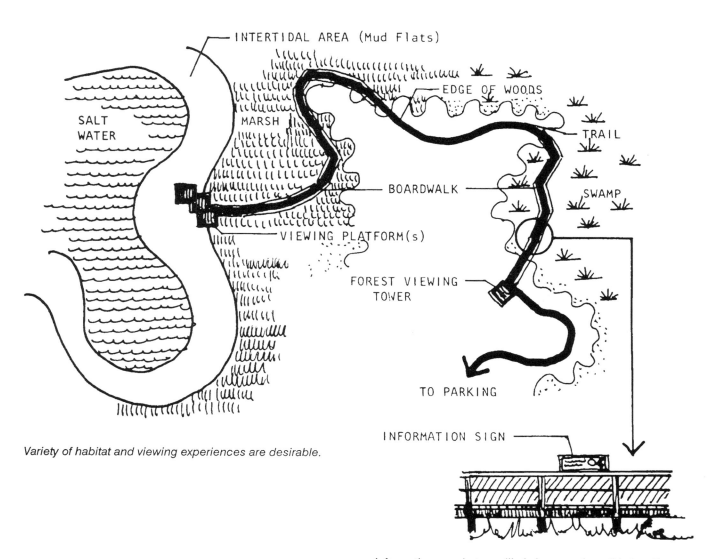

Variety of habitat and viewing experiences are desirable.

Information on what can likely be seen from this location.

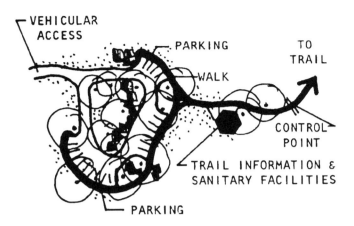

Parking and trail head facilities.

- Trails.
- Solid waste collection and disposal system.

DESIRABLE

- Information at the parking lot on what can be seen on the site.
- Exhibits.
- Sanitary facilities.
- Potable water.
- Observation platform(s) and/or tower(s).

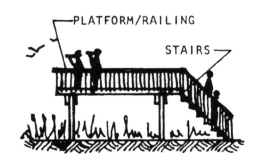

Platform -- good in wet and marshy areas.

High towers -- especially useful in forested areas enabling the viewer to observe life at different levels from floor to canopy.

- Photography and observation blinds.

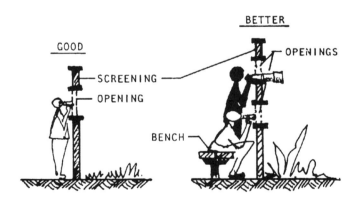

Blinds.

- Interpretive signs along trails.

In some situations special conditions are present which lend themselves to boat trails, boardwalks and one-way, low speed car trails. It is interesting to note that wildlife does not seem to be adversely affected by slow moving vehicles, and, in fact, wildlife observers who stay in their cars can observe much more at closer range than can those walking on a trail.

162

DRIVING TRAIL

Required

- One-way road [12' (3.6 m)] wide.

- Numerous pull-offs at likely wildlife observation areas.

- Road to be inconspicuous visually.

Desirable

- Habitat improvement at designated observation areas.

- Interpretive signs which can be read from the cars.

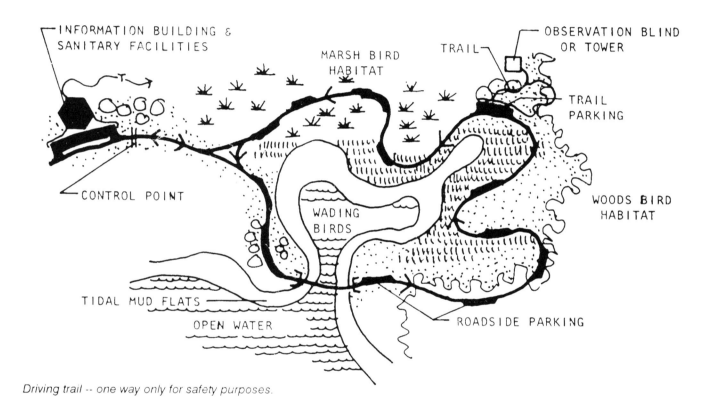

Driving trail -- one way only for safety purposes.

OTHER NON-CONSUMPTIVE WILDLIFE RECREATION ACTIVITIES

WILDLIFE VIEWING (other than birding)

The requirements are the same as for birding except where special habitats require modifications, i.e. under-water viewing. Best done from vehicles either on a self-guiding basis like Assateague National Preserve in Virginia, on Ding Darling Preserve in Florida; or on mini-buses with guides such as is done on wildlife safaris in Africa or the larger school buses in Denali National Park in Alaska.

FISH VIEWING

Glass bottom boats (usually available for a fee which includes a guide). Tours of this type are currently done at many natural underwater features such as John Pennekamp State Park in Florida and Green Island in the Great Barrier Reefs in Australia.

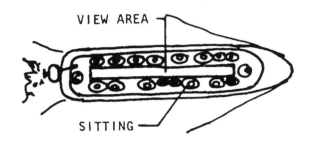

PLAN

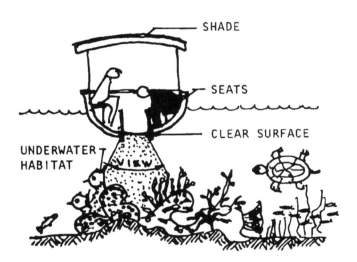

"Glass bottom" boats are an excellent way to view fish.

Underwater observatories are another option. These exhibits are extremely popular and resemble an aquarium exhibit without the habitat maintenance requirements.

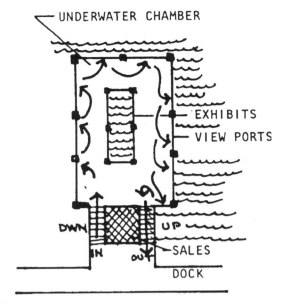

PLAN

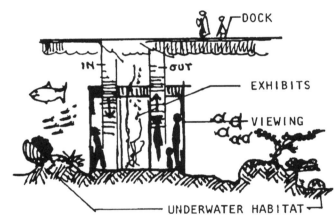

Underwater observatories are very exciting ways to view fish and their habitats.

PHOTOGRAPHY

Wildlife and plant photography have the same basic requirements as birding, wildlife, and nature viewing. The only modification to these requirements would be to provide additional space for the photographer (who usually takes considerable time setting up his equipment and waiting for the right picture) so that he does not interfere with the normal flow of traffic.

164

WILDLIFE FEEDING

This activity is usually done only to increase the number and type of animals in a given area. Many wildlife specialists consider this an undesirable activity because the wild animals' normal habitats are distorted, and if the feeding were to be interrupted for any extended time period, the birds and animals would find it very difficult, and frequently impossible, to adjust to "natural" conditions.

Special care needs to be taken to insure the type of food provided to the animals attracted will be what is needed by them and that the food will not be harmful.

HABITAT ENHANCEMENT OR MODIFICATIONS

This work is also done to increase the number and types of animals (or plants) in a given area.

• The installation of salt licks is very useful in bringing wild animals to areas where people can view them. This is extensively done in game parks in some regions of Africa.

• Water holes in dry areas are another type of habitat improvement that is very useful in concentrating all types of wildlife in dry climates.

• Creating edge type environments can greatly enhance the number and variety of wildlife and for that matter plant life.

• Proper management of grazing lands can help increase the number and variety of wild flowers.

• Grain and other forage crops can be planted.

• Management agreements with surrounding farms (where present) can be prepared which will enhance their wildlife carrying capacity.

The last two items are especially useful in migratory bird stopping areas such as is done at Pymatuning State Park and Game Preserve in Pennsylvania and in many other state and national game preserves.

Visitor control guidelines and an ongoing habitat management plan will be necessary to insure a long-term success of any wildlife or plant viewing area.

Chapter 26
ADMINISTRATION AND SERVICE AREA

SERVICE AREA

All parks need some type of service area. The size and complexity of a service area increases as the size and complexity of the park increases. Before locating or designing a service area it is necessary to have a preliminary park master plan. A study of the service needs should be completed in cooperation with the park operator.

Some factors to consider:

• Access from a good, all-season road to all areas of the park. If the park has controlled access it is desirable to have a separate entrance to the service area from public roads. This will permit material deliveries to the maintenance area when the park is closed and may reduce circulation conflicts between maintenance functions and park users.

• Adequate power, water and sewage disposal.

• Storage space, both inside buildings and outside. Exterior storage space should be much larger than most planners believe necessary. All kinds of things are stored -- tables, trash cans, gravel, old equipment, salvaged lumber, etc.

• Screening from roads and use areas.

• Employee parking, either inside or outside the fenced space.

• Security fencing around service areas is a necessity as these facilities are frequently the target of thieves and vandals.

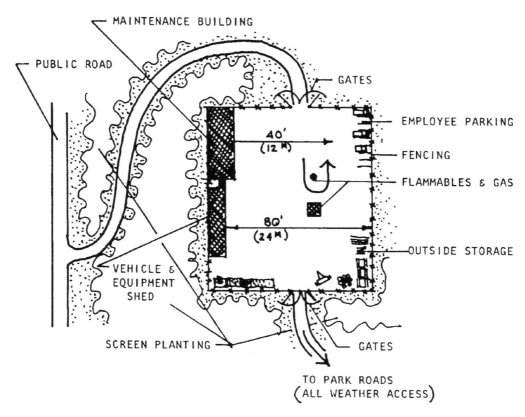

Service area.

- Space to load and unload heavy equipment.

- Indoor and outdoor work and repair space.

- Park vehicle storage space.

- Fuel pumps.

- Flammable materials storage structure.

- Office space.

- Night lighting for entire fenced area.

- Employee lunch area.

- Employee locker space and shower(s).

Large parks sometimes require sub-maintenance areas for efficient operation.

ADMINISTRATION

Parks with heavy attendance, or parks which are located at a considerable distance from the park system's headquarters, will normally need administrative facilities.

LOCATION

Adjacent to a public road and generally before any visitor entrance station to permit park business to be handled easily without conflicts with users.

PARKING

- Employee.

- Visitor -- if boating and/or camping are permitted in the park provide for car and trailer parking.

Administration and maintenance facilities are frequently located within a short walking distance, 300 feet (100 m) of each other.

RESIDENCE

There are three reasons for park employee housing: remoteness, reduction of vandalism, and protection of historic buildings and settings.

REMOTENESS

Where parks are located in areas remote from sources of housing for employees, provision must be made for their needs in the park.

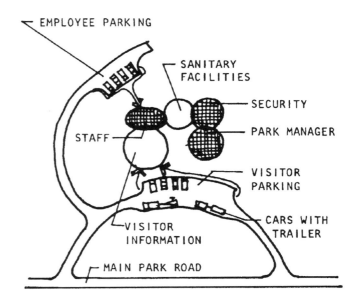

Administration -- public contact.

Requirements

- Locate away from public-use area.

- Access is needed to public roads outside of any park control point if possible.

- It is desirable to have easy access to the park office and/or maintenance area.

REDUCTION OF VANDALISM

Some parks subject to vandalism may need housing as a protective measure. Parks with overnight accommodations need 24-hour access to park personnel, which may require on-site housing.

Requirements

- Must have visual control of park access.

- Provide residence some degree of privacy.

- Overnight areas should have reasonable access to park residence or have 24-hour protection at camp entrance station.

PROTECTION OF HISTORIC BUILDINGS AND SETTINGS

Where buildings of historic or visual significance are to be preserved in the park it is necessary to keep them occupied to prevent vandalism.

Requirements

- Unobtrusive parking.

- Some privacy.

168

Appendix A
REFERENCES FOR COST ESTIMATING INFORMATION

Building Construction Cost Data, Robert Snow Means Co., Construction Consultants and Publishers, P.O. Box 6, Duxbury, Massachusetts 02332.

Building Construction Estimating Standards, Richardson Engineering Services, Inc., P.O. Box 370, Solana Beach, California, 92075.

Cost Data for Landscape Construction (the latest available edition), by Kathleen W. Kerr, Kerr Associates, Inc., Minneapolis, Minnesota.

Dodge Construction Processing and Scheduling Manual, Dodge Building Costs Services, McGraw-Hill Information Systems Co., 330 West 42nd Street, New York, N.Y. 10036.

Basically -- check with suppliers and contractors in area for assistance with details.

Also, for up-to-date construction costs, see the **Engineering News-Record Magazine,** and McGraw-Hill's **Construction Weekly.**

Appendix B
GLOSSARY OF COMMONLY USED RECREATION PLANNING TERMS

ACCESS AISLE: An accessible pedestrian space between elements such as parking spaces that provide clearances appropriate for use by the [handicapped]. [78]

ACCESS ROAD: The road serving as the route of vehicular travel between an existing public thoroughfare and the recreation area.

ACCESSIBLE: A site, building, facility or portion thereof that meets the Federal Accessibility Standards and that can be approached, entered and used by the physically handicapped. [78]

ACCESSIBLE ROUTE: A continuous unobstructed path connecting all accessible routes in a facility, and may include parking access, aisles, curb ramps, walks, ramps and lifts. [78]

ACTIVITY DAY: A measure of recreation use by one person in one facility or area for one day or part of a day. One person may exert more than one activity day per day. The activity day is probably most useful for apportioning total use to single uses and for sizing various parts of a given recreation development.

ACTUAL OR PRACTICAL CAPACITY: The number of people that can use the area, considering the requirement of dual usage, traffic, vacant units, and the capacity of the land to support the people without deterioration of the resource.

ADMINISTRATIVE AREA: An area set aside for facilities used by an operating agency in administering a park or recreation area; may include office building, kiosks or visitor centers.

ANGLE OF REPOSE: The angle at which a given soil or rock will remain stable, i.e., 1:1, 2:1, 3:1.

ANNUAL CAPACITY: The total capacity for use in a given year, considering the daily, weekly and seasonal variations in density of use.

BACKSTOP: (When used in conjunction with ranges) - A device (usually a barrier) to stop or redirect bullets or arrows fired on a range.

BAFFLES: (When used in conjunction with ranges) -- Barriers to contain bullets and arrows and to reduce/redirect sound waves.

BEACH: An area of shoreline which is developed and/or designated for swimming use.

BERM: (When used in conjunction with ranges) - An earth embankment used for restricting bullets or arrows to a given area or as a divider between ranges.

BOAT DOCK: A facility located in or adjacent to the water which is designed and constructed to provide for the mooring and/or storage of boats.

BOAT LAUNCHING AREA: An area for boat launching and removal. Area could include a launching ramp, maneuvering and rigging area and/or other launching facilities such as a crane, tramway, etc.

BOAT LAUNCHING RAMP: A graded and surface-stabilized facility designed and constructed to allow for the launching and removal of boats from the waterway by means of boat trailers.

BUFFER AREA: An area set aside to preserve the integrity of an adjacent recreation area and to prevent physical or aesthetic encroachment on the area.

BUNKER: See "Sand Trap."

BURSLEY'S FORMULA: A method to determine the design load of an individual recreation area; no longer used.

"C" CURVE: Maximum flood level. This is a much greater height than that typically known as the flood plain for one hundred year floods.

CAMPGROUND: A portion of land surface within a recreation area or recreation site which is designated and at least partially developed for camp use. Includes camp units and/or camp site, roads, parking, sanitary facilities, water supply, etc. **Note:** Camp areas, campgrounds, campsites, camp units and camp facilities are usually planned for family use. In general, the unmodified term "camp" implies family use (or use by other than a large group). Consequently, the modifier "group" should be used if group use is planned.

CAMPING: Overnight recreation use which involves sleeping one or more nights in the "out-of-doors." In this definition, "out-of-doors" implies outside of an established dwelling.

CAMPSITE: An area which is constructed to accommodate camp use, e.g., a table, a camp stove, a fire ring, a tent site, a trailer space, etc.

CARRYING CAPACITY: The amount of use that land can support over a long period without damage to the resource. It is measured in terms of recreation use per time unit (usually a day or a year), and varies with the conditions of rain, topography, soil, climate and vegetative cover. It can be increased by protective measures which do not in themselves harm the resources. It can be decreased by the harmful effects of use greater than the safe capacity.

CIRCULATION ROAD: A public road for vehicular traffic within the recreation area.

COMFORT STATION: See "Restrooms."

CONCESSION AREA: That portion of the recreation area or facilities which is to be operated by private parties and may include ski areas, food service, marina, motels, etc.

CONSULTANT: An individual or organization hired to perform professional advisory or design services. Usually refers to architects, engineers, landscape architects, planners, etc.

COURTESY DOCK: A facility located on the water adjacent to a boat-launching facility and provided for the convenience of those using the launching and retrieving facilities.

CURB RAMP: A short ramp cutting through a curb or built up to it. [78]

DAILY CAPACITY: The number of people who can use an area in a day, considering the rate of turnover.

DAY USE: Recreation use of an area for one day or less. Day use may include participation in a number of recreation activities, e.g., picnicking, play, water sports, sightseeing, etc., but excludes overnight use.

DAY USE AREA: A portion of a recreation area which is designated for recreation use by recreationists remaining in the area for one day or less. Does not include overnight use. Commonly a day-use area will be developed to accommodate a number of recreation activities, e.g., picnicking, sightseeing, water sports, etc.

DESIGN LOAD OR INSTANTANEOUS CAPACITY: The theoretical number of people the area can accommodate at a given moment.

DEVELOPED AREA PLAN: A drawing showing the existing and proposed development of a unit within a park, generally at a scale of 1 inch = 200 or 400 feet (1:20 or 1:40).

DEVELOPMENT PLAN: A plan showing development proposals for a given park or portion thereof.

DISTANCE ZONE: Also known as "Service Area Zone" or "Travel Zone." Approximately concentric areas are delineated around a recreation resource, measured by units of distance or travel time. The distance zone is used for defining populations from which users of a recreating resource come or will come. A better designation method is actual travel time and becomes free form shapes.

FIRING DISTANCE: The distance between the firing line and targets.

FIRING LINE: A line parallel to the targets from which firearms or arrows are discharged.

FISH CLEANING FACILITY: A structure designated and constructed to provide for the cleaning of fish and for the sanitary disposal of the unwanted fish parts.

FLOOD PLAIN: Those areas subject to periodic flooding; usually defined as the "100 year flood."

GARBAGE DISPOSAL SYSTEM: Those sanitary facilities which are normally necessary to receive and dispose of garbage and refuse; also known as solid waste disposal.

GENERAL DEVELOPMENT PLAN: A drawing showing the existing and proposed development of a unit of the park system, generally at a scale of 1 inch = 500 feet (1:50) or larger.

GREEN: In golf, it is the place where each hole ends; sometimes called a putting green.

HANDICAPPED ACCESS AISLE: See "Access Aisle."

HANDICAPPED ACCESSIBLE: See "Accessible."

HANDICAPPED ACCESSIBLE ROUTE: See "Accessible Route."

HANDICAPPED RAMP: A walking surface to an accessible space that has a slope greater than 5 percent (1:20).

HOLE: In golf, it has two definitions; first, it is the entire combination of a tee, a fairway, roughs, hazards and a green which make up one unit of play. There are 18 holes on a normal golf course. The second definition is the hole in the ground located on the green which is the ultimate target of each "hole" played.

INITIAL STAGE DEVELOPMENT: That portion of the total recreation development which is constructed first. Ideally, the initial stage should be planned and constructed to accommodate a predicted level of visitation, e.g., an initial stage recreation development which will accommodate the predicted visitation in the tenth year of park operation.

KIOSK: A building or shelter so located in reference to the recreation area that it may be operated for the collection of fees, as a checkpoint for control of use and/or for the dissemination of information.

LAND USE MAP: A map showing in a diagrammatic fashion the existing land use.

LAND USE PLAN: A plan showing in a diagrammatic fashion the proposed park uses.

LEISURE TIME: A person's time not required for the necessities of life and with which he can do what he wants, i.e., watch T.V., play football, go to a concert, play cards, etc.

LOOP TRAIL: A trail which returns the user to the original beginning point.

MARINA: A combination of facilities which might include a boat launching area, boat launching facilities, boat dock, boat rentals, and boat service facilities (gas, oil, repairs, snack bar, etc.). The connotation is a general boat-associated facility which may be operated by a concessionaire.

M.G.D.: Millions of gallons per day.

MASTER PLAN: The document guiding the development of a park.

MANAGEMENT PLAN: The controlling document which establishes direction for development, operation, programming and maintenance of a park.

MOORING RAIL: A device to secure boats located along the edge of a body of boating water.

NATURAL AREA: An area, sometimes within a park, which is left generally undeveloped for passive recreation use and generally serves the function of enhancing the aesthetic quality of the overall recreation development.

ON-SHORE RECREATION FACILITY: A recreation facility which is provided in relation to a water-associated recreation area.

OVERLOOK: A sightseeing and/or observation area so located and constructed that visitors can view the dam, reservoir, lake, surrounding countryside and/or other objects or areas of interest.

OVERNIGHT USE: A portion of a recreation area which is designated for recreational use which includes camping. An overnight use area will usually be developed with a campground or motel-type area and may include other facilities primarily for the use of campers, e.g., boat ramp, trails, etc.

PARK SEASON: The time of year when the heaviest park use occurs.

PARKING AREA: An area designated and constructed for the parking of vehicles. Implies parking developed for a number of automobiles, i.e., a parking lot. A specialized type of parking area is needed for buses and in connection with a boat-launching area.

PARKING SPUR: An area designated and constructed for the parking of an automobile. In a campground, it implies a parking area for one to three automobiles or a trailer and one or more automobiles.

PEAK LOAD DAY: The day of maximum use, usually the Fourth of July or some other major holiday.

PERCENT (%) GRADE: A figure used in determining the rise or fall of the ground. Vertical change (distance) divided by horizontal distance = % grade.

PHASING (PHASED DEVELOPMENT): The construction of recreation facilities in stages. The basis for phasing or phased development may be recreation demand (for types and/or numbers of facilities), availability of money, etc.

PHYSICAL FITNESS AREA: An area, usually for young adults, provided with gym-type facilities -- usually located along jogging trails and sometimes adjacent to swim areas which serve a large number of young adults.

PHYSICALLY HANDICAPPED: An individual who has a physical impairment, including impaired sensory, manual or speaking abilities, which results in a functional limitation in access to and use of a facility.

PICNIC: A type of day-use recreation which includes at least one meal in the open air. **Note:** Picnic areas, picnic grounds, picnic sites, picnic units and picnic facilities are usually planned for either family use or group use. In general, the unmodified term ''picnic'' implies family use (or use by other than a large group). Consequently, the modifier ''group'' should be used if group use is planned.

PICNIC AREA: That portion of land surface within a recreation area or recreation site designated or zoned for picnic use.

PICNIC FACILITY: A device which is constructed to accommodate picnic use, e.g., a table, a stove.

PICNIC UNIT: A group of facilities developed to accommodate picnic use.

PLAY AREA: A space, usually with play apparatus, and generally for young children ages 3 to 12.

PLAY FIELD: Open play space for activities such as frisbee, softball, volleyball, football, etc.

POTABLE WATER: Water than can be used for drinking.

QUASI-PUBLIC: Agencies which are open to the public and are owned and/or operated by a non-profit organization like the YMCA, religious groups, Elks, etc.

RECREATION: An activity beyond that required for personal or family maintenance or for material gain; that is, for enjoyment rather than for survival.

RECREATION AREA: That portion of land and water surface which is designated for recreation use.

RECREATION DEMAND: The measured, implied or predicted ability and desire of the people in a designated recreation area to expend (exert) recreation in a designated recreating resource. It may be latent, as in an undeveloped area which would be used if it were developed. It may be expressed or measured in units of use plus units turned away.

RECREATION FACILITY: A specific device provided to accommodate recreation use, e.g., a table, a stove, a road, etc.

RECREATION SITE: A parcel of land within a recreation area which has recreation potential and is designated for recreation development and use. Does not imply specific development for the type of designated recreation use.

RECREATION UNIT: A grouping of recreation facilities which are constructed to provide a type of recreation accommodation, e.g., a camp unit is a type of recreation unit and is developed with the following facilities: a table, camp stove, parking spur, tent or trailer space, etc.

RECREATION USE: The occupation, utilization, consumption or enjoyment of a recreation resource, or of a particular part of a recreation resource.

RESTRICTED USE ZONE: A portion of a recreation area which is designated to serve a specified recreation function or functions to the exclusion of other activities.

RESTROOM OR COMFORT STATION - WASHHOUSE: A building designed and constructed as a portion of the sewerage system which contains toilet facilities. A washhouse contains, in addition to toilet facilities, laundry facilities and showers.

ROUGH: In golf, it is an area outside the fairway which is still within the course playing area and which can be rough and have little care.

SAFETY ZONE: The area needed to insure the safety of shooters, spectators and other people. This is the zone where bullets or arrows will impact taking into consideration the installed protective berms, baffles, etc.

SAND TRAP: In golf, it is an area void of vegetation and filled with sand. They are strategically placed around a golf course to make the game more challenging; sometimes called bunkers.

SANITARY FACILITIES: Those developments or services which are necessary for the disposal of human wastes in a manner which will protect the public health and environment.

SECTION: A drawing of a slice through a structure or natural feature showing how it is or should be made.

SERVICE AREA: An area set aside for facilities used in routine operation for maintaining a park or recreation area; may include equipment yards, shops and dwellings. A second definition is the area served by the park/recreation facility.

SERVICE ROADS: Vehicular roads within a park/recreation area used primarily for maintenance vehicles. These roads may also serve as public pedestrian paths and fire trails.

SEWAGE DUMPING STATION: A facility for the disposal of human wastes from camp trailers.

SEWAGE SYSTEM: Those sanitary facilities which are normally necessary to dispose of waste products of the human body, food preparation, showers and laundry facilities.

SHOOTING RANGE: Places where people may participate in recreation, competition, skill development and/or training with firearms, archery equipment and/or air guns.

SHORELINE MOORING: An area designated for boat tie-up along the shore of a body of water. Frequently requires grading and a mooring rail.

SIZING: The level, capacity, volume, magnitude of development within a stage of development, e.g., a given facility may be sized for a larger capacity than is needed in initial stage development. Initial stage development sizing is primarily a function of economic considerations.

SOLID WASTE: Rubbish, trash, etc. (see "Garbage Disposal System").

STABILIZED TURF: An area which has been constructed for occasional use for parking or vehicular access. Usually requires grading, improved drainage and generally a gravel surface chocked with fines and seeded.

SOUND BASIN: An area where sounds can be heard -- usually the line of site, excluding vegetation, from the source of the sound.

SWIMMING: A general term which includes actual swimming, water play, wading, etc.

SWIMMING AREA: That portion of a body of water designated specifically for swimming use.

SWIMMING IMPOUNDMENT: A portion of a reservoir, lake or stream which is specifically constructed for swimming and/or swimming use, e.g., an arm of a reservoir which may be diked to form a sub-impoundment for swimming use.

TEE: In golf, it is the place from which each hole starts. It is frequently different for men and women.

TRAIL: A pathway or roadway designed and constructed to carry other than normal vehicular traffic. Use of a trail may be as restricted as is desired by the recreation operator. For example: A trail may be used by hikers or hikers and cyclists, or motorized vehicles, etc.

TRAILHEAD: A developed area that serves as the beginning point of a trail and includes at least parking, trail information, rubbish containers and water and sanitary facilities.

TRANSIENT CAMPER: A camper who is staying in an area for less than a day while en route to his ultimate destination.

TURNOVER RATE: The number of times a given facility is used during a given period of time, usually a day.

VISITOR DAY: A measure of recreation use by one person for one day or part of a day. It may be brief or it may be as long as 24 hours. Brief views, as from a highway, are not visits in this sense nor are brief stops at such places as overlooks. So far as accuracy of data permits, one person will log only one visitor day at a given recreation resource during any 24-hour day. The visitor day is probably the most convenient unit for purposes of economic analysis; it is probably less convenient when used for sizing recreation facilities and apportioning total use to various activities.

WATER-ASSOCIATED RECREATION: Recreation which is carried on, at, near, in, under, or because of the presence of, standing or running water.

WATER HAZARD: In reference to a golf course, it is a water course (even when containing no water) or any other areas of water, i.e., ponds lakes, reservoirs, rivers, streams, and even drainage ditches. [71]

WATER SYSTEM: Facilities, including developments for supply, treatment, storage and distribution, which supply water to the recreation area and/or recreation sites.

XERISCAPE: The use of water-conserving landscape practices.

Appendix C
BIBLIOGRAPHY

1. **Interpretive Prospectus for the Pennsylvania Department of Forests and Waters,** Bureau of State Parks, Jonathan Wert, January 1979.

2. **Recreation Surveys, 1965,** Recreation Contract Services, Beaches and Parks, State of California, George E. Fogg.

3. **Recreation Surveys, 1966,** Recreation Contract Services, Beaches and Parks, State of California, Ralph McCormick.

4. **Survey of Folsom Lake, Summer, 1966,** Reservoir Development Unit, Beaches and Parks, State of California, George E. Fogg.

5. **Survey of Millerton Lake State Recreation Area, 1958-59,** Beaches and Parks, State of California, D. Knoefler.

6. **Survey of Folsom Lake Peninsula Campground, 1966,** Beaches and Parks, State of California, D. Knoefler.

7. **Survey of Alminor Campground,** National Forest Service, 1966.

8. **Recreation Use Surveys of Several Reservoirs in California, 1964-66,** U.S. Army Corps of Engineers.

9. **Recreation Information Management Surveys,** U.S. Forest Service, Bob Mace.

10. **Oroville Dam Overlook Attendance Records,** July 1965 to July 1966, Beaches and Parks, State of California.

11. **Recreation and Wildlife Summary, 1966,** U.S. Bureau of Reclamation.

12. **Pine Flat Reservoir and Isabella Reservoir,** U.S. Army Corps of Engineers, Recreation Use Survey, 1964, Boating Use.

13. **Outdoor Recreation Research in the U.S. Forest Service,** Walter S. Hopkins, Jr.

14. **Ratios and Distances Between People, Land and Facilities on Recreation Areas,** U.S. Bureau of Reclamation (a summary from other "reliable sources").

15. "Footpaths and Bike Routes," Oregon State Highway Division, Published in **Guidelines,** Vol. 2, No. 2, March/April 1972.

16. **Rules and Regulations,** Commonwealth of Pennsylvania, Department of Health, Chapter 4.

17. **Standards for Particular Recreational Activities and Facilities,** U.S. Department of the Interior, Bureau of Outdoor Recreation, Northeast Region.

18. **Survey for Pennsylvania State Park Planning,** "Campgrounds", National Campers and Hikers Association, 1967.

19. **Sewage Report,** Prince Gallitzin State Park, Pennsylvania State Park System.

20. **Pennsylvania State Park Attendance Reports,** Department of Forests and Waters, Bureau of State Parks.

21. **Battelle Survey, Summer 1967,** Bureau of State Parks, Department of Forests and Waters, Penn. and Battelle Memorial Institute.

22. **Summer Recreation Survey, 1968,** Bureau of State Parks, Department of Forests and Waters, Commonwealth of Pennsylvania.

23. **Park Road Standards,** U.S. Department of the Interior, National Park Service, May 1968.

24. **Snowmobile Manual,** Commonwealth of Pennsylvania, Department of Forests and Waters, Bureau of State Parks, Ralph A. Romeo.

25. **Camper Survey,** National Campers and Hikers Association, U.S., 1971.

26. **Camper Survey,** National Campers and Hikers Association, Pennsylvania, 1969.

27. **Facts and Trends,** Recreational Vehicle Industry Survey, 1969.

28. **Summer Survey, 1969,** Bureau of State Parks, Department of Forests and Waters, Pennsylvania.

29. **Traffic Control Sign Program,** Department of Forests and Waters, Bureau of State Parks, March 1969, Commonwealth of Pennsylvania.

30. **Ski,** September 1970.

31. **Analysis of Water Used in Camp Areas in Pennsylvania,** Division of Outdoor Recreation, Department of Environmental Resources, Commonwealth of Pennsylvania.

32. City of Los Angeles, Department of Parks and Recreation.

33. **Summer Survey, 1971,** Bureau of State Parks, Department of Forests and Waters, Commonwealth of Pennsylvania.

34. **Camper Survey, 1973,** Bureau of Resources Programming, Division of Outdoor Recreation, Commonwealth of Pennsylvania.

35. **Summer Survey, 1972,** Bureau of State Parks, Division of Planning and Development, Commonwealth of Pennsylvania.

36. **Sanitary Fixture Requirements for Pennsylvania Park Facilities-Day Use,** Engineering Report, Division of Outdoor Recreation, Department of Environment Resources, 1973.

37. **N. P. S. Recreation Symbols,** a pamphlet, July 1970.

38. **State Park Attendance, 1971-72,** Summer Recreation Survey, Pennsylvania State Parks, Planning and Development Division, an unpublished report.

39. **Concept Design Standard for Culvert Underpass,** Larry Sharer, 1973, an unpublished report.

40. **Sailing Facilities,** Larry Sharer, October 1973, an unpublished report.

41. **Recreation Symposium Proceedings,** United States Department of Agriculture, Northeast Forest Experiment Station, Upper Darby, Pennsylvania, 1971.

42. Commonwealth of Pennsylvania, Bureau of Resources Programming, Unpublished research papers by Cyrus A. Yoakam, assisted by Pamela J. Werner, Division of Outdoor Recreation based on 1971, 1972 and 1973 summer recreation surveys and other Pennsylvania state park user information.

43. **Watershed Recreation Research Project, OWRR Project No. A-033-Pa.** Annotated bibliography on recreation users, Betty van der Smissen and Monty L. Christiansen, Institute for Research on Land and Water Resources, Pennsylvania State University, State College, Pennsylvania, 1973.

44. **Beach Capacities,** Brij Garg, Pennsylvania Department of Environmental Resources, Division of Outdoor Recreation, 1973, an unpublished report.

45. **Swimming Pool Guidelines,** Department of Environmental Resources, Commonwealth of Pennsylvania, Bureau of State Parks, Swim Pool Task Force, 1973, and unpublished report.

46. **Prediction of Day Use in Eastern State Parks,** Allyn P. Bursley, United States Department of the Interior, April 1953.

47. **Conversations with Kenneth Okorn,** biologist, fisherman and hunter.

48. Standards adopted and used by the National Golf Foundation.

49. **The Interpreter's Handbook,** Russell K. Grater, edited by Earl Jackson, published by Southwest Parks & Monuments Association, 1976.

50. Surveys conducted in Pennsylvania State Parks in 1978, 1979 & 1980, Jack Shindler, Research Staff, Pennsylvania Bureau of State Parks.

51. **1975-1977 Summer Recreation Survey of Pennsylvania State Parks,** June 1979, Division of Outdoor Recreation, Commonwealth of Pennsylvania.

52. 1977 & 1980 Summer Recreation Survey Questions on the effect of increased gas prices on visits to state parks, analysis by George Fogg.

53. **1981 Construction Cost Summary,** Division of Recreation Services, D.N.R., Michigan, P. O. Box 30028, Lansing, Michigan 48909.

54. **Non-Motorized Trails -- An Introduction to Planning & Development,** June 1980, Division of Outdoor Recreation, Commonwealth of Pennsylvania, Robert Hershey.

55. **Motorized Trails -- An Introduction to Planning & Development,** June 1980, Division of Outdoor Recreation, Commonwealth of Pennsylvania, Robert Hershey.

56. "Trail Construction", N.P.S as shown in **Park Practice,** October 1975.

57. **The Recreation Trailbike Planner,** Vol. II, No. 1.

58. **American National Standard,** ANSI A.117.1-1980.

59. **The Park Practice Program,** July 1973, U.S. Army Engineers, A-1257.

60. "Skiing Trends", **Proceedings -- 1980 National Outdoor Recreation Trend Symposium,** Vol. 1, U.S. Department of Agriculture, Forest Service, Charles R. Goeldner & Stacy Standley.

61. "An Important Industry Source of Camping Information", **Proceeding -- 1980 National Outdoor Recreation Trend Symposium,** Vol. II, U.S. Department of Agriculture, Forest Service, Woodall Publishing Company, Curtis Fuller, Paul Foght & Linda Profaizer.

62. 1981 figures used by Department of Environmental Resources, Commonwealth of Pennsylvania, for estimating state park projects.

63. "Off Road Vehicle Trends", **Proceedings -- 1980 National Outdoor Trend Symposium,** Vol. II, U.S. Department of Agriculture, Forest Service, Garrett E. Nicholas.

64. 1979 Summer Survey, Bureau of State Parks, Commonwealth of Pennsylvania, unpublished computer runs.

65. **Management Planning for Park & Recreation Areas,** George E. Fogg and J. William Shiner, National Recreation and Park Association, Alexandria, Virginia, 1983.

66. **The 1988 Bicycle Market in Review,** Bicycle Manufacturers Association, Washington, D.C.

67. **Recap of International Travel To and From the United States in 1987,** U.S. Department of Commerce, Washington, D.C., July 1988.

68. **Recreation Standards for Comprehensive Planning in Florida,** Stephen M. Holland, Department of Recreation and Parks, University of Florida, Gainesville, Florida, December 1988.

69. **The New World Atlas of Golf,** Pat Ward-Thomas, et. al Gallery of Books, New York, N.Y., 1988.

70. **Recreation, Park and Open Space Standards and Guidelines,** ed. by Roger Lancaster, National Recreation and Park Association, Alexandria, Virginia, 1983.

71. **Rules of the Game** (The Complete Illustrated Encyclopedia of All Sports of the World), Bantam Books, New York, N.Y., 1980.

72. The Sports Fan's Ultimate Book of **Sports Comparisons,** The Diagram Group, St. Martin's Press, New York, N.Y., 1982.

73. **The Range Manual,** National Rifle Association, Washington, D.C., 1988.

74. National Golf Foundation, North Palm Beach, Florida, 1987 data.

75. Ed Rogers, Superintendent, Bonita Bay Club, Bonita Springs, Florida.

76. **1985 Survey of Fishing, Hunting and Wildlife Associated Recreation,** U.S. Department of the Interior, Fish and Wildlife Service, November 1988.

77. **Guidelines to Improve the Aesthetic Quality of Roads in Pennsylvania,** Pennsylvania Department of Transportation and the Pennsylvania Department of Environmental Resources, June 1980.

78. **Uniform Federal Accessibility Standards,** General Services Administration, Department of Defense, Department of Housing and Urban Development and U.S. Postal Service, as printed in the Federal Register, Vol. 49, No. 153, August 7, 1984.

79. **Highway Noise,** prepared for U.S. Department of Transportation, 1974.

80. **Playground Design,** Aase Eriksen, Van Nostrand Reinhold Company, New York, 1985.

81. **Playing, Living, Learning,** Cor Westland and Jane Knight, Venture Publishers, State College, Pennsylvania, 1982.

82. **Childs Play,** David Aaron and Bonnie P. Winawer, Harper & Row, New York, 1965.

83. **Perceptual and Motor Development in Infants & Children,** 2nd Edition, Bryant J. Cratty, Prentice Hall, Inc., 1979.

84.   **Equestrian Sports,** Sally Gordon, et. al, Pelham Books, London, UK, 1982.

85.   **Trends,** Vol. 26, No. 2, 1989, U.S. Department of the Interior, National Park Service/National Recreation and Park Association, Washington, D.C., "Trends in Private and Public Campgrounds 1978 to 1987," McEwen & Profaizer.

86.   **Design for Sport,** Gerald A. Perrin, Butterworths, London, UK, 1981.

87.   **A Site Design Process,** George E. Fogg, National Recreation and Park Association, Alexandria, Virginia, 1986.

88.   Original manuscript provided by Dennis Pagen, board member of United States Hang Gliding Association.

Appendix **D**
U.S.-METRIC EQUIVALENT CHART

This chart compares units of measure within and between the U.S. standards and metric system. To convert U.S. units to metric units, multiply the number of U.S. units by the metric equivalent. For example: to convert 5 yards into meters, use the fact that 1 yard = .9144 m, 5 yards x .9144 m/yd = 4.5720 m.

U.S. UNIT   METRIC EQUIVALENT

Length

1 mi. = 1,760 yds. = 5,280 ft. = 1.609 km = 1609 m
1 yd. = 3 ft.   = .9144 m = 91.44 cm
1 ft. = 12 in.   = 30.48 cm
1 in.   = 2.54 cm

For approximate quick conversion use the following:
1' = 30 cm or 1 yd. = 90 cm
1" = 2.5 cm therefore a 2" x 4" would be 5 cm x 10 cm

Area

1 sq. mi. = 640 ac   = 2.59 sq. km
1 ac. = 4840 sq. yd. =
   43,560 sq. ft.   = .4047 ha = 4047 sq. m
1 sq. yd. = 9 sq. ft.   = .8361 sq. m
1 sq. ft. = 144 sq. in.   = 929 sq. cm
1 sq. in.   = 6.542 sq. cm

Volume

1 ac. ft. = 1613 cu. yd. =
   43,560 cu. ft.   = 1233.49 cu. m
1 cu. yd. = 27 cu. ft.   = .7646 cu. m
1 cu. ft. = 1728 cu. in. = .02832 cu. m
1 cu. in.   = 16.39 cu. cm
1 gal.   = 3.8 l

Temperature

degrees Fahrenheit   = degrees Celsius =
                         5/9 after subtracting 32

Mass

1 ounce   = 28 g
1 lb.   = .45 kg
1 ton   = .9 Mg

METRIC UNIT   U.S. EQUIVALENT

Length

1 km = 1000 m   = .6214 mi. = 1094 yd.
1 m = 100 cm   = 1.094 yd. = 3.281 ft.
1 cm = 10 mm   = .3937 in.
1 mm   = .03937 in.

Area

1 sq. km = 100 ha   = 247.1 ac.
1 ha = 10,000 sq. m
   (100 m x 100 m)   = 2.471 ac.
1 sq. m = 10,000 sq. cm   = 1.196 sq. yd. =
                         10.76 sq. ft.

A quick approximation 1 ha = 2.5 ac

Volume

1 cu. m =
   1,000,000 cu. cm   = 1.308 cu. yd. =
                         35.31 cu. ft.
1 l   = 0.26 gal. = 1.056 qt.
A quick approximation 1 l = 1 qt.

Temperature

degree Celsius   = degree Fahrenheit =
                         9/5 then add 32

Mass

1 g   = .035 oz.
1 kg   = 2.2 lb.
1 Mg   = 1.1 tons

ABBREVIATIONS

ac = acres	ha = hectare	m = meter
cm = centimeter	in = inch	Mg = megagram
cu = cubic	kg = kilogram	mi = mile
ft = foot	km = kilometer	mm = millimeter
g = gram	l = liter	sq = square
gal = gallon	lb = pound	yd = yard